The Emperor Caligula in the
Ancient Sources

The Emperor Caligula in the Ancient Sources

ANTHONY A. BARRETT
and
J. C. YARDLEY

OXFORD
UNIVERSITY PRESS

OXFORD
UNIVERSITY PRESS

Great Clarendon Street, Oxford, OX2 6DP,
United Kingdom

Oxford University Press is a department of the University of Oxford.
It furthers the University's objective of excellence in research, scholarship,
and education by publishing worldwide. Oxford is a registered trade mark of
Oxford University Press in the UK and in certain other countries

Published in the United States of America by Oxford University Press
198 Madison Avenue, New York, NY 10016, United States of America

British Library Cataloguing in Publication Data
Data available

Library of Congress Control Number: 2022948820

ISBN 978–0–19–885456–2 (hbk.)
ISBN 978–0–19–885457–9 (pbk.)

DOI: 10.1093/oso/9780198854562.001.0001

Printed and bound by
CPI Group (UK) Ltd, Croydon, CR0 4YY

Preface

This is in some ways a rather unconventional book. But that is probably as it should be—it is, after all, a book about an unconventional character. The Roman emperor Gaius Caesar, more recognizable by his childhood nickname, Caligula, provoked fear and despair during his own lifetime, some two thousand years ago, and in his own special way he still does, although admittedly it is now only academic historians who are made to suffer. Their grief arises from the inescapable recognition that Caligula represents an insoluble paradox. There can surely be few historical figures who have made such a powerful impact on the popular imagination. He has long been a hot topic in films and TV, where an unwritten rule guarantees that his depiction will be exaggerated to the point of absurdity, ranging from his demented antics in the notorious Penthouse *Caligula* (1979) to our personal favourite, the less well-known but wonderfully weird Italian-French co-production *Caligule et Messalina* (1981), which offers only minimal hints of historical reality. Even the BBC's distinguished and broadly authentic series *I Claudius* (1976) relaxed for the portrayal of this particular emperor, with its particularly gruesome scene of Caligula disembowelling his sister/mistress Drusilla, for which there is not a shred of ancient evidence.

Academics may feel that they rise above such tawdry entertainments in their noble mission of reconstructing some semblance of narrative truth from the ancient evidence. But this is where Caligula is so frustratingly paradoxical. The source material available for this quest for the truth is plentiful, even lavish, by the standards of antiquity. The problem lies not so much in the *quantity* of evidence available, but in its *quality*. The historian Tacitus, the most reliable ancient chronicler of this period, did write an account of Caligula's brief reign as part of his celebrated *Annals*, but, frustratingly, the relevant sections are lost without trace. To fill the gap we are obliged to draw on the colourful *Life of Caligula* of Suetonius, a writer quite incapable of resisting an entertaining anecdote. Along with Suetonius we can draw upon the almost complete account of the much later Greek historian Cassius Dio, unfortunately also a lover of anecdotes (although, sadly, not nearly so entertaining, at least not the way Dio tells them), and exhibiting far less critical analysis than we would expect of today's historians. We can supplement these two with various strands of information derived from other, generally no more reliable, ancient literary sources. As a consequence we end up with a rich abundance of information, and a disheartening scarcity of knowledge. That is the Caligulan paradox.

The broad outline of Caligula's imperial career is in fact very straightforward. He came to power in early AD 37 in a wave of enthusiasm, by 39 things had gone seriously wrong, by early 41 he had been assassinated. That much can be agreed. But within that general framework there is hardly a detail that the modern historian can present without deep reservations about its reliability. What then is that historian to do? In recent years we have seen a string of biographies of Caligula. These certainly have their place, but they do risk creating what is in essence an illusion, that a biography of Caligula, in the regular modern sense of the word, is possible. The true Caligulan biography is in fact a quintessential mare's nest—the most we can hope from them is a summary personal interpretation by an individual historian of a mass of incoherent and often inconsistent material. There might be a case to be made for going to the opposite extreme and for directing anyone seriously interested in the topic straight to the raw material of the ancient sources. That to some extent is one of the objectives of this book. We provide over three hundred translated passages of ancient text, taken mainly from literary sources, and also from coins and inscriptions. References to the catalogue of these sources are made using the simple format of, e.g., 1.1 for Chapter 1, Passage 1, and so on. But perusing this raw material works only at a limited level. The information that has survived is often inconsistent or downright contradictory, and navigating it calls for a fairly mature understanding of the period. For better or for worse, readers do need guidance, or at the very least some reassurance that the seemingly impenetrable character of whatever truth is lurking beneath the tangle of confusing testimonies reflects the nature of the beast and not any intellectual shortcomings on the part of the reader. Hence we accompany our translations with relatively extensive introductions and/or notes, to place the events and institutions in their historical contexts, or sometimes simply to provide what we hope will be interesting secondary observations. Any guidance that we provide on these matters is of course bound to be infected by our own views—it simply cannot be otherwise—but at least those potentially tainted observations are throughout subservient to the sources themselves.

There is in fact a bright side to all of this. While Caligula perhaps does not lend himself well to a biographical approach, he is, on the other hand, the perfect tool to assist students of history in practising their trade (we use the word "student" here in the broadest sense). Perhaps better than any other historical figure Caligula constitutes a sort of historical laboratory where the student is confronted by a mass of contradictory, inconsistent, and at times nonsensical data. He obliges us to confront head on the stark reality that what we read in our sources is not necessarily the truth and that it is consequently a massive challenge to use this jumble of material to reconstruct and understand the past—particularly the ancient past, but the principles can be applied to almost any period of history. Arguably better than any other historical figure Caligula brings home the degree to which the monuments of our understanding of history are built on often unstable foundations.

We begin with what is in essence a fairly conventional biographical essay. The remainder of the book in a way deconstructs that essay and tries to demonstrate how wary in fact one should be of taking any account of the reign at simple face value. The eight central chapters, of which Chapters 1–4 and 8 are more or less chronological, 5–7 thematic, consist generally of a series of introductory paragraphs, each followed by the relevant passages, sometimes with extensive annotation. What must be acknowledged here, and it is acknowledged without apology, is that there is no attempt at a sustained uniformity of approach; indeed, we feel that strict uniformity would compromise the usefulness of the book. In places a lengthy introduction to a given series of passages seems essential, in others the briefest prefatory comment suffices. Some passages are heavily annotated, others seem hardly to need any explanatory notes. Often a passage will fit under several rubrics: generally in such cases the catalogue number assigned to each passage will be used to make cross-references, but occasionally, very rarely, it has seemed more appropriate simply to repeat a line or two. Also, the book reflects the very wide range of its potential users. It is, of course, directed at what might be broadly defined as "serious readers." Among those serious readers some may have only a general, even amateurish, interest in Caligula and will no doubt focus their attention on the translated passages and the introductory sections. They will also find the basic glossary of Roman terms useful but probably will only rarely dip into the notes. Classicists whose acquaintance with antiquity is cultural rather than philological, as well as readers who have not passed through a traditional Classical curriculum but have a specialist training in related academic disciplines like history or archaeology, may well want to pursue some topics in depth, and the detailed notes are intended to serve them. Our desire to cater to readers from this variety of academic backgrounds may create apparent inconsistencies in how the material is presented. We at times provide fairly elementary data, and will repeat such basic information as family relationships or insert what might on occasion seem otiose "BC" or "AD" definitions to years. Also, as noted above, we provide a basic glossary of unfamiliar terms. Because the translated passages are in most cases extracted from larger contexts we occasionally replace ambiguous pronouns with proper names. To avoid confusion we refer throughout to the almost ubiquitous familiar Jewish ruler by the technically incorrect but hallowed by usage "Herod Agrippa," and we refer to the emperor Tiberius' grandson by his cognomen "Gemellus," rather than by the potentially confusing form most often used in the literary sources, "Tiberius." All of this in an effort to guide the beginner through the basic events of the period. Yet at other times we challenge the reader with problems that call for a fairly sophisticated way of looking at the evidence. We see no real contradiction in providing this more advanced material. Readers of this book will inevitably have gaps in their knowledge, but gaps in knowledge do not preclude those same readers, with responsible guidance, from applying to historical problems intelligence, insight, ingenuity, or simply the fundamental curiosity that lies at the heart of the study of history.

It goes without saying that all academic endeavours are greatly indebted to the work of their scholarly predecessors. In the case of this book in particular it should not be left unsaid. We have made an effort to reflect recent ideas about the many contentious issues of Caligula's reign in the notes and introductory sections and our debt there to the achievements of other scholars is enormous, although in most cases shortage of space has precluded our recording the specific sources of much of the current thinking. We are also much indebted to the staffs of libraries where we have been fortunate enough to carry out our own work, the Library of the University of British Columbia, Vancouver, the Robarts Library of the University of Toronto, the Sackler and Bodleian libraries in Oxford, the Universitätsbibliothek and the Institute libraries of Alte Geschichte, of Klassische Philologie, and of Anglistik in Heidelberg. The staff of Oxford University Press, most notably Charlotte Loveridge, Karen Raith and Cathryn Steele, have been helpful and encouraging from the outset. Friends, families, and colleagues have been consistently supportive and we are grateful to them all.

As in the past Kornelia Roth has come to our assistance, with drawings of the young Caligula and of one of the calendar inscriptions from Ostia. Valerie Louis provided invaluable help with computer-related challenges and contributed a constant flow of perceptive insights into the complex historical problems that we encounteed throughout the project.

Contents

List of Illustrations

List of Abbreviations

Abbreviations follow the standard format prescribed by *Année Philologique*. In addition:

EJ   Ehrenberg, V. and A. H. M. Jones. 1955. *Documents Illustrating the Reigns of Augustus and Tiberius*. 2nd edition, Oxford: Clarendon Press.

Smallwood Smallwood, E. M. 1967, reprinted 2011. *Documents Illustrating the Principates of Gaius Claudius and Nero*. Cambridge: Cambridge University Press.

Important Events in Caligula's Life and Reign

Glossary

aedile A magistrate holding office after the quaestorship. His duties generally involved various aspects of city administration.

Armenia A kingdom with a strong sense of independent identity, bordering Parthia, in the mountainous area south and southwest of the Caucasus and east of the Euphrates. It was a constant source of contention between Romans and Parthians.

Arval brotherhood A priestly college that recorded its rituals in stone inscriptions, preserved, with gaps, for the period 21 BC to AD 304. The college consisted of twelve men in addition to the emperor.

Asia A province that came into being in 129 BC after the Romans inherited the kingdom of Pergamum in northwest Asia Minor, on the death of its last king, Attalus III. It was hugely wealthy, and the governorship was much coveted.

assemblies Gatherings of Roman citizens convened to carry out specific tasks, usually related to elections and the passing of legislation.

augur An official belonging to one of the four Roman priestly colleges. His area of expertise was divination inspired by the characteristics and behaviour of birds.

auxiliaries Approximately half of the total Roman military forces, recruited locally but posted throughout the Roman frontier area. Citizens normally served in the legions, a distinct body, while auxiliaries were usually, although not exclusively, non-citizens.

Cappadocia A rugged area in eastern Anatolia, stretching from the Taurus mountains to the Black Sea.

centurion A legionary officer in command of a "century," originally consisting of one hundred men, eighty by the imperial period.

Cilicia A mountainous area extending along the Mediterranean coast of southeast Asia Minor, gradually incorporated by Rome from 103 BC on.

cognomen The third element of a Roman name (such as Cicero, in Marcus Tullius Cicero). Sometimes it reflected supposed ancestral attributes, or it could be a title bestowed after an achievement, such as "Germanicus."

cohort A unit of the Roman army. A legion consisted of ten cohorts. The term is used also of units of the auxiliaries, and of military/quasi-military units in Rome like the Praetorians, the Urban Cohorts, and the Vigiles.

colony (*colonia*) At the outset a settlement made up of Roman citizens, often veterans. Later the status could be granted to other types of towns to convey enhanced status.

Commagene A region between the west bank of the Euphrates and the southeast edge of the Taurus mountains. An independent kingdom was established there in the second century BC, incorporated by Rome in AD 18.

consul The highest Roman official. Emperors regularly held the office. Two consuls were elected together, originally for a period of one year. After 5 BC it was routine for consuls appointed at the beginning of the year (*ordinarii*) to resign during their term of office, to be replaced by "suffects" (*suffecti*), who might in turn later resign in favour of further suffects. Consular rank was attainable after the praetorship, normally when the candidate had reached the age of forty-two, but a previous consulship in one's family allowed entry much sooner, perhaps by the age of thirty-two. Members of the imperial family did not even have to wait that long, or to have held a previous praetorship (Caligula was twenty-four when he held his first consulship, Nero seventeen).

dictator A magistrate elected during the republic to deal with an emergency. The term of office was six months.

donative A distribution of cash by the emperor, usually to mark a special occasion.

equestrian (*eques*, pl.*equites*, also**knights**) Originally this term was applied to an order that served in the cavalry, later more generally to the commercial middle class, with a property qualification of 400,000 sestertii. Equestrians could not maintain their rank and be simultaneously members of the Roman senate, but they did play an important role in imperial administration, holding a number of key offices, the most notable being the prefectures of Egypt and of the Praetorian guard.

Fasti Ostienses A calendar of significant events from 49 BC to AD 175, preserved in stone in Ostia.

freedman A former slave who had earned his freedom, often staying in the service of the home where he had been a slave. Imperial freedmen were a distinctive feature of the Julio-Claudian period.

Germany In the early imperial period Germania (Germany) and Germani (Germans) are applied loosely to the regions east of the Rhine and north of the Danube, although these should not be envisaged as constituting a strict border. Rome established two military districts on the Rhine, which were in place during the Caligula period, Upper (south) and Lower (north) Germany, each housing four legions.

imperium The power to command, vested in magistrates at a certain rank.

knight *See* equestrian.

legate A flexible term with three common meanings: (a) someone assigned a particular task; (b) a commander of a legion; (c) a governor of an imperial province.

legion The main unit of the Roman army, commanded by a legate chosen by the emperor, consisting of between five and six thousand Roman citizens.

maiestas Maiestas laesa ("injured majesty") was an offence against the dignity of the state, later against the person or character of the emperor and his family, broadly "treason." It embraced verbal abuse and slander. Under the republic the *maiestas* laws were directed against incompetence rather than criminality; under the principate they were applied more broadly and were a considerable source of fear and resentment. By the latter part of Tiberius' reign, banishment or the death penalty were frequent penalties.

Moesia A region inhabited by Thracians to the south of the lower Danube, west of the Black Sea. It was incorporated by Rome in about 29 BC, initially as part of Macedonia, and later became an independent province, possibly under Claudius.

nomen The main element of a Roman name (such as Tullius, in Marcus Tullius Cicero), indicating the holder's *gens* (family).

Ovation A lesser Triumph, granted when the victory did not meet all the requirements for a full Triumph—if not won on a sufficient scale, or not against formal enemies of Rome in a declared war, or against unworthy foes, such as against slaves or pirates. The victorious general did not enter the city in a chariot drawn by four horses, as he did during a Triumph, but on foot or horseback in a simple toga, wearing a wreath of myrtle rather than of laurel.

Pannonia A Roman province bordered by the Danube, consisting of what is now western Hungary, as well as parts of Austria, Slovenia, Croatia, and Serbia.

plebeian Originally, a member of the lower grade of citizens, as opposed to the patricians. The distinction ceased to be important, and by Caligula's time there were several prominent plebeian families. Literary sources sometimes use the term casually of the mass of people of Rome who were not members of either the equestrian or the senatorial class.

pontiff (*pontifex*) A member of one of the four priestly colleges of Rome. The senior priest held the title of pontifex maximus, an office occupied by the emperor from 12 BC.

praenomen The first element in the name of a Roman man (such as Marcus, in Marcus Tullius Cicero), roughly equivalent to a "given" name, but there was a very limited choice.

praetor A magistrate second in seniority after the consuls, holding office after the aedileship or the quaestorship. His main task in the imperial period was the administration of the courts. Under Tiberius and Caligula the number elected annually was sixteen.

Praetorianguard The imperial guard, consisting in Caligula's day of nine cohorts, commanded by a prefect or sometimes a pair of prefects. Stationed in Rome and elsewhere in Italy, they enjoyed certain privileges, such as higher rates of pay than those of the legionary soldiers. They often played a key role in the accession of any given emperor.

prefect (*praefectus*) A broad term with the basic sense of "the person placed in authority" used in a wide range of military and civilian contexts. The most important military prefects were (a) the commander of an auxiliary unit; (b) commander of the fleet; (c) prefect of the camp, ranking second to the legionary legate and in command in the legate's absence; and (d) the commander of the Praetorian guard or the Vigiles. The main administrative prefects were (a) the prefect of Egypt; (b) the prefect of the grain supply; and (c) governors of smaller districts like Judea (called "procurator" from Claudius on).

The ancient office of (d) city prefect (*praefectus urbi*) was unique in being occupied by a senator of consular rank, while other prefects were equestrian. The largely ritual duties of this prefect were enhanced by Augustus, and the city prefect became responsible for maintaining order in Rome, through command of the Urban Cohorts; he was granted summary justice in minor criminal cases and, later, in more serious ones.

princeps ("holding first rank") The conventional designation of the Roman emperors, endorsing the fiction that they were simply the leading citizens in what was in essence a republican system.

Princeps Iuventutis ("leader of the youth") The title is found in the republic but given a formal and constitutional status under Augustus when his grandsons Gaius and Lucius Caesar were hailed as such by the equestrian order and granted spears and silver shields. Subsequently it was applied generally to intended successors to the principate.

proconsul The governor of a "public" province, chosen by lot from the most worthy senators, and administrating with the authority of an ex-consul.

procurator A very flexible term with a long history. A procurator could be a private agent or bailiff on an estate. Procurators also administered the imperial properties in the provinces, and sometimes assumed an official role as "provincial" procurators. From the Claudian period on, the term is used for the governors of small districts like Judea (previously "prefects").

propraetor The governor of a province, with the status of praetor. Legates of imperial provinces governed with this status even if they were ex-consuls and their province was an important one, so as not to seem to challenge the consular authority of the emperor.

province (*provincia*) The term referred originally to a magistrate's sphere of competence. It came to acquire a more specifically geographical character, designating external territories subject to Rome. After the Augustan settlement of 27 BC overseas provinces were either (a) "imperial," housing Roman legions and administered by legates appointed directly by the emperor (Egypt was an exceptional major imperial province, governed by an equestrian prefect); or (b) "public" (sometimes called "senatorial"), which with rare exceptions did not house legions, and were administered by proconsuls of senatorial rank chosen by lot from pre-selected candidates.

quaestor A magistrate whose duties were mainly financial. Twenty were elected annually, and candidates needed to be in their twenty-fifth year. The holder of the office gained entry to the senate.

senate The senior judicial, executive, and deliberative body of the Roman state, consisting of ex-magistrates who had held at least the rank of quaestor, or others deemed especially worthy, originally by a senior official known as a censor and later by the emperor. There would have been some six hundred senators in Caligula's time, each holding property worth 1,000,000 sestertii. Decrees of the senate (*consulta*) did not then have the force of law, and had to be confirmed as laws by a popular assembly (essentially a formality).

sestertius (pl. sestertii, or sesterces) The highest-valued of the base metal Roman coins, made of brass, an alloy of zinc and copper. It is the standard used by Romans to express monetary values (with the symbol HS). Value in modern terms is very difficult to define, but the annual pay of a regular legionary soldier during the Julio-Claudian period was 900 HS.

toga The traditional public garb of the Roman male, made of fine white wool. Young boys wore the *toga praetexta*, distinguished by a purple border. At about the age of fourteen, they put this aside for the plain white version, the *toga virilis*, in a ceremony marking the transition to manhood. The *toga praetexta* was resumed by those who attained high office.

tribune An office holder. The most familiar was the tribune of the plebeians, a powerful magistrate of the republican period, whose person was sacrosanct and who had the right to veto and to initiate legislation, appointed historically to protect the lower orders, but in the imperial period occupying a routine office between the quaestorship and praetorship. The term also appears in military contexts. Six military tribunes were assigned to each legion. Also, a tribune commanded each of the nine cohorts of the Praetorian guard.

tribunician authority Emperors did not become tribunes of the plebeians *per se*, but assumed the tribunes' authority (*tribunicia potestas*) and their sacrosanctity. This conferred a number of privileges, the most significant being the right to convene the senate and the popular assemblies and to initiate or veto legislation. Tribunician authority was in a sense the foundation of the imperial system, and emperors dated their accession from the day of its bestowal.

Triumph The procession led by a commander, after a major victory, through Rome up to the Temple of Jupiter on the Capitoline hill. The procession would be accompanied by war booty and prisoners of war. The event conferred enormous prestige on the celebrant. In the imperial period the Triumph gradually became restricted to members of the imperial family.

Troy, Game of(*Ludus Troiae***)** A complicated cavalry manoeuvre, supposedly of great antiquity, performed by young men of noble families. By tradition it was brought from Troy by Aeneas, founder of the Roman people (Verg. *Aen.* 5.543–603). The ritual became popular after its revival by the dictator Sulla in the late republic. Its further popularity under the Julio-Claudians is explained to some degree by the fictitious connection between Iulus (son of Aeneas) and Iulius Caesar.

Vestal Virgins Priestesses of Vesta. The order was founded by tradition by King Numa and consisted originally of two Vestals, gradually increased to six. Recruited as children, they took a vow of chastity and served for thirty years. Their duties included maintaining the sacred fire in the "public hearth" and participation in celebrations of state cults. They held certain privileges, such as special seats at the games and transportation in the *carpentum* (two-wheeled carriage). They enjoyed considerable prestige and state documents were entrusted to their care.

Vigiles Members of the Roman fire service established by Augustus in AD 6, organized in seven cohorts, each with responsibility for two of Rome's fourteen *regiones*. Occasionally the Vigiles were called upon for broader duties related to law and order.

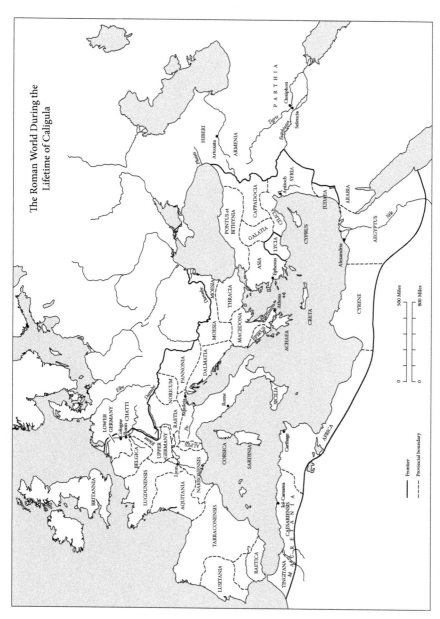

The Roman World During the Lifetime of Caligula

PARTHIA

HIBERI
ARMENIA
Artaxata
Tigris
Euphrates
Seleucia
Ctesiphon

PONTUS et BITHYNIA
CAPPADOCIA
Antioch
SYRIA
GALATIA
CILICIA
LYCIA
ARABIA
ASIA
JUDAEA
Ephesus
CYPRUS
COS
AEGYPTUS
Alexandria
Nile

Danube
THRACIA
MOESIA
MACEDONA
EPIRUS
Athens
ACHAEA
CRETA
CYRENE

Danube
NORICUM
PANNONIA
DALMATIA
RAETIA
Po
Aquileia
Rome
SICILIA
Carthage
AFRICA

Elbe
LOWER GERMANY
Cologne
Bonn CHATTI
UPPER GERMANY
Rhine
Süd IV
BELGICA
Lyon
NARBONENSIS
LUGDUNENSIS
AQUITANIA
CORSICA
SARDINIA
Iol-Caesarea
Caesarea
CAESARIENSIS
MAURETANIA

BRITANNIA
TARRACONENSIS
LUSITANIA
BAETICA
TINGITANA

Frontier
Provincial boundary

0   500 Miles
0   800 Miles

Map of the Roman empire at the time of Caligula.

Family tree

Spouses and siblings omitted in places.

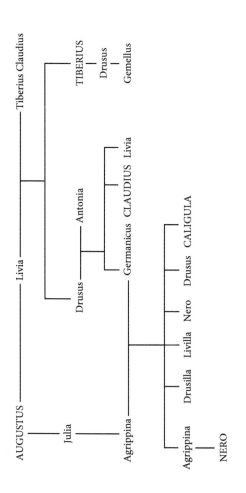

Introduction

The social and political milieu in which Caligula lived and reigned was arguably the outcome of a lengthy process of historical evolution, but the more immediate events that made a phenomenon like him possible can reasonably be traced back to the aftermath of the assassination of Julius Caesar, in March 44 BC. This celebrated event initiated a period of political chaos, leading to the rise of Caesar's grandnephew and heir, Octavian. In 27 BC, after the defeat of his arch-rival Mark Antony, he was granted the title of "Augustus" by the Roman senate. The senate also assigned him an enormous "province," in the form of authority over those Roman possessions requiring a military presence, not unalterably fixed but consisting basically of Gaul, Syria, and most of Spain; the remaining public/senatorial provinces were generally administered by proconsuls selected from the senate. It is at this point that we conventionally date the beginning of the Roman "empire," in the sense of a system of government (Rome had, of course, already long possessed a physical empire of overseas territory).

We commonly refer to Augustus as an emperor, Rome's first, but he sought to clothe his imperial regime with the veneer of republicanism, and with the pretence that he was essentially no more than a leading citizen, a *princeps*, in essence a regular magistrate, albeit one with unusual power and privileges. He showed his true monarchical colours, however, through his efforts to ensure that he would be succeeded from within his own family. In the event, he and his wife, the celebrated Livia (from the Claudian line, despite her name, "Livia," acquired through adoption), had no surviving children. Augustus' previous wife, the supposedly shrewish Scribonia, had given him a daughter, the strong-minded Julia, who was summoned to duty and obliged to marry Augustus' old lieutenant, Marcus Agrippa, bearing him five offspring. The next four Roman emperors came from the lines of Augustus, a Julian through his legally dubious posthumous adoption by his maternal great-uncle Julius Caesar, and of Livia, a Claudian by descent. Hence they are commonly referred to as the Julio-Claudians.

None of Augustus' close male relatives survived him (females were excluded from the process), and, reputedly with reluctance, he marked out Tiberius, Livia's son by a previous marriage, as his successor. Tiberius came to power in AD 14, but although he had earlier enjoyed a distinguished military career he proved to be a morose and uncharismatic emperor. By the time he died in March 37 his only son Drusus had already perished (perhaps murdered by his wife) and his sole close blood relative was his young grandson, Drusus' son, Gemellus. The situation was

The Emperor Caligula in the Ancient Sources. Anthony A. Barrett and J. C. Yardley, Oxford University Press.
© Anthony A. Barrett and J. C. Yardley 2023. DOI: 10.1093/oso/9780198854562.003.0001

much different from that following Augustus' death in AD 14. On that earlier occasion there had been an experienced administrator waiting in the wings—Tiberius himself, previously associated in high office with his predecessor and thus marked out unmistakably to follow him. No clear candidate was apparent on Tiberius' death in AD 37. Gemellus had not yet reached the formal age of manhood. But Tiberius also had a grandson through adoption, Gaius Caligula, relatively youthful, at twenty-four, and politically inexperienced. Beyond designating both as his joint heirs to his private estate (3.3–6), the punctilious Tiberius gave no hint of who should succeed as emperor, presumably intending to leave any such decision to the senate. The resolution of this issue had a profound effect on the subsequent course of Roman history.

Early Years

Caligula was the son of Germanicus, himself the son of Tiberius' brother Drusus (not to be confused with Tiberius' son, also Drusus). The elder Drusus was an accomplished commander who had died on campaign in Germany in 9 BC. In AD 4 Germanicus was adopted by his uncle Tiberius (no doubt under pressure from Augustus), and was thus technically Tiberius' son when his own son Caligula was born, in AD 12. Caligula's mother was Agrippina (the Elder), granddaughter of Augustus, through his daughter Julia and Marcus Agrippa. Caligula was born at Antium in the imperial villa (1.4) and given the name "Gaius." He shortly afterwards joined his father, who held military command over the Rhine district; there he was dressed up as an infant soldier by his mother and acquired his nickname of Caligula, from the Latin word for leather military boot (*caliga*) (1.5–8). On the death of Augustus, in AD 14, Tiberius became emperor, and in 17 transferred Germanicus from his command in Germany to a special commission in the east, where the little Caligula accompanied him, winning over audiences with his precociously delivered speeches (1.17–19). Tragedy struck in late 19, when Germanicus died in Syria (1.21–2), and Caligula returned with his mother, Agrippina, to a Rome fraught with political intrigue (2.1). There, Agrippina and her two eldest sons fell victim to the machinations of Sejanus, the sinister commander of the Praetorian (imperial) guard (2.2, 10, 12–16) and all three ultimately lost their lives. Caligula may have been too young to be seen as a serious threat, and he was in any case removed from danger in AD 31, when summoned to join Tiberius, by now living in self-imposed exile on Capri (2.17–20).

The literary sources regale us with scenes of decadent self-indulgence on Capri, but Caligula's life there was probably an unexciting one, while he was prepared for future responsibilities. In 33 he held a quaestorship and in that same year was married to Junia Claudia (2.23–6), from a distinguished aristocratic family. Junia died not much later, giving birth (the child also died). Two other individuals seem to have been particularly close to Caligula on the island. Agrippa (popularly known as Herod Agrippa, to be distinguished from Marcus Agrippa), a grandson of Herod the Great of Judaea, was a charming character, with considerable energy and ambition, who somehow managed to be both shady and flamboyant. Caligula also caught the eye of Macro, the prefect of the Praetorian guard. Macro had apparently concluded that Caligula had the best chance to succeed Tiberius, and courted his favour, even reputedly pandering his own wife Ennia (2.21–2).

Accession

Caligula had been living on Capri for some six years when Tiberius died, in March 37. He would have been largely unknown to most Romans, but he had two distinct advantages. He was the son of the still immensely popular Germanicus, a man of supposedly enlightened political convictions, inherited in turn from Germanicus' own father, Drusus, Tiberius' brother—their early deaths meant that neither man had actually been called upon to put those supposed convictions to the test. Perhaps even more importantly, Caligula enjoyed, through Macro, the backing of the Praetorian guard, inadvertently establishing a precedent for later imperial claimants throughout the course of Rome's subsequent history.

Macro went into action when it was clear that Tiberius was on the point of death. He informed the military and civilian authorities in the provinces that they had a new emperor. To ensure a smooth transition he made a hasty journey to Rome. There he announced Tiberius' passing to the senate (3.2, 4). No doubt he also brought up the issue of the succession, but the details are hazy. The senators were given the opportunity to go through the motions of validating the next emperor and they seem to have done so enthusiastically, perhaps in the belief that they would be able to manipulate someone so youthful and inexperienced. In any case, on March 18, a mere two days after Tiberius died, the senate proclaimed Caligula *Imperator* (3.7).

These formal measures were topped off by a series of orchestrated events celebrating the return of Caligula to Rome, along with the body of his late predecessor, when large crowds gathered on the route to show their devotion to a young man who had been almost completely unknown a few days before. They were vociferously enthusiastic (5.5). Caligula reached Rome at the end of March and met the senate, who granted him "power and authority over all things" (3.9–11). He was the first emperor to have complete imperial authority conferred upon him by an official act of the senate at the very outset of his reign.

First Months

However outrageously Caligula might have behaved later, his behaviour during the first few months of his reign was impeccable. He was the epitome of tactful deference, and made a point of showing senators in particular enormous respect, taking Augustus as his model. He strengthened his support base among other segments of society, by paying off and, in some cases, increasing the bequests specified in Tiberius' will, even though that will had in fact been annulled (3.4,15–18). In a gesture of reconciliation he declared an amnesty for exiles and made a great show of destroying all the documents relating to the earlier proceedings taken against members of his family (3.19–20). He adopted Gemellus, implying that he considered him his successor in the event of his own death (3.20). Above all, Romans would have been relieved by the suspension of one of the major causes of fear and resentment under Tiberius, trials for *maiestas*, acts against the state, and, more troubling, against the emperor himself (3.19–20).

Family piety was highly important to Romans, and there would have been broad approval of Caligula's efforts to show his devotion to his closest relatives. He recovered the ashes of his mother and his brother Nero and placed them alongside those of his father Germanicus inside the mausoleum of Augustus (3.26–8, 31–2). Special honours were bestowed on his sisters, and they, and his parents, were featured on his coinage (3.34–6).

These extravagant gestures were accompanied by a large-scale building programme, in contrast to the tight-fisted policy of Tiberius, who had disapproved of expensive public works. Outstanding among Caligula's projects was the completion of the magnificent Temple of Augustus, decreed after that emperor's death but left in abeyance under Tiberius, to be opened within months of Caligula's accession in a grandiose spectacle (3.44–7). In September Caligula accepted the symbolically potent title of Pater Patriae ("Father of the Fatherland") (3.50–2).

Early Tensions

After his sheltered existence on Capri, Caligula must surely have found his early months as emperor a dizzying experience, and also a draining one. At some point in early autumn he fell seriously ill (3.53–5). When he recovered, the news was celebrated enthusiastically across the Rome world. But the happy improvement in his health heralded a far less happy change in the general ethos of the new regime, and there are signs of tensions within the imperial court, possibly fuelled by suspicion of some sort of conspiracy. Several people closely connected with the emperor lost their lives in the months that followed, including Gemellus and Caligula's father-in-law, Junius Silanus (4.1–8). Most alarmingly, perhaps, at some later point Caligula turned on Macro, perhaps on suspicion of involvement in some sort of plot with Gemellus and Silanus (the course of events during these months is particularly murky) (4.11–18).

Caligula took a second wife (her name is uncertain) shortly after his recovery (4.9–10), only to divorce her soon afterwards, and later married Lollia Paulina, one of Rome's wealthiest women (4.33–4). But he seems to have remained closest to his three sisters, Agrippina (the Younger), Livilla, and Drusilla, leading to persistent rumours of incest (2.6–8). He was devastated when Drusilla, possibly his favourite, died, in AD 38. A period of public mourning was decreed and, even more remarkably, she was deified, with her own temple and priesthood (4.25–32).

Crisis

Although the exact process is far from clear, the political atmosphere had unquestionably darkened even further by the beginning of AD 39, when Caligula entered the senate and engaged in a bitter denunciation of the members, taunting them as agents of Sejanus and blaming them for the deaths of his mother and brothers. Perhaps most alarmingly he announced that *maiestas* trials would resume (4.35–8). It is during this period of increasing tensions that the literary sources generally locate some of the more blatant manifestations of outrageous behaviour. It was almost certainly in this year that his famous pontoon bridge was built across a section of the Bay of Naples (4.39–43).

Conspiracy

Towards the end of 39 the simmering tensions between emperor and senate burst into the open. Caligula removed the two serving consuls from office (4.44–9), but the most striking evidence of some sort of power struggle was the clear effort to undermine a number of military commanders (4.55). The most significant of these was Cornelius Lentulus Gaetulicus, legate of Upper Germany. He was a lax disciplinarian, but mere incompetence alone does not explain his downfall. In October 39 a formal celebration was held in Rome to mark the exposure of his "nefarious plots" (4.53–4, 65). And the conspiracy may have extended right into the heart of Caligula's family. In late 39 he travelled north, accompanied by his surviving sisters, Agrippina and Livilla, as well as by Lepidus, the husband of his late sister Drusilla, reputedly a very close friend. At some point in the journey Lepidus was executed, possibly for conspiring with Gaetulicus. Moreover both sisters were somehow implicated, and were banished to the Pontian islands (4.56–65). Also in 39 Caligula divorced Lollia and remarried. His new, and final, wife was Milonia Caesonia, who gave birth to a daughter a month after the marriage (4.50–2). It may be that this marriage, and the birth of a child, made his sisters feel sidelined, provoking them to associate themselves with Lepidus in some sort of attempted putsch.

Britain and Germany

The dismissal of Gaetulicus was the prelude to one of the most notorious chapters of Caligula's career, his campaigns against Germany and his planned invasion of

Britain. As the literary sources tell the story he left Rome in 39 without any serious preparations, took part in some foolish skirmishes in Germany, and on several occasions led his troops over the Rhine, only to withdraw in panic (7.18, 19). He then progressed to the English channel. There he mustered his troops, went out in a ship, returned, and then told the soldiers to march into the ocean and collect shells, to be carried back to Rome as victory spoils (7.16, 18–20). This campaign is generally depicted as a bout of reckless folly.

Africa

Major developments were taking place in another part of the world, on the coast of North Africa. An anomalous situation, whereby the senatorial governor of the province of Africa commanded a legion, was brought to an end and the troops were placed under an imperial legate (7.4–5). To the west lay the vast kingdom of Mauretania. Caligula summoned its king, Ptolemy, a loyal ally, to Rome, where he was imprisoned and executed, for reasons unknown. The process by which Mauretania was subsequently incorporated as a Roman province was initiated, although it was probably not finalized until the reign of Claudius (7.6–10).

The Jewish World

One of the most intractable problems faced by Caligula was the relationship with the Jews. Two separate Jewish communities became the focus of unrest. In Alexandria tensions between Jews and Greek nationalists led to riots, causing widespread destruction and death (7.23–6). In Judaea, Jewish extremists tore down an altar to the imperial cult in Jamnia in AD 39, and in retaliation Caligula threatened to have his statue installed in the Temple at Jerusalem. There were demonstrations throughout Judaea and serious danger of a popular uprising, aborted supposedly by the deft handling of the situation by the governor of Syria, Publius Petronius (7.29–31). After Caligula's death the new emperor Claudius imposed a temporary calm by a combination of tact and firmness (7.27–8).

Assassination

Caligula returned to Rome from his northern campaigns in early 40, and entered the city in late August, when he celebrated an Ovation (lesser Triumph) (8.1). Relations with the senate grew ever worse. Caligula's demands to be recognized as a god are generally dated to this period (6.19, 29). Numerous trials and executions are recorded, some of them reputedly horrific (8.2–5). Details are not clear but already in AD 40 an embryonic conspiracy may have been formed. Matters reached their perhaps inevitable conclusion in January 41, when Caligula was assassinated by members of his own imperial guard during a festival on the Palatine, as he made his way to the palace for lunch through an underground tunnel. The details of how the plot came about, who was involved, and who masterminded it are unfortunately very obscure. The fatal blow was struck by a tribune, Cassius Chaerea (8.7–8, 12), but there is much speculation that more powerful figures, perhaps even Caligula's uncle Claudius, were pulling the strings in the background (8.8–11, 15–17).

The Sources

Literary Sources

Literary sources lie at the very heart of this book and it is appropriate to provide some background information on those ancient writers who supply the bulk of the information about Caligula, and on the issues raised by their texts. This section can hardly do justice to the complexity of Caligulan historiography, and what follows is essentially elementary information for the general reader.

Some important caveats must be made at the outset. It is essential to bear in mind that the aims of ancient Greek and Roman historians were fundamentally different from those of their modern counterparts. Modern historians generally see it as an important part of their mission to aspire to objective truth, fully conscious, of course, of the difficulties of avoiding bias and preconceptions absorbed through cultural backgrounds. They will be expected to cite their sources and to be candid about which statements reflect their own speculations. Moreover, while modern historians might strive to write clearly and pleasingly, they will generally see their endeavours primarily as works of science and scholarship rather than of refined literature. The ancient historians, by contrast, saw themselves very much as creative writers. Their historical accounts are inherently literary, replete with devices that often border on the poetic. Also, while they may have believed that they were conveying a truth, it was a truth very much as they saw it, and they seem generally unconscious of their own bias. Moreover they seem broadly indifferent to the dangers of hearsay and unsubstantiated gossip, rarely citing their sources, but content often to retail what they perceive as popular opinion. All history should be read with caution; ancient historians need to be read with extreme caution, and we must resist any temptation to see them as authoritative.

Added to our concern over the reliability of ancient authors, we must always be conscious that information derived from translated passages has passed through a cultural filter. Every language has its unique nuances and idiosyncrasies, which have no proper equivalents in other languages. Hence the translated text, no matter how accurate, can never be more than an approximation of the original. Moral or political concepts are especially problematic: Latin words like *potestas*, *pietas*, *auctoritas* may seem superficially simple, even self-evident, but in a very real sense they are untranslatable. This problem is of course insoluble, but we do hope that the background information that we provide will alleviate it somewhat.

Finally, it is important to realize that there can be no such thing as "the text" of an ancient author. In antiquity works were composed usually by dictation to a scribe. Mistakes would quite likely enter into the texts at this initial stage, but if they did not they most certainly would do so during the subsequent stages, when copies were made of the original version, then copies were in turn made of those copies, a process repeated throughout the centuries, during the course of which the early versions would be lost, leaving us with only later manuscripts that are copies of copies of copies of copies with additional errors inserting themselves at each stage. One of the most challenging tasks facing the Classical scholar is to reconstruct the history of the transmission process and to produce a text that comes as close as possible to the intentions of the author. There is no pretence that the exact original text has, or can, ever be created—we can at best achieve approximations of what the author originally wrote or dictated. This is not unique to ancient works: we often cannot reconstruct the exact writings of more recent authors too—Shakespeare is a famous case in point. But the problem is especially severe before the age of printing, when the manuscripts were, as the Latin elements of the word indicate (*manu*, "by hand," *scriptum*, "a written thing"), written out by hand, often by weary monks working in poor light in draughty and uncomfortable cells.

Neither of our two major sources for the events of Caligula's reign, Suetonius or Cassius Dio (see below for both), was a contemporary of Caligula, and both were obliged to rely on earlier writers. Most of the writers alive in the Julio-Claudian period have survived only as shadowy names, figures like Cluvius Rufus, Fabius Rusticus, Servilius Nonianus, or Alfidius Bassus, and their contributions to the story of Caligula are far from certain. The debt of later authorities to these for material relating to Caligula, and even the issue of whether they in fact wrote specifically on him, is highly contentious. As noted earlier, ancient historians only rarely thought it necessary to name their sources.

In the introductory section of his *Annals* Tacitus states that the histories of the Julio-Claudian period were infected by flattery during the lifetimes of the subjects, and by hatred after their death. Any favourable reports of Caligula's reign are long lost. We are in a far better position when it comes to the negative authorities. Two of those unsympathetic authors, Seneca and Philo, were actually present in Rome in the relevant period. Philo certainly met Caligula, and Seneca most likely did too. The reliability of their reports might be questionable, but they do at any rate serve to illustrate how he was viewed by hostile contemporaries.

The dramatist and philosopher **Seneca the Younger** (before AD 1–AD 65) was born in Cordoba, Spain, around the end of the first century BC and taken to Rome as a child, where he built up a considerable reputation as a writer. He is not a historian as such but does occasionally preserve useful historical information in his philosophical essays, and alludes often to Caligula. He committed suicide in AD 65, after being implicated in a plot against the emperor Nero. Many of the negative aspects of Caligula, such as his brutality and extravagance, make their first appearance in Seneca, which does not, of course, necessarily mean that Seneca was the source, at least the direct one, of hostile information for later writers like Suetonius or Dio.

It is important to remember that most of what Seneca wrote about Caligula was composed during the reign of his successor, Claudius, who had a vested interest in seeing his ousted predecessor depicted as cruel and despotic, or even mad. It is also important to acknowledge that Seneca was prone to grovelling flattery, happy always to malign a previous ruler to win favour with the current one. Also Seneca's personal experiences under Caligula could have clouded his judgement. Caligula derided Seneca's literary style, and reputedly even thought of executing him (4.66, 5.18).

Philo of Alexandria (*c*.30 BC–AD 45) led a delegation of Alexandrian Jews to Rome near the end of Caligula's reign and there he met the emperor in person. Philo was a prolific writer, and two works, written in Greek, are particularly significant for this reign, the *In Flaccum*, an account of Avilius Flaccus, governor of Egypt when Caligula came to power, and an untitled work conventionally known as the *Legatio* (Embassy). Both are intended to illumine the difficult experiences of the Jews, and Philo naturally strives to describe his own community in the most favourable terms. He stresses their sufferings, for which he assigns responsibility both to Caligula and to the Greek population of Alexandria. In Philo's narrative Caligula is presented as a sinister enemy of the Jews, although there are few concrete or substantiated charges made against him.

The pro-Roman Jewish writer **Josephus** was born in 37/8, shortly after Caligula came to power. His *Jewish War*, an account of the Jewish uprising of AD 66–70, with an extensive introduction to the historical events leading up to the great rebellion, was written first in Aramaic and appeared in a Greek version in AD 75–9. Caligula is mentioned there only occasionally. The *Jewish Antiquities*, apparently written in Greek from the outset, is a broad account of the Jews down to the time of the rebellion, and appeared in AD 93–4. It provides the most detailed narrative of any episode of Caligula's reign, the events leading to the emperor's death, and its aftermath. The account is so detailed that scholars generally assume that Josephus had access to Roman material, but much of his information about Caligula is thought to be based on a richly embroidered and historically imaginative later anonymous *Life of Agrippa*, now lost, of the emperor's close friend, Herod Agrippa, a work that much inflated Agrippa's influence on events in Rome. Although Josephus is a useful source where he deals with exclusively Jewish matters, he often seems confused when he covers more exclusively Roman topics, and the problems are aggravated by the very corrupt state of his manuscripts. Hence his narrative of the assassination is confused and muddled and in places inconsistent, and he does not seem to have properly reconciled his different and sometimes contradictory sources.

For Josephus, Caligula's downfall had a double moral significance, in that it delivered the Jews from their destruction and also provided clear proof that divine justice will punish moral failings. Like Philo, Josephus saw Caligula as the irreconcilable enemy of the Jewish people.

Pliny the Elder (AD 23/4–79) was a young man when Caligula died. He makes a number of references to the emperor but there is no indication that he had ever actually set eyes on him. Pliny was an irremediable collector of facts, and an immensely learned individual; he met his end during the famed eruption of Vesuvius. His great encyclopaedia, the *Naturalis Historia*, was published in thirty-seven books in AD 77, and is a rich source of information on almost every aspect of antiquity, including Caligula, who is referred to throughout in uniformly negative terms, with emphasis on his savagery and mental vagaries. Pliny also wrote a traditional history in thirty-one books, the *Historiae*, now lost but occasionally cited by Tacitus, as well as an account of the German wars, particularly the campaigns of Caligula's grandfather Drusus, and a life of Pomponius Secundus, pardoned in Caligula's general amnesty early in his reign. Suetonius refers to Pliny on the issue of Caligula's birthplace (presumably using one of Pliny's lost works, since the topic does not appear in the *Naturalis Historia*), but any other specific borrowings are speculative.

The pre-eminent chronicler of the Julio-Claudian regime, **Cornelius Tacitus** (AD mid-50s–after 118), offers frustratingly little information on Caligula's reign. His final and most famous work, the *Annals*, was designed to cover events from the succession of Tiberius, AD 14, to the death of Nero in AD 68 (it breaks off in AD 66). But Books 7–10 and the early part of Book 11, that is, from the death of Tiberius to about midway in Claudius' reign, have been lost. Apart from the occasional casual comment, the information that can be drawn from Tacitus is restricted to Caligula's family background and his early years, before his accession, covered in books of the *Annals* that are still extant. It is not Tacitus' supposed impartiality that is missed—his hostility to Caligula is patent from the brief passing comments he makes in related historical contexts. But the loss of that key part of the *Annals* seriously hampers any effort to reconstruct a clear and coherent picture of the reign.

This leaves us with the two surviving major literary sources for the Julio-Claudians. **Suetonius** (AD 70?–130s?) was born around AD 70, most likely in Africa. He occupied several imperial offices under Trajan and Hadrian and was a prolific writer, best known for his *Lives of the Caesars*, Rome's rulers from Julius

Caesar to Domitian (died AD 96). The emperor Commodus reputedly fed a man to wild beasts just for reading Suetonius' *Life of Caligula*, but in Suetonius' defence it has to be said that for a time under Hadrian he had access to important imperial archives and when he conducted his own research he could achieve impressive results. He is often the most convincing of the major literary authorities on specific points of detail. He certainly does not seem to have been in the habit of fabricating material. In his discussion of Caligula's birth, which seems at least in part intended to expose the shortcomings of previous accounts, his version is far more convincing than Tacitus'. At times he can be very much on his guard against the excesses of his sources; he declares that he would find it hard to repeat the stories of Tiberius' sexual perversions when on Capri in the company of Caligula, never mind give them any credence. It does not stop him, however, from going ahead and repeating them anyhow. The passages on sexual oddities and perversions constitute a relatively small portion of the *Lives*, even though to the modern general reader they are the most familiar (and popular) feature of Suetonius' work. But that said they invariably find their place, whether the emperor was one Suetonius despised or admired. We might want to attribute this to some theoretical principle of biography, that a person's sexual behaviour provides an insight into their deepest character, but we cannot discount the simple allure of tittle-tattle, and that Suetonius sensed that humanity finds the sex lives of celebrities wonderfully entertaining.

When Suetonius relies on material provided by others, he is often lacking in mature judgement, and is quite happy to accept whatever has been passed down in the tradition, no matter how implausible, and he was addicted to engaging anecdotes and frivolous gossip, happy to leave it to the reader to decide how much faith to place in them. He can also be quite blatantly inconsistent. Hence, in the *Caligula*, the preliminaries for the campaigns against Britain and Germany in AD 39 are reduced to little more than a farce, while in the *Galba* they involve serious military preparations. He also has a habit of taking what are almost certainly specific, and isolated, incidents and characterizing them as part of the general and consistent conduct of his subject. Nor is there any evidence that he was possessed of a broad sense of history or was interested in the great political questions of the day unless they related directly to the character or personality of his subject.

Another difficulty is that Suetonius wrote biography, rather than history, and treated his material thematically, rather than in chronological order. Apart from providing the family background, education, and early life of the emperor at the beginning of the individual *Life*, and his death and funeral at the end, there is very little effort to follow chronology. In between we have physical attributes, personal oddities, and civil and military activities. Here Suetonius generally arranges his account by topic rather than by chronological sequence. Also, frustratingly, he seems to presume a general familiarity of the reader with the basic course of events. Hence he does not provide a complete and coherent account of Caligula's reign and we cannot rely on him to place the events of the reign in any sort of structured order.

There has been much discussion about whether Suetonius borrowed from Tacitus, or if the relevant books of the *Annals* were even completed and accessible when Suetonius wrote his *Caligula*. Generally Suetonius seems to have gone back to earlier sources rather than deriving his information directly from his celebrated contemporary. That said, he does at times seem to go out of his way to imply that he was the better researcher of the two, as in the debate over the birthplace of Caligula (1.4). Also in his favour, Suetonius is clearly not motivated by the strong hostility towards the imperial system that drives Tacitus. In the *Caligula* he actually assigns some chapters to the positive features of the reign (*Cal.* 13–21), contrasting them with the actions of the monster, to which he dedicates the bulk of the nearly forty remaining chapters.

The other major source for Caligula, **Cassius Dio** (AD 165?–235?), was a Greek-speaking Roman citizen, born in Bithynia in Asia Minor. He held Roman consulships in about AD 205 and in 229. He wrote his history, in Greek, over a period of twenty-two years (ten in accumulating the material, twelve in writing it out), beginning with the early kings and going down to AD 229, in the reign of Severus Alexander (222–35).

Dio primarily accumulates information. While he does seek to show why Roman politics evolved as they did, and to demonstrate that the monarchical system is the superior one—provided always that the ruler is responsible and competent—his historical framework is so extensive that he is hard pressed to develop this theme consistently. Hence he rarely attempts deep analysis and his opinions seem usually to be elicited from the situation at hand. It is, however, fair to say that the general assessment of his abilities as a historian has grown more favourable of late.

Dio almost never reveals his sources (Augustus and Hadrian are the only two authors actually cited), although references to writers like Livy indicate that he presumably made use of them. Also he frequently displays a lack of critical judgement in assessing his material, and seems to make little effort to determine what is reasonable and what is ridiculous, or to eliminate material that is patently biased. He approaches his topics very much from the viewpoint of a senator, which he was, and it is thus hardly surprising that he was not sympathetic towards Caligula.

Because of the loss of the relevant books of Tacitus' *Annals*, Dio can be useful for the reign of Caligula in that unlike Suetonius he arranges his material in a broad chronological sequence, and he offers the only surviving annalistic account (material arranged by year) of Caligula's reign. That said, the annalistic scheme is not adhered to strictly. It has been observed that in some respects Dio exhibits traits of a biographer, and sometimes treats topics by theme, out of their chronological context. In a sense his approach is almost a hybrid of that of Suetonius and Tacitus. Hence Caligula's progress towards divine status is treated as one comprehensive item under AD 40, but some of the details belong without question to the early period of the reign. Also Dio has a tendency to lump together at the end of a given year items that he has not previously covered, as he does with Caligula's marriage to Caesonia in AD 39, possibly a key factor in the conspiracy of that year and whose precise date would be of great value to the historian.

In places there are gaps in the text which have to be filled by epitomes (summaries) made in the Byzantine period. This proves less of a problem for the reign of Caligula than of, say, Nero, but there is a gap in Dio's account after AD 39 and four pages of the manuscript of the events leading to Caligula's death are missing and the narrative proper does not return until Book 60, by which time Claudius has replaced him. For most of AD 40 and early 41 we must rely on the epitomes of Xiphilinus of the eleventh century and of Zonaras of the early twelfth. The epitomators tend often to select rather than summarize, leading at times to the total omission of important sections, such as the absorption into the empire of Mauretania in AD 40, an event preserved only in the Index.

Dio is biased against Caligula, but, like Suetonius, he does not share Tacitus' general hostility towards the imperial system as such. His main deficiency is rather a general lack of historical curiosity. Some events are treated quite differently by Dio and Suetonius. Where they are in agreement, it is broadly felt that Dio did not use Suetonius directly but that they used the same common source.

Coins and Inscriptions

Coins are a valuable tool for the historian. Intended primarily as units of currency, they are a means for governing authorities to broadcast ideas among the populace at large, and to keep selected issues and items in the public eye. There is considerable debate on the degree to which the Roman emperor controlled the images that appear on official coins produced by the imperial mints, but those images would presumably have met with his approval or at the very least not have encountered his active disfavour. Coins that depict the ruler are also useful at the basic level of giving us an idea of what he looked like. There is bound, of course, to be some degree of idealization, but in the case of Roman emperors images produced by the official Roman mint, certainly after the reigns of Augustus and Tiberius, do maintain a high level of realism, with portraits that are often far from flattering. This applies of course only to the official mint, where pieces were struck for wide distribution throughout the empire. There were also numerous provincial and city mints, where, especially at the city level, central control seems to have been non-existent and where the images can be generic and often crude. The denominations of Caligula's official coins were essentially those of his predecessors, but the images were highly innovative, and a number of the coins illustrated in this book broke new boundaries.

Inscriptions are another rich source of information. Unlike coins, they were for the most part one-off affairs, usually, though not always, made in a single copy, and most have been lost. They are found throughout the Roman world, and their content, created at the local level, may not conform to the central Roman practice. Errors in titles and nomenclature are not uncommon, as are mistakes in dates. Relatively few inscriptions have survived for Caligula's reign, but two groups are particularly useful. The Fasti were essentially calendars of official events, and as such contain a wide range of information about important state occasions, including the names of presiding magistrates. The Fasti for the city of Ostia have survived, and albeit brief they contain much valuable information for AD 37 and 38 (Figure 1). Even more significant for this period is the record of the Arval brothers. The centre of this cult was located some four miles west of Rome at the shrine of Dea Dia, although occasionally the rites were performed in Rome proper. The Arvals consisted of a college of the emperor and twelve additional members. They recorded their proceedings on stone, and this record has survived for the period from 21 BC to AD 304, often in a very fragmentary state. The imperial family figures largely in their rituals, and significant anniversaries like birthdays are noted. The Arval record often provides such basic information as whether the emperor was in Rome at a particular point, or whether a local political figure was still in favour.

The Problem

What are the consequences of all the above observations? To illustrate the difficulties that can arise when we try to reconstruct events from purely literary sources we can usefully note, as one of many possible examples, the accounts of Caligula's reforms in Africa, a public/senatorial province that housed a legion, the command of which was moved by Caligula from the control of the senate. Tacitus provides the name of the last senatorial commander, Marcus Silanus, and offers a plausible reason for his candidacy (7.4). But Dio suggests a different individual, and his explanation is equally plausible, Lucius Piso (7.5). The cases to be made for both are equally strong, and frustratingly the truth evades us, as it often does throughout Caligula's reign.

When the literary sources can be enhanced by epigraphic and/or numismatic material the situation becomes more complex but usually much more satisfactory. Take the familiar crux of Caligula's attitude towards one of his ancestors. Marcus Vipsanius Agrippa was a loyal though humbly born lieutenant of Augustus, who married the emperor's daughter Julia, and produced, among other offspring, Agrippina the Elder, mother of Caligula. Agrippa never succeeded in escaping

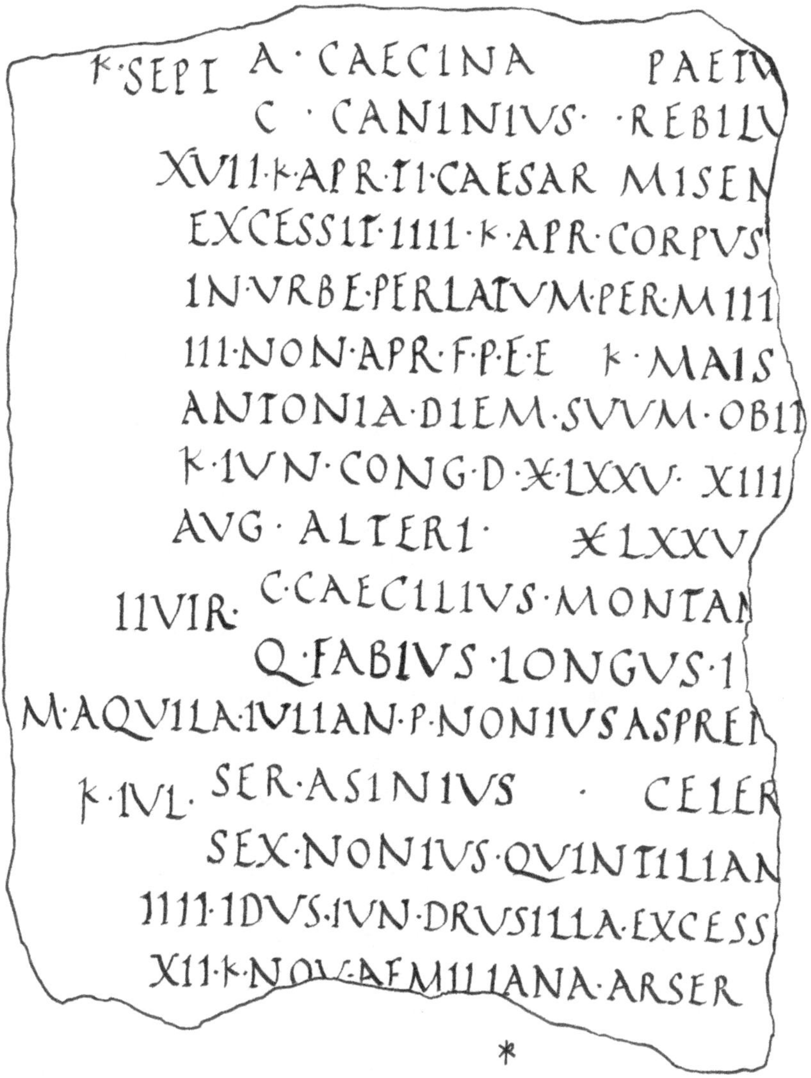

K·SEPT A·CAECINA   PAETV
        C · CANINIVS· ·REBILV
    XVII·K·APR·TI·CAESAR MISEN
    EXCESSIT·IIII·K·APR·CORPVS
    IN·VRBE·PERLATVM·PER·M III
    III·NON·APR·F·P·E·E   K·MAIS
    ANTONIA·DIEM·SVVM·OBII
    K·IVN·CONG·D·X·LXXV· XIII
    AVG· ALTERI·   X·LXXV
    IIVIR· C·CAECILIVS·MONTAN
         Q·FABIVS·LONGVS·I
    M·AQVILA·IVLIAN·P·NONIVS ASPREN
    K·IVL· SER·ASINIVS   · CELER
        SEX·NONIVS·QVINTILIAN
    IIII·IDVS·IVN·DRVSILLA·EXCESS
    XII·K·NOV·AEMILIANA·ARSER

                    *

Figure 1 Fasti of Ostia for years AD 37 and 38. Kornelia Roth.

from the shadow of his humble family background, and was not generally accepted by elite Romans, even after a distinguished career—members of prominent families even declined to attend the festivals that followed his funeral.[1] Suetonius reports that Caligula shared this aversion and declined to be considered

---

[1] Vell. Pat. 2.96.1, 129.2; Tac. *Ann.* 1.3.1; Dio 54.29.6.

Agrippa's grandson, even to the extent of claiming that his mother was not Agrippa's daughter but the result of an incestuous affair between Augustus and his daughter Julia (3.37). So Suetonius. But when we consider another piece of literary evidence, the *Legatio* of Philo, we find there a supposed letter from the Jewish friend of Caligula, Herod Agrippa (unrelated to Marcus, of course), to Caligula about how he ought to respect the sanctity of the Temple of Jerusalem. He cites two precedents, Augustus and Marcus Agrippa, and significantly he calls Agrippa Caligula's *pappos* (grandfather) (3.38). Of course Philo is not always reliable on details, and we cannot be sure if this letter was quoted accurately or even if it actually existed, but Philo had spent considerable time in Rome and had met the emperor. As an ambassador he would surely have made himself familiar with any such prejudices of Caligula. The suspicions aroused by Philo that Suetonius is misleading on this point are fortified by the numismatic and epigraphic evidence. The most common coin of Caligula's reign, the "Agrippa As," may well have been minted by other emperors too, but it was certainly issued by Caligula and clearly honours Agrippa unreservedly (3.39). Also the sestertius issued to commemorate Caligula's mother Agrippina (3.30) identifies her unequivocally as the daughter of Marcus. Epigraphic evidence bears this out. The inscription that accompanied the urn containing Agrippina's ashes, almost certainly in the mausoleum of Augustus, carries the very same nomenclature, "daughter of Marcus Agrippa." Inscriptions from two provincial cities, Aphrodisias in Asia and Mytilene in Achaea (Greece), follow the same pattern.[2] Thus the numismatic and epigraphic evidence, reinforced by Philo, seems to indicate overwhelmingly that Marcus Agrippa was acknowledged, and even honoured, by Caligula as his grandfather. Does this mean that Suetonius' testimony is to be rejected? The situation is more subtle. It is very possible that Caligula made some sort of passing witticism about his origins, and that this involved some off-colour fantasy about Augustus' relationship with his daughter and a facetious comment at Agrippa's expense. That much can perhaps be assumed. Where Suetonius might be misleading us is in his prefatory comment, based possibly on this single witticism, that as a *general and established part* of his character and personality Caligula refused to acknowledge his relationship to Agrippa. The point about Caligula objecting to Agrippa being included among the Caesars may also simply reflect Caligula's academic pedantry, since Agrippa, despite his marriage to Julia, was never adopted into the Julian line. This is an excellent example of the type of challenge consistently presented by the sources for Caligula.

---

[2] Aphrodisias *AE* 1980.874; Mytilene *IGR* 4.79–80.

1
Family and Childhood

Romans believed that ancestry played a significant role in the formation of a person's character. Certainly, in Caligula's case, his family background was a key factor in marking him out as the prime candidate to succeed Tiberius in AD 37. His paternal grandfather, Drusus, son of Augustus' wife Livia, through her previous husband, and the brother of the future emperor Tiberius, gained a formidable reputation as a military commander in Germany, taking Roman arms as far as the Elbe. Before his death in 9 BC this Drusus had married Antonia, the much-admired daughter of Mark Antony. Three of their children survived infancy: (a) the future emperor Claudius, (b) a daughter Livilla, and (c), most significantly for the present context, Caligula's father, Germanicus (born in 15 or 16 BC).

Little is known of Germanicus' early life, but in AD 4, just before Tiberius was adopted as son and, by implication, successor by a reputedly reluctant Augustus, Tiberius was himself obliged to adopt Germanicus. It seems likely that Augustus intended that the succession would fall in due time to Germanicus, and as further evidence of this broad objective Germanicus had been required, before his adoption, to marry Agrippina (the Elder), the daughter of Julia (Augustus' daughter) and of Augustus' loyal lieutenant Marcus Agrippa. Agrippina would no doubt have had considerable influence on her son Caligula's formative years. She was proudly conscious of her distinguished lineage and unabashedly ambitious, not directly for herself—women could exercise influence but not formal power in the Roman political system—but on behalf of her husband, then, after his death in AD 18, of her three surviving sons, Caligula and two others, named, confusingly for us, Nero (to be distinguished from his nephew, the later emperor) and Drusus (to be distinguished both from his grandfather and from Tiberius' son). She also had three daughters, one of whom, to sustain the confusion, was the like-named Agrippina (the Younger), who would become the mother of the emperor Nero.

In AD 11, the year before the birth of his youngest son, Caligula, Germanicus replaced his uncle Tiberius as military commander of the campaigns against Germany. As depicted by the sources, Germanicus and Caligula represent two different sides of the coin. Whereas Caligula receives an almost uniformly negative press, the same sources generally do their best to inflate Germanicus' military talents, as well as his personal qualities of tact and diplomacy. The latter qualities may have been genuine, although an early death largely precluded the opportunity for any more unattractive aspects of his temperament to show. But in the sphere of competence as a military commander it is not too difficult to read between the

The Emperor Caligula in the Ancient Sources. Anthony A. Barrett and J. C. Yardley, Oxford University Press.
© Anthony A. Barrett and J. C. Yardley 2023. DOI: 10.1093/oso/9780198854562.003.0002

lines of his admirer Tacitus, whose reservations about Germanicus' competence in the field peep through.

The death of Augustus in AD 14 was the catalyst for serious mutinies among the legions of the Rhine and in Pannonia. Tiberius' son, Drusus, was despatched to deal with the latter and brought things under control with commendable efficiency. Germanicus proved far less adept at handling the disturbances among the German legions, where he seemed if anything weak and indecisive and where matters got seriously out of hand. He combined this diffidence with rash and irresponsible overconfidence after the mutinies, when he committed troops to campaigns in Germany that came very close to disaster. Tiberius was obliged to withdraw him, probably in late 16, almost certainly because he felt that Germanicus' aggressive strategy was dangerous, rather than, as the sources insist, because he was jealous of his military successes.

Father: Germanicus

1.1 Suet. *Cal.* 1.1 Germanicus, the father of Gaius Caesar,[1] was the son of Drusus and the younger Antonia[2] and was adopted by his paternal uncle Tiberius. After holding the quaestorship five years before the statutory age,[3] he advanced from there immediately to a consulship and was assigned to the army in Germany.[4] There, after the announcement of Augustus' death,[5] all the legions,[6] after persistently refusing to accept Tiberius as emperor, offered Germanicus supreme command of the state, but he restrained them, though whether that was more by appealing to their loyalty or by firmness is uncertain;[7] and later he defeated the enemy and celebrated a Triumph.

---

[1] Suetonius begins the *Life of Caligula* with the words *Germanicus, C. Caesaris pater* (Germanicus, Gaius Caesar's father), juxtaposing the names of the two, as if to emphasize the contrast between them and to stress the paradox that a monster like Caligula could be the son of such a great man.

[2] The younger of the two Antonias, borne by Octavia, the sister of Augustus, to Mark Antony. Antonia Minor's fame eclipsed that of her older sister Antonia (Major), who married Lucius Domitius Ahenborbarbus and thereby became grandmother of the future emperor Nero.

[3] Germanicus held the quaestorship in AD 7 (Dio 55.31.1).

[4] Germanicus apparently skipped the praetorship and proceeded directly to the consulship, which he held in AD 12 (Dio 56.26.1). Suetonius omits Germanicus' previous service, perhaps because he was under the command of Tiberius, operating both in Pannonia and in Germany. Strictly speaking Germanicus had later been appointed to govern the "Three Gauls," Aquitania, Belgica, and Lugdunensis. The office embraced overall command over the eight legions stationed in the two military zones on the Rhine frontier, Upper and Lower Germany.

[5] Augustus died on August 19, AD 14 (*EJ* p. 50; Suet. *Aug.* 100.1).

[6] Suetonius clearly overstates the case here. At most it was the four legions of Lower Germany who wanted to shift their allegiance to Germanicus, with the grievances largely limited to Legions I and XX, according to Tacitus, and even at that involving only certain elements within the legions (Tac. *Ann.* 1.35). There is no claim elsewhere that there was any movement for Germanicus in Upper Germany.

[7] Suetonius' delicate language reflects the awkward tension between Germanicus' general image and his incompetence in handling the mutinies.

1.2 Suet. *Cal.* 3.1 It is generally accepted that Germanicus had all the fine physical and intellectual qualities to a degree unparalleled by any other man: superlative looks and strength; outstanding talent in the oratory and learning of both cultures;[8] unprecedented graciousness; and an amazing and successful proclivity for winning people's regard and earning affection. The skinniness of his legs did not match the rest of his physique, but those also gradually filled out with persistent horse riding and eating.[9]

1.3 Suet. *Cal.* 4.1 From these virtues Germanicus won a rich bounty, the approval and affection that he received from his kin being such that after much hesitation Augustus (for I omit other relatives) passed him on to Tiberius for adoption, earmarking him as his successor.[10] So popular was he with the masses that, according to many authors, when he reached or left a place he sometimes faced mortal danger from crowds rushing to meet him or bid him farewell; and when he was returning from Germany after suppressing the mutiny there, all the praetorian cohorts actually went out to meet him despite orders that only two should go, and all the people of Rome, whatever their sex, age, or class, flooded out as far as the twentieth milestone.[11]

Birth of Caligula

Suetonius' account of the birth of Caligula is in its own way a very remarkable document. The date of the birth, August 31, AD 12, is undisputed, but there was evidently a major difference of opinion among ancient authorities about the place,

---

[8] Germanicus, like other members of the imperial family, was an accomplished *litterateur*, writing, as Suetonius observes, in both Latin and Greek. He composed Greek comedies (Suet. *Claud.* 11.2), and his translation into Latin of the Greek astronomical work, the *Phaenomena* of Aratus, has possibly survived (authorship of the extant text is disputed)—and he even wrote an epigram marking the funeral of Augustus' horse. He was admired by the poet Ovid (*Fast.* 1.1; *Pont.* 2.5.41–76, 4.8.65–6); admittedly in his lonely exile Ovid had a vested interest in flattering important relatives of the emperor. After Germanicus' death, Tiberius personally dedicated an image of him among those of the great orators that adorned the library attached to the Temple of Apollo on the Palatine (Tac. *Ann.* 2.83.3). His skill in oratory was apparently inherited by Caligula (see 5.14,16), but it is striking that Caligula's literary achievements are simply recorded, without attracting the breathless admiration garnered by his father's.

[9] Suetonius made a show of striking some sort of balance by mentioning negative physical characteristics. He does the same with the short-lived emperor Titus, son of Vespasian, commenting, among his laudatory remarks, that Titus was short and had a protruding belly (Suet. *Tit.* 3.1). In Germanicus' case even this modest shortcoming is turned into something positive.

[10] Tiberius was adopted on June 26, AD 4, as Augustus' son, and received tribunician *potestas*. Before the adoption he had been obliged to adopt Germanicus. Interestingly, here Suetonius is keen to boost the attractiveness of Germanicus and to stress Augustus' reluctance to see power go to Tiberius. But in the biography of Tiberius (Suet. *Tib.* 21), Augustus is positive about Tiberius' fitness for the succession.

[11] It seems to have been regular practice that three Praetorian cohorts could be assigned to special duties within the imperial family. Two would later accompany Germanicus' ashes through Italy to Rome (Tac. *Ann.* 3.2.1). Tacitus makes no mention of the visit and the warm welcome described here. We in fact have no other evidence that Germanicus left Germany until he was in Rome to celebrate his Triumph in AD 17.

and Suetonius' discussion of this problem is the most thorough treatment of conflicting historical theories known in any Roman writer. Roman texts tend to identify specific sources rarely. Here Suetonius provides the uncommon spectacle of an authority enumerating in detail the shortcomings of both named and unnamed rivals.

Seasoned literary magician that he is, Suetonius waits until well into his performance to pull out the conclusive piece of evidence, the actual record of the birth, from his scholarly hat. His case is persuasive, and one might ask why he should feel the need to defend his conclusion with such vigour. It all smacks of academic gamesmanship and a deliberate display of superior research. It is striking that both Tacitus and Seneca make what Suetonius characterizes as the erroneous claim that Caligula was born in a legionary camp, but neither is identified here by name. Could it be that Suetonius is treating them with silent contempt? Possibly, but it should be noted that in fact nowhere in any of his *Lives* does Suetonius explicitly mention Tacitus by name.

1.4 Suet. *Cal.* 8.1 Gaius Caesar was born on August 31st in the year when his father and Gaius Fonteius were consuls.[12] Where he was born the various accounts leave uncertain. Gnaeus Lentulus Gaetulicus writes of him as born at Tibur, but Pliny the Elder has him among the Treveri in the village of Ambitarvium-above-Confluentes; and he further adds as evidence that altars are to be seen there inscribed "For Agrippina's delivery."[13] Verses circulated early in his reign suggest his life began in the legionary winter quarters:

> In the camp born, among his father's weapons raised,
> Already it was an omen of a forthcoming ruler[14]

2 I find his birthplace in the records as Antium.[15] Gaetulicus is refuted by Pliny, who says that he lied to flatter him (sc. Caligula), even using the city sacred to

---

[12] Caligula's birthdate, on August 31, AD 12 (the year of his father's consulship), is confirmed by Dio 59.6.1, who provides his exact age at accession, and by two surviving official calendars preserved in inscriptions (Fasti Vallenses and Fasti Pighiani).

[13] Gaetulicus served as military commander of Upper Germany under Tiberius and, until 39, under Caligula. He was removed from office and executed for conspiracy when Caligula visited Germany in late AD 39 (4.53, 54); Gaetulicus' flattering words about the emperor's birthplace may have been part of a welcoming address delivered on the latter's arrival in that year. Gaetulicus had a reputation as a poet (Pliny *Ep.* 5.3.5; Mart. *Praef.* 1.12; Sid. Ap. *Carm.* 9.259; *Ep.* 2.10.6); his forte seems to have been erotica. Three lines of his are preserved by the late grammarian Probus (on *Georg.* 1.227), referring to a constellation that can be seen in the north, where Probus comments that Gaetulicus is referring to Britain. This might have been in a flattering composition delivered before Caligula's projected invasion in AD 39, containing some reference to the emperor's birthplace.

The Treveri inhabited the area around the lower Moselle; their tribal centre was Trier. Ambitarvium (or Ambitarvius) cannot be identified, although it clearly stood north of where the Moselle joins the Rhine, the "Confluence," modern Coblenz.

[14] Seneca (1.5) and Tacitus (1.6) claim that Caligula was born in the camp.

[15] Suetonius presumably found his evidence in the *Acta Diurna*, the gazetteer of important public events, or possibly in the registry of births preserved in the treasury (the *Aerarium Saturni*). As noted in

Hercules[16] to promote the arrogant young ruler's reputation, and that he was all the more outrageous in his lying because about a year earlier a son had been born to Germanicus at Tibur (and of the young boy's lovable nature and premature death I have written earlier[17]). Pliny is wrong in his chronology. **3** For historians of Augustus agree that Gaius was already born when Germanicus was sent to Gaul at the end of his consulship.[18] Nor can Pliny's view find any support from an altar inscription, since Agrippina twice gave birth to daughters in that region, and any birth at all, whatever the child's sex, is called *puerperium* because older generations would always call girls *puerae*, just as they called boys *puelli*.[19] **4** There also survives a letter of Augustus about this Gaius written to his granddaughter Agrippina a few months before he died (for there was no other child of similar name still alive at the time). It reads: "Regarding the boy Gaius, I arranged yesterday that, if the gods so will, Talarius and Asillius should bring him on the 15th day before the Kalends of June.[20] I am also sending with him one of my slaves, a doctor whom I have in a letter told Germanicus to keep if he wishes. Farewell, dear Agrippina, and be sure you reach your Germanicus in good health."

5 I think it perfectly clear that Gaius could not have been born in some place to which he was first taken from Rome when he was almost two years old.[21] Confidence in the verses is also undermined by these same facts, all the more so by their having no author. One must therefore follow the only remaining possibility, namely, the public record, especially since Gaius always set Antium above all other areas and resorts as though it were his native soil, and it is even on record that, weary of the city, he had intended to transfer there his imperial seat and residence.[22]

the Introduction, Suetonius could make use of the imperial archives, and was adept at this type of research.

Antium (modern Anzio), south of Rome, was an ancient coastal colony, a favourite resort of the Julio-Claudian family. It was the birthplace not only, apparently, of Caligula, but also of both Nero and Nero's daughter, Claudia Augusta. There are traces there of an imperial villa with terraces, a good candidate for the precise location of Caligula's birth.

[16] Tibur (Tivoli), located to the northeast of Rome, was particularly associated with the worship of Hercules ("Herculaean Tibur" in Mart. 4.62.1 and Prop. 2.32.5).

[17] Suet. *Cal.* 7 reports that the child died in infancy; he had been the favourite of Augustus, who kept his statue in his room and kissed it each time he entered.

[18] Suetonius does not provide the names of the historians, which is in fact typical ancient historical practice.

[19] The information is not found in the *Historia Naturalis* and presumably was covered in Pliny's work on the German wars. In Pliny's defence we cannot be sure that he did rest his case on the meaning of *puerperium*—given his prodigious range of learning we would expect him to know what the word meant.

[20] May 18 (AD 14).

[21] An excellent demonstration of Suetonius' archival research. The fact that Caligula was later sent out to join his father does strengthen the case against birth in Germany, but it is by no means conclusive, since he could have been sent to Rome shortly after his birth.

[22] Suetonius might have been wiser to close his case with the archival evidence. Caligula's apparent affection for Antium proves little and the story of his plans for a new seat of empire was told also about Alexandria (Suet. *Cal.* 49.2). There is no other evidence that Caligula was devoted to Antium. Apart

1.5 (see also 5.11) Sen. Cons. 18.4 Since he was born in the camp and was the "baby" of the legion, that (sc. Caligula) was what he was usually called.

1.6 (see also 1.9) Tac. Ann. 1.41.3 ... the infant, born in the camp and brought up in the legions' barracks, the boy to whom they gave the soldiers' nickname "Caligula" ...

1.7 (see also 1.11) Suet. Cal. 9.1 The cognomen Caligula he inherited from the military camp because he was raised among the troops wearing the clothes of the common soldier.

1.8 (see also 1.12) Dio 57.5.6 The son they used to call Caligula because he had for the most part been brought up in military camps and wore soldier's boots rather than city shoes.[23]

Germanicus and the Mutinies

The death of Augustus was the catalyst for serious mutinies among the legions of the Rhine and in Pannonia. During the very thick of the disturbances, Caligula, just under two years old, was staying with his mother in the settlement of the Ubii (Ara Ubiorum) on the Rhine (the later site of Cologne). Agrippina was pregnant, and as the unrest among the troops grew more serious Germanicus decided to move his family to the protection of a friendly local tribe, the Treveri. We are given dramatic accounts of Agrippina clasping Caligula close to her as she left, accompanied by the wives of Germanicus' officials. At this juncture the literary authorities provide different versions of events. In Dio's account (1.12) the soldiers seize Agrippina and Caligula. When they discover that she is pregnant, they release her, but at first refuse to give up the child. They come to recognize that their holding him hostage will achieve nothing and they release him too, which defuses the situation and marks the first stage in the gradual ending of the mutiny. Suetonius hints at this same version of events much later, reporting that at the close of his German campaigns in AD 40 Caligula intended to punish his own soldiers because they had seized him during the mutiny.[24] In Tacitus' version (1.9), supported by Suetonius in his account of these specific events (1.11), the troops are ashamed that a fine lady like Agrippina should feel she had no option but to take her son, the favourite of the soldiers, to seek asylum among the Treveri.

---

from being married there (presumably Tiberius' decision) he is recorded as visiting the town only once, just before the end of his life, when a small fish, the *echineis*, attached itself to his ship's rudder and brought it to a halt on the way there. This was considered a bad omen (Plin. *NH* 32.4).

[23] Dio is much more cautious than Seneca and Tacitus, claiming only that Caligula had been *raised* in the camp, and leaving open the question of where he in fact was born.

[24] Suet. *Cal.* 48.1.

Tacitus has them see the error of their ways and regret their mutiny. Suetonius adds in this context that what finally persuaded them to give up their rebellion was the spectacle of little Caligula. It may be that these accounts originate from a different source than the one behind Dio's humiliating version (echoed in Suetonius' alternative account), although Dio's may be the true one while Tacitus' could represent a pro-Germanicus recasting of events, perhaps circulated later by Agrippina. But there are also several common elements in all three authorities and the differences may spring from the differing prejudices of the authors. In any case the action apparently took the wind out of the mutineers' sails; from that point resistance all but collapsed and authority was gradually restored. Germanicus now belatedly took decisive action and eventually managed to regain control.

1.9 Tac. *Ann.* 1.40.1 In this alarming situation there was general criticism of Germanicus for not proceeding to the upper army, where obedience and assistance against the rebels could be found. Enough and more than enough damage had been done, it was thought, by granting discharge and by cash payments, and by easygoing policies.[25] **2** Even if he thought little of his own safety, why keep his little son and why keep his pregnant wife amid madmen who violated all the laws of humanity?[26] Those at least he should send back to the boy's grandfather and the state.[27] Germanicus vacillated for a long time. His wife rejected the idea: she was descended from the deified Augustus, she said, and was not his inferior in facing danger, but with copious tears Germanicus finally embraced his wife's womb and the son they shared and made her leave.

A pitiful column of women began moving out, the commander's wife a refugee clasping to her breast her tiny son, and around her uttering cries of grief were wives of Germanicus' staff-members who were being dragged along with her. And those left behind were no less despondent.

41.1 Rather than a picture of a successful Caesar in his own camp, it was what might be seen in a captured city; and the groaning and lamentation caught the soldiers' ears and eyes. They came from their tents. What was this weeping, they asked themselves, what was this sad procession? These were women of distinction, with no centurion, no common soldier to guard them, and there was nothing appropriate to a commander's wife, no sign of her usual retinue—they were going to the Treveri, under the protection of foreigners!

---

[25] Germanicus made a number of concessions to the mutineers. They were voided by Tiberius (Tac. *Ann.* 1.78.2; Dio 57.6.5).

[26] None of the birthdates of Agrippina's surviving children fits into this date sequence, and it seems that she lost the child.

[27] The grandfather is of course Tiberius, by virtue of his adoption of Germanicus.

2 Shame and compassion followed, and recollections of Agrippina's father Agrippa, and Augustus her grandfather; they thought of her father-in-law Drusus, of the woman herself and her outstanding fertility and renowned chastity;[28] they thought of the infant, born in the camp and brought up in the legionary barracks, the boy to whom they gave the soldiers' nickname "Caligula," because to win the support of the ordinary soldiers he was usually shod with this sort of footwear.[29] But nothing affected them as much as their envy of the Treviri: they appealed, blocked the way, asked them to come back and stay, some standing in Agrippina's way, but most going back to Germanicus. And he, smarting with hurt and anger that was still fresh, spoke as follows to the men around him...

[42–3 Germanicus' appeal to the troops]

44 This turned the men to entreaty, and admitting the truth of his reproaches they begged him to punish the truly guilty, to pardon those who had made a mistake, and to lead them against the enemy; his wife should be called back, they said, and the legions' foster child should return to them and not be surrendered to the Gauls as a hostage.

1.10 (see also 1.13) Tac. Ann. 1.69.4 Agrippina already had greater influence with the armies than the legates and generals, and it was by a woman that a mutiny which the emperor's name could not end had been suppressed.

1.11 Suet. Cal. 9 The cognomen Caligula he acquired from the military camp because he was raised among the troops in the clothing of a common soldier. How much affection and good will he further garnered through being brought up in an environment providing this sort of upbringing is best seen from the fact that, when the men were mutinous after Augustus' death, and, at the point of frenzy, it was clearly he who calmed them, merely by appearing before them. For they did not halt until they realized that it was because of the danger posed by their mutiny that he was being taken away and entrusted to the closest town; only then, overcome with regret, did they block and hold back the carriage and beg pardon for the disgrace that would come to them.

1.12 Dio 57.5.6 They almost murdered some of the legates and they put pressure on Germanicus to the point of seizing his wife Agrippina, daughter of Agrippa and Augustus' daughter Julia, and their son when both were being

---

[28] Agrippina had nine children, of whom six survived infancy. No hint of sexual scandal ever attached itself to her name. Drusus fought a series of distinguished campaigns in Germany and his name was held in high honour.

[29] Caligula's nickname "little boot" is derived from the diminutive of the distinctive leather half-boots (caligae) worn by Roman legionaries.

sent away by Germanicus. The son they used to call Caligula because he had been mostly raised in military camps and wore soldier's boots rather than city shoes. 7 Agrippina, who was pregnant, they released after an appeal from Germanicus, but they held on to Gaius. But as time went on and they were getting nowhere, they settled down on this occasion, too; and they experienced such a change of feeling that they themselves readily arrested the most aggressive among them. Some they killed, and the rest they brought together before their assembled multitude and, following the majority decision, either cut their throats or let them go.

Mother: Agrippina

Germanicus seems to have determined that the soldiers' aggressive energies might best be diverted to military activity. A limited foray into German territory was conducted later in AD 14, with some success. In the following year he embarked on a more ambitious project, of emulating the campaigns of his father Drusus with an advance to the river Elbe. He was initially successful, and in the Teutoburg forest carried out ceremonies in honour of those who had died there in AD 9, when Rome suffered one of her greatest ever military disasters with the loss of three legions under the command of Quinctilius Varus. But Germanicus then made the mistake of advancing too far, and had difficulty extricating himself. His troops retreated and poured over the river at Vetera, where they were greeted by the almost certainly pregnant Agrippina, who had reputedly intervened to maintain the bridge and to hand out supplies to soldiers as they returned. Tacitus' inconsistency should be noted here. He usually takes a dim view of women who involve themselves in military affairs—Plancina, the wife of Calpurnius Piso, Germanicus' rival in Syria, for instance, is scathingly rebuked for participating in cavalry exercises and infantry parades.[30] By contrast Tacitus chooses to find such conduct by Agrippina admirable, and puts any criticism of her in the mouth of Tiberius, egged on by the Praetorian prefect Sejanus (on whom, see Chapter 2).

Germanicus was a tactful and diplomatic individual, so we are led to believe, and had circumstances been different he might have inculcated these social skills into his son. But he died when Caligula was only seven and his influence was probably minimal. Caligula was looked after by his mother until he was fifteen and her impact on her son's personality would have been much greater. This description of Agrippina's stubbornness at the Rhine crossing gives us some insight into the role model she would have provided Caligula.

[30] Tac. *Ann.* 2.55.6.

1.13 Tac. *Ann.* 1.69.1 A rumour had meanwhile spread of the army being cut off and Gaul being attacked by a bellicose German column heading for Gaul; and had Agrippina not prevented a bridge over the Rhine from being demolished there were men who were ready from fear to commit such an outrage. But the immensely courageous woman took on a leader's role throughout that time and dispensed clothing or dressings to all the needy or wounded among the soldiers.[31] **2** Gaius Plinius, author of *The German Wars*, records that Agrippina stood at one end of the bridge praising and thanking the returning legions.[32] **3** That deeply impressed Tiberius: this solicitude of hers was no ordinary thing, and it was not against foreigners that support from the soldiers was being sought! **4** Commanders were left with nothing to do, he mused, when a woman inspected maniples, appeared before the standards, tried distributing largesse— as if she were not sufficiently courting popularity by carrying her son around dressed as a common soldier and wanting him called "Caesar Caligula"![33] And she already had greater influence with the armies than did the legates and generals; and it was by her, a woman, that a mutiny which the emperor's name could not end had been suppressed. **5** Such thoughts were inflamed and aggravated by Sejanus who, well acquainted with Tiberius' character, was sowing seeds of hatred for later use, hatred the man would now hide and bring out when it matured.[34]

Germanicus' Recall and Triumph

Germanicus had campaigned in Germany between AD 14 and 16 with mixed military results, including a withdrawal of troops by sea from the mouth of the Ems that ended in disaster. Despite Tacitus' suggestion (1.14) that the war in Germany was all but won, Tiberius clearly felt serious qualms about further

---

[31] If the commonly accepted date for the birth of Agrippina the Younger (mother of Nero), November 6, AD 15, is correct, Agrippina the Elder would have been pregnant at the time of the incident at the bridge.

[32] A relatively uncommon instance of Tacitus' citing his source by name.

[33] The general complaints of Tiberius are echoed later when Aulus Caecina Severus, in a famous debate about the proconsulship of Africa in AD 21 (Tac. *Ann.* 3.32–5), spoke disdainfully in the Roman senate about the behaviour of the wives of Roman governors who accompanied their husbands to their provinces. It is perhaps no coincidence that the troops apparently rescued by Agrippina's actions at the bridge were under the immediate command of that very same Caecina!

Caligula's name at birth would have been Gaius Julius Caesar Germanicus (the "Julius" is in fact never attested). Tiberius might have taken offence at his being acclaimed by the soldiers as "Caesar," with its imperial associations when used in an acclamation, rather than "Gaius." The "Caligula" element seems harmless enough, and Caligula even supposedly found it demeaning (5.9), but it does have military connotations.

[34] The general theme of the *Annals* after the death of Germanicus is the hostility of Sejanus towards Agrippina and her sons, with the possible exception at the outset of Caligula, perhaps too young to be seen as an obstacle to Sejanus' ambitions.

military adventures. Germanicus' recall from Germany was arranged in such a way that there was no loss of face. He was granted a Triumph in AD 17 for military actions on the Rhine frontier that had been less than stellar, possibly, in Tiberius' judgement, risky. As a passing detail Tacitus mentions that Germanicus was accompanied in the procession of the Triumph by his five children. This enables us to place Caligula squarely on the scene (with his brothers, Nero and Drusus, and two older sisters, Agrippina and Drusilla, Livilla being as yet unborn). He would have been close to five years old and just beginning to have conscious memories of events. Thus one of the earliest of those memories would have been of him progressing through Rome, surrounded by the great mass of adulating crowds and standing at the centre of attention. This can only have served to reinforce his later narcissistic sense of the world.

1.14 Tac. *Ann.* 2.26 There was no doubt that the enemy was wavering and considering plans to sue for peace, and that with another campaign the following summer the war could be ended.[35] But in a flurry of letters Tiberius kept advising him to return for the Triumph that had been decreed for him—there had been enough successes, enough misfortune. His battles had been great victories, he said, but he should also bear in mind losses brought on by the winds and waves—losses which, while no fault of the leader, were nevertheless heavy and serious. He himself had been sent into Germany nine times by the deified Augustus, he added, and had achieved more by diplomacy than force.

1.15 Dio 57.6.2 So while Germanicus could actually have gained the supreme power (for he clearly had the support of all the Romans and their subjects), he demurred. Tiberius praised him for this and sent both him and Agrippina many agreeable messages, but he was not in fact pleased with his conduct and feared him all the more for having the attachment of the troops. **3** For because of his own proclivity for saying one thing and doing another he surmised that this was not really how Germanicus felt, and he was suspicious of him and suspicious of his wife, too, for she had a will that matched the importance of her ancestry.[36]

1.16 Tac. *Ann.* 2.41.2 In the consulship of Gaius Caelius and Lucius Pomponius on the 26th of May, Germanicus Caesar celebrated a Triumph over the Cherusci, Chatti, Angrivarii, and all other tribes as far as the Elbe. Spoils, prisoners, and representations of mountains, rivers, and battles were in the procession; and because Germanicus had been forbidden to finish off the war it was deemed finished. For the onlookers the spectacle was enhanced by

---

[35] Tacitus describes the situation after the campaigning season in AD 16, and anticipates that Germanicus' subjugation of Germany could be achieved with only one more campaign, in AD 17.
[36] Dio here stresses the image of Tiberius the hypocrite.

Germanicus' handsome appearance and the chariot with its cargo of five children.[37] But there was also subliminal apprehension, when they remembered that the favour of the crowd had not been to his father Drusus' advantage, that his uncle Marcellus had been swept away in his youth despite the ardent support for him among the common people, and that the Roman people's love affairs were short-lived and ill-starred.[38]

Germanicus' Eastern Commission

Germanicus was transferred to a sensitive diplomatic mission in the east, where a number of problems had arisen that called for diplomatic, rather than military, talent, in particular the need to reach a settlement with Parthia over the disputed kingdom of Armenia (see Chapter 7). The challenge was ideally suited to Germanicus' talents. After celebrating his Triumph in Rome he set out for Syria with his wife and the young Caligula. The journey was a huge public relations success, and Germanicus was warmly welcomed throughout the eastern provinces. In early AD 18 Agrippina gave birth to her third daughter, Livilla, on the island of Lesbos, and probably remained there while her husband made a visit to northwest Asia Minor. At some point they joined up together and made their way to Rhodes, where they encountered Gnaeus Calpurnius Piso, governor of Syria, who would in short order become Germanicus' *bête noire*.

We might have expected Germanicus to leave his children in Rome. But in describing the return of Agrippina to Rome in early AD 30 Tacitus says that she was accompanied by *two* children, one of whom must be Livilla, born on the journey out (2.1). We have only a single literary indication of the identity of the other child, when Suetonius says in a terse statement that Caligula accompanied his father to Syria (1.17). Why Caligula alone should have taken on the journey is not made clear but we have striking confirmation of Suetonius' notice in the form of an inscription from Assos, a prosperous city located on the northwest coast of Asia Minor in the Roman province of Asia, particularly associated with Aristotle. Some years later, in AD 37, Assos sent an embassy to Caligula to congratulate him on becoming emperor, and the decree that they issued has survived in this inscription. It is dated precisely by the convention of the consular year, and the consuls named are the two who held office when Caligula succeeded in 37; it must therefore belong to the period before they left office, namely before July 1 of that year, which is in complete harmony with the contents. The

---

[37] The casual reference to five children is what enables us to place Caligula at the event.
[38] Drusus the Elder was twenty-eight years old when he was crushed by his horse in Germany in summer 9 BC. Marcellus was born in 42 BC, the son of Gaius Claudius Marcellus and Octavia, the sister of Augustus. He was thus the half-brother of Germanicus' mother Antonia, daughter of Octavia and Mark Antony. Marcellus had been earmarked by Augustus as his successor, but died in 23 BC.

inscription offers a valuable insight into how the Roman world responded enthusiastically to the succession of Caligula. It is to be assumed that other cities throughout the empire would have sent similar embassies to Rome on the accession of the new emperor. It also reveals how comfortable the eastern provinces were with recognizing their rulers as gods, explicitly identifying Caligula as such. But it also illustrates nicely how it is often the incidental information that is the most interesting contribution made by an inscription. This one nicely confirms Suetonius' assertion that Caligula went to Syria with his parents. And it also records Caligula's first active role on the historical stage. We cannot date that event *precisely* but it was probably early in AD 18, when he was five years old and made some sort of speech during his father's visit to the city. His expression of "concern" for the city of Assos suggests a diplomatic rather than genuine display of affection, but it is of course highly unlikely in any case that Caligula wrote the lines himself. The public exploit-ation of endearing young family members by politicians is clearly not exclusive to our own age. This is Caligula's first recorded public foray into oratory, in which he and his father both reputedly excelled.

It is possible that an image of Caligula has survived from around this time, on a famous cameo, the Grand Camée de France (Figure 2).[39] The various scenes depicted on the cameo are much disputed, but there is a fairly large scholarly consensus that it is Germanicus and his family who are portrayed at the far left of the middle frieze (on the eve of their departure for the eastern mission, it has been argued), in which case we would have a likeness of Caligula at about the age of five, appropriately dressed as a little soldier in a cuirass, carrying a miniature shield. It must be stressed that the identification, while very plausible, cannot be definitive. It is only with his succession in AD 37 that we begin to have indis-putable examples of Caligula's image, on his coin issues.

1.17 Suet. *Cal.* 10.1 Caligula also accompanied his father on his Syrian expedition.

1.18 Assos. Inscription. Greek. *IGR* 4.251 (Smallwood 33). AD 37 In the consulships of Gnaeus Acerronius Proculus and Gaius Pontius Petronius Nigrinus. A decree of the people of Assos in accordance with the will of the people.

Since the principate of Gaius Caesar Germanicus Augustus has been pro-claimed as hoped by the payers of all humanity, and the universe has found no limit to its joy, and since the whole city and the whole community has been eager to witness the god and since the sweetest era is now upon humanity, the

---

[39] Grand Camée de France: https://fr-academic.com/dic.nsf/frwiki/1952426 accessed December 30, 2022.

*

Figure 2 Image of young Caligula. Kornelia Roth.

council and those Romans who have business among us and the people of Assos
have resolved to appoint an embassy made up of the best and most prominent
Greeks and Romans to convene with him and celebrate with him and to beg
him to remember and have concern for the city just as he undertook to do when
he entered the province of our city for the first time with his father Germanicus.

The Oath of the People of Assos.

We swear by Zeus Soter and the deified Caesar Augustus and the ancestral
sacred Maiden[40] to be loyal to Gaius Caesar Augustus and to his entire house
and to deem as friends whomsoever he might choose and deem as enemies
whomsoever he might choose. May it be well with us if we swear honestly, and
the opposite if we swear falsely.

---

[40] Assos was famed for its Temple of Athena, built in the sixth century BC.

Germanicus in Syria

Germanicus continued to Syria, where he put his diplomatic skills to maximum use, and further successes followed. The old kingdom of Cappadocia
was organized as a province, and Commagene was incorporated into Syria.
Parthia consented to the establishment of a pro-Roman king, Zeno, in the
contentious realm of Armenia. These were clear successes. But there were dark
clouds on the horizon. Germanicus found himself treading on the toes of the
legate of Syria, Calpurnius Piso, and after a serious clash in AD 19 Piso
withdrew from his province. Worse was to come. In October of that same
year tragedy struck, when Germanicus died, in Antioch, Syria. The cause of
death was probably natural but reputedly there were widespread suspicions
that he had been murdered by Piso, acting on the instructions of Tiberius and
his mother Livia.

1.19 Suet. *Cal.* 1.2 Later Germanicus was elected consul for a second time,[41]
and before entering office he was sent off to establish a settlement of the east;
and then after defeating the king of Armenia[42] and organizing Cappadocia as
a province[43] he died at Antioch following a protracted illness, in his thirty-
fourth year, not without suspicion of poisoning. For in addition to discolor-
ations all over the body and frothing from the mouth, his heart was also
found intact among his bones, something thought unable to be consumed by
fire if poisoned.[44]

1.20 Tac. *Ann.* 2.72 Turning then to his wife, Germanicus begged her by her
memory of him and the children they shared to set aside her pride, submit to
the cruelty of fortune, and after her return to Rome avoid enraging those
stronger than her by competing for power.[45] This he said openly, other things

---

[41] Germanicus held his second consulship in AD 18 (his first fell in AD 12), and was in Greece
when he entered office at the beginning of the year. His colleague in the second consulship was
Tiberius.

[42] As it stands, Suetonius' text indicates that Germanicus defeated (*devicisset*) some unknown king,
who reigned before Zeno. It may be that the manuscript reading is corrupt and that the text originally
indicated that Germanicus *appointed* the king (perhaps *dedisset* or *delegisset*, or the like).

[43] Germanicus succeeded in persuading Parthia to recognize Zeno, the son of the Roman client king
of Pontus, as king of Armenia. Zeno changed his name to Artaxias and ruled successfully for sixteen
years.

The annexation of Cappadocia as a province created considerable revenues for Rome. It was
eventually incorporated into the province of Syria.

[44] Germanicus died on October 10, AD 19. Syria was particularly unhealthy and his death need not
be sinister. Tac. *Ann.* 2.73.4 is sceptical about the body providing proof of poisoning, noting that the
symptoms could be interpreted either way, depending on one's prejudices.

[45] Tacitus is generally very sympathetic towards Agrippina, whom he sees as a victim of the imperial
system, but he concedes here that she was a highly ambitious woman, and that her open ambition could
be irksome (a characteristic he explicitly condemns in other women of the imperial house, such as
Agrippina's like-named daughter).

privately, in which he was thought to have alerted her to the threat posed by Tiberius.[46] Not much later he died, bringing great sorrow to the province and its surrounding peoples.

1.21 Suet. *Cal.* 5.1 However, there were far greater and more positive assessments of him at the time of his death and after his death. On the day he died[47] stones were hurled at temples, altars of the gods overturned, and household gods thrown into the streets by a number of people, and their wives' newborn children exposed.[48] Indeed they even say that barbarians at war, whether allied with us or against us,[49] agreed to a truce as if sharing one domestic tragedy; and a number of chieftains are said to have rid themselves of their beards and shaved their wives' heads to show their heartfelt sorrow; and even the king of kings abandoned his hunting expeditions and banqueting with his noblemen, something equivalent to the *iustitium* for the Parthians.[50]

Birth of Tiberius Gemellus

The death of Germanicus in AD 19 was followed shortly after by the birth of Caligula's only potential rival to his succession, when Tiberius' son Drusus became father to twins, of which one was so identified, with the name Tiberius Gemellus ("Tiberius the twin," hereafter, simply "Gemellus"). The other died in infancy.

1.22 Tac. *Ann.* 2.84 Now while grief for Germanicus was still fresh, his sister Livia, who was married to Drusus, gave birth to twins of male sex.[51] This, being an unusual and happy occurrence even for lowly households, brought such

---

[46] Frustratingly, as often, the historian provides no information on what the sources are for these *private* communications.

[47] October 10, AD 19. It would have taken some time for the information to be broadcast, and consequently Suetonius seems to suggest that the scenes of excessive reaction were limited to Antioch. Suetonius is the only source to record this behaviour and the account is unconvincing.

[48] Suetonius stresses that the reaction was both public (temples and altars) and private (tutelary gods, the Lares, and exposed children). Exposure of children is certainly well attested in antiquity but there seems to be no parallel for the kind of mass exposure described by Suetonius.

[49] Artabanus had reached a settlement with Rome, brokered by Germanicus himself. It is not clear who the other enemies were. Suetonius is perhaps a little unconvinced by the claim, and points out here that he is reporting the assertions of others—"they say."

[50] The *iustitium* was the formal suspension of business, when in response to the death of a prominent individual it lasted normally from the day of the death to the day of the burial. In Germanicus' case there was a delay—the Fasti of Ostia indicate that the suspension of business began on December 8, two months after the death (*EJ* p. 41).
The king in question is Artabanus III, who ruled Parthia *c.*AD 12–*c.*38. During the early part of his reign he pursued a policy that was reasonably friendly to Rome, but he held Tiberius in low regard and shifted his loyalties. He came to terms with Caligula at the beginning of the latter's reign (7.1–3).

[51] Tacitus' date for the birth of the twins (AD 19) has been questioned, since Gemellus, who survived infancy (the other twin died in AD 23 [Tac. *Ann.* 4.15.1]), is said not to have reached puberty by March, 37 (the grounds for invalidating Tiberius' will [3.4]), even though he would have been seventeen by

great joy to the emperor that he could not refrain from boasting to the senators that no Roman of such high rank had ever before been blessed with a twin birth—for he would turn everything, even chance events, to self-glorification. But to ordinary people, given the circumstances, this also brought pain, since they felt that the increase in Drusus' children put greater pressure on the house of Germanicus.[52]

Further Reading

Humphrey, J. W. 1979. "The Three Daughters of Agrippina Maior." *American Journal of Ancient History* 4: 125–43.

Hurley, D. W. 1989. "Gaius Caligula in the Germanicus Tradition." *AJP* 110: 316–38.

Hurley, D. W. 2003. "The Politics of Agrippina the Younger's Birthplace." *American Journal of Ancient History* 2: 95–117.

Pelling, C. 1993. "Tacitus and Germanicus." In *Tacitus and the Tacitean Tradition*, edited by T. J. Luce and A. J. Woodman, 59–85. Princeton, NJ: Princeton University Press.

Williams, K. 2009. "Tacitus' Germanicus and the Principate." *Latomus* 68: 117–30.

---

then. Such an erroneous date would be a curious mistake for Tacitus to make, given that he makes much capital from the coincidental events. It could be that Gemellus was not very advanced for his age and had a late puberty.

[52] The expectations of Germanicus' sons would be reduced by the birth of sons to Tiberius' son, Drusus.

2

Young Caligula

We know that Caligula accompanied his father Germanicus on the journey out to Syria in AD 17–18. When we next meet him it is by inference only, when his mother Agrippina returned to Italy in early AD 20 after the death of her husband. Her ship sailed into Brundisium (Brindisi), and when Tacitus tells us that she dramatically appeared, carrying the ashes of her husband and accompanied by "her two children," these two can only have been have been Julia Livilla, born in AD 18 in Lesbos, on the journey out to Syria, and the seven-year-old Caligula.

From Brundisium the family travelled into Rome in a spectacular *coup de théâtre* that garnered much sympathy. The next decade would prove a turbulent one for them.

2.1 Tac. *Ann.* 3.1 Once the fleet was sighted out at sea, it was not only the harbour and areas closest to the seas that filled up with crowds of mourners but so also did the city walls and roofs of houses and any points from which a distant view could be had, as these people asked each other whether they should receive Agrippina in silence as she stepped ashore or with words of some kind. They were still not in agreement on what suited the occasion when the fleet gradually approached, not with the usual vigorous rowing but with everything arranged suggesting sadness. When Agrippina together with her two children stepped from the ship holding the funeral urn, she kept her eyes down, and a concerted groan arose from the whole gathering, and one could not tell relatives from strangers, men's lamentations from women's, except that Agrippina's attendants, exhausted from protracted grief, were surpassed in expressing it by those who met them and whose pain was fresh.

2 Tiberius had sent two Praetorian cohorts and also relayed instructions for the magistrates of Calabria, together with the Apulian and Campanian officials, to pay their last tributes to his son's memory. Germanicus' ashes were thus carried on the shoulders of tribunes and centurions, and before the procession the standards were unadorned and the fasces reversed.[1] And when they passed through the *coloniae*, the common people dressed in black and knights in the

---

[1] Fasces were bundles of rods, often surrounding an axe, representing a magistrate's authority. They were carried ahead of him by attendants (lictors).

The Emperor Caligula in the Ancient Sources. Anthony A. Barrett and J. C. Yardley, Oxford University Press.
© Anthony A. Barrett and J. C. Yardley 2023. DOI: 10.1093/oso/9780198854562.003.0003

trabea,[2] there were burning garments, incense, and other traditional funerary offerings, according to the district's resources. Even those from faraway towns came to meet them, and offering sacrificial victims and altars to the spirits of the dead made clear their pain with tears and lamentations.[3]

Political Tensions

Agrippina's pride and ambition would in themselves have almost guaranteed that she would at some point clash with Tiberius, and the situation was much aggravated by the machinations of a figure of considerable notoriety, the sinister Praetorian prefect Sejanus. This man took command of the guard in AD 15, the year after Augustus' death. Probably not long after Agrippina's arrival in Rome he created a formidable power base in the city by amalgamating the scattered units of the guard into a single garrison. He clearly entertained lofty political ambitions of his own, not compatible with the advancement of the sons of the late Germanicus, or indeed of Tiberius' own natural son, Drusus. Sejanus reputedly seduced Drusus' wife, Livilla (sister of Germanicus, hence aunt of Caligula), and contrived Drusus' murder by poison, in AD 23. He was then able to focus his efforts on bringing down Agrippina and her sons.

2.2 Tac. *Ann.* 4.12 Now when Tiberius delivered his son Drusus' eulogy from the rostra,[4] the senate and people assumed the demeanour and tones of mourning but with more pretence than inclination, and they were secretly pleased with the revival of the house of Germanicus. This renewed popularity, however, and Agrippina's failure to conceal her ambition only accelerated the family's destruction. For when Sejanus saw that Drusus' death brought no punishment to his killers and no grief to the public, he became brazen in his criminal designs, and his early success led him to ponder ways of destroying Germanicus' children, whose succession was now assured. Poison could not be dispensed to all three;[5] their bodyguards' loyalty was exceptional and Agrippina's virtue unassailable. He therefore proceeded to target her wilfulness and to work on Livia Augusta's long-standing hatred of the woman[6] and

---

[2] The *trabea* was a short toga-like garment, mainly purple, worn on formal occasions by members of the equestrian order.

[3] The transportation of Germanicus' ashes from the east coast to Italy to Rome is described in terms of an elaborate funeral procession. It would have reminded people of the progress of the corpse of his father, Drusus, who had died in Germany in the service of Rome, and had been brought home amidst considerable spectacle. Tacitus would have wanted to emphasize the association of father and son, both charismatic individuals.

[4] Drusus, son of Tiberius, died on September 14, AD 23.

[5] Tacitus suggests here that Caligula also had now become a target of Sejanus' campaign.

[6] This seems implausible. The likelihood that Livia would have collaborated with Sejanus is surely very remote. Moreover, the children of Agrippina and Germanicus were Livia's great-grandchildren by

Livilla's recent complicity.[7] He prompted both of them to criticize Agrippina in Tiberius' presence; her pride in her fertility and her support amongst the people were giving her imperial ambitions, they were to say.

Sejanus' Machinations

After Agrippina's return to Rome, down to her initial detention in AD 27, we have literally only one very brief notice of Caligula, that on coming back from Syria he lived with his mother (2.4), which is what we might have expected. Because Caligula was still young, Sejanus' focus would presumably have been on undermining the two eldest sons, Nero and Drusus, and he would in fact have been indirectly aided in this by Agrippina herself, who was incapable of concealing her ambitions, and, despite the earlier deathbed pleas of Germanicus (1.20), equally incapable of curbing her brash manifestations of pride. A brief but fascinating comment of Tacitus also reveals serious tensions between Caligula's two brothers. Drusus, it emerges, deeply resented Nero's position as the oldest brother and was apparently even willing to conspire against him.

> **2.3 Tac. Ann. 4.60.1** Nero harboured no criminal thoughts, but occasionally trenchant and ill-considered remarks would emerge from him and those assigned to watch him took note of them and exaggerated them in their reports, while Nero was given no chance to defend himself. So various forms of anxiety began to manifest themselves. **2** One would avoid meeting him; another would exchange a greeting and immediately turn away; some would break off speaking in mid-conversation—while Sejanus' supporters who were present just stood by laughing. As for Tiberius, he would meet Nero with a grim expression or false smile; and whether the young man spoke or said nothing, silence showed his guilt and so did talking. Even night was not safe since his wife disclosed to her mother Livilla his waking moments, his sleep times, and his sighs, and Livilla would disclose them to Sejanus.[8] Sejanus had also brought Nero's brother Drusus over to his side, offering him hope of the supreme position if he removed his elder brother, who was already in difficulties. **3** In addition to his lust for power and the usual hatred between brothers, Drusus had a frightful

blood, through her son Drusus, father of Germanicus, and she would presumably have had a natural interest in their potential succession. In any case, if we are to accept Tacitus' own account, Livia had very little influence over her son Tiberius.

[7] The reference here is to Livilla's supposed complicity in the murder of her husband Drusus, son of Tiberius (see the next note).

[8] Drusus, son of Tiberius, had married his cousin Livilla, daughter of his uncle Drusus, brother of Tiberius; their daughter Julia married Nero, brother of Caligula, probably in AD 20 (Tac. Ann. 3.29). Presumably Julia passed on the information to her mother Livilla in innocence, not realizing that the mother was Sejanus' mistress.

character that was further inflamed by envy over his mother Agrippina's preference for Nero. Even so, Sejanus' backing of Drusus was not such as to prevent him sowing the seeds of *his* future destruction, too, for he saw he was particularly headstrong and could be more easily trapped.

Life with Livia and Antonia

In AD 26, Tiberius, weary of the unrelenting political intrigues, left Rome, never to return, and spent most of the remaining years of his reign on the island of Capri. His departure gave Sejanus much greater freedom of action. The record of the prefect's final efforts against Agrippina is murky, but it seems that at some point in AD 27 she was removed from Rome and restricted to her villa in Herculaneum in Campania.[9] Nero seems to have been placed under restraint also, perhaps in some sort of house arrest in Rome. Caligula had probably just turned fifteen, but had still not yet received the toga of manhood (normally granted in the previous year), perhaps deliberately, to lower his profile. He now moved from the orbit of his proud and ambitious mother into that of the two most powerful women of the period, powerful not because of office or constitutional position, but because of their personal prestige and extensive connections. They were in their own ways possibly no less ambitious than Agrippina, but they both had the political acumen to appreciate that in Rome a woman could not exercise influence directly, but by tact, diplomacy, and a good deal of cunning.

Caligula moved in first with his great-grandmother Livia, presumably in her house on the Palatine, in the latter part of AD 27. She died in 29, most likely early in the year, at the age of eighty-six, and he would thus have spent about a year and half with her. Livia had been a major player in the political life of Rome for over fifty years. Although her role was curtailed when her husband Augustus died and her son Tiberius came to power in AD 14, she continued to maintain an influential nexus of friends and clients, and had a keen sense of how the political power game was played. Caligula much admired her, despite a very dubious anecdote retailed by Suetonius (2.5). When she died in AD 29 he gave the funeral oration. Also, when he came to power he honoured her legacies, which had been left unpaid by Tiberius.

After Livia's death Caligula moved into the home of another powerful woman, his grandmother Antonia, the widow of Tiberius' late brother Drusus. He remained some two years with her until Tiberius summoned him to Capri in AD 31 (Antonia was still alive). As the daughter of Mark Antony, Antonia may well have instilled in her grandson the respect for her father's talents and

---

[9] Sen. *Ira* 3.21.5.

achievements that Caligula himself later enunciated (4.46). She had many close ties with ruling families of the east, in particular with the house of Herod, which would have allowed Caligula as a boy to make useful personal contacts (most notably with Herod's grandson, Herod Agrippa). We do get a glimpse of his youthful activities in this period in an inscription from Cyzicus on the Hellespont (Smallwood 401), in which we learn that the three sons of the king of Thrace were "brought up with him as his companions," which may well have helped them later, since as emperor he bestowed kingdoms on all three. His sisters presumably were living with him, as indicated by the later stories of incest (2.6–8). His oldest brother Nero seems to have been placed under arrest in AD 27 or soon after. We do not know for certain the whereabouts of his second brother, Drusus, but he may well have been on Capri with Tiberius.

2.4 Suet. *Cal.* 10.1 After returning from Syria he lived first with his mother and then, when she was exiled, with his great-grandmother Livia Augusta;[10] and on her death he gave the eulogy from the rostra although he was still a boy.[11] He then passed into the care of Antonia, his grandmother...

2.5 Suet. *Cal.* 23.2 Repeatedly referring to his grandmother Livia Augusta[12] as "Ulysses in a stola,"[13] he even presumed, in some letter to the senate, to accuse her of humble origin, claiming that she was descended from a maternal grandfather who had been a decurion,[14] although it is clear from the public

---

[10] When Augustus was still emperor, Livia brought up the father of the later emperor Otho (Suet. *Oth.* 1).

[11] Suetonius' text says *praetextatus*, that is, he was still young enough to be wearing the *toga praetexta*, which was put aside after the ceremony of manhood, usually at about the age of fourteen. The Julio-Claudians had a tradition of very young men delivering such speeches for their late distinguished seniors; Julius Caesar, Augustus, and Tiberius all performed similar services.

[12] Livia was granted the title of Augusta after the death of her husband Augustus. Her name appears inconsistently in various forms in the sources after that date, with or without "Augusta," but it may be that Suetonius here deliberately uses the potent title to stress what he sees as Caligula's disrespect for her.

[13] Ulysses/Odysseus was notorious for his clever scheming—where other heroes evaded danger by courage Ulysses succeeded through trickery. The expression is often translated as "Ulysses in petticoats," which misses much of the point. Caligula did not see Livia as a feminist icon. The *stola* was a long woollen dress and was for women the equivalent of the male toga, hence the symbol of the *matrona*, the dignified woman of high status. Caligula's point was that behind the veneer of traditional respectability Livia was an inveterate and successful schemer. His assessment may not have been far from the mark.

[14] Caligula supposedly asserted that Livia's father, Aufidius Lurco, was a decurion (member of a local council) of the town of Fundi. This is a curious claim. One suspects that it might have its origin in a Caligulan joke, but the reference to the letter to the senate (Suetonius makes good use of archival material) might seem to suggest that something more substantial was involved. There were certainly unsubstantiated stories that *Tiberius*, Livia's son, was born in Fundi, located near the coast on the Via Appia, between Rome and Naples, and Suetonius *Tib.* 5 records that this belief may have originated from the fact that Livia's *mother* came from Fundi. But there is something not quite right in Suetonius' account here in the *Caligula*. Inscriptions (*CIL* 2.1667, 9.3661; *IGR* 4.983) indicate that Livia's grandfather was not Suetonius' Aufidius, but a Marcus Alfidius, who held office in Rome. Aufidius

records that the man, Aufidius Lurco, had held important positions in Rome. He refused his grandmother Antonia's request for a private meeting unless his prefect Macro could attend, and it was through slights and offensiveness of this sort that her death came about, although according to some she was given poison.[15] And on her passing he showed her no respect, and looked out on her burning pyre from his dining room.[16]

Sisters

During the first two years or so after he became emperor Caligula showed great favour to his sisters. Nor is this surprising. It might be expected that after losing both parents and both brothers he would have looked to his sisters for family affection. And it is also perhaps not surprising that some of the literary sources would have presented that affection in the worst possible light. Incest has traditionally been a convenient charge to make against one's enemies, ranging from Napoleon to Hitler, because it is one almost impossible to disprove. Suetonius and Dio report such claims about Caligula and his sisters, as do other sources,[17] and by the fourth century it was even supposed that Caligula fathered a child by one of them.[18] But we should exercise caution. Countering such assertions, it is to be noted that Seneca and Philo, who both place heavy emphasis on moral conduct and who were both in Rome at the time, and were inveterate foes of Caligula into the bargain, do not even hint at any rumour of impropriety between the emperor and his sisters. Moreover, although we have lost that part of Tacitus' *Annals* where he might have dealt with the claim, and we therefore cannot know for certain if he did in fact address it, we do know that in a later section of the *Annals* he found fault with one of the sisters, Agrippina, for committing incest with her son Nero,

Lurco, who is attested in late republican Rome, seems to have been someone quite different (Cic. *Pro Flacco* 86f.; *Att.* 1.16.13). Either Caligula deliberately and mischievously transposed the names, which seems unlikely, or Suetonius has simply made an error.

[15] Dio reports similarly (59.3.6) that Caligula was offended by Antonia after she rebuked him, and he obliged her to commit suicide. This is implausible. Antonia died on May 1, AD 37 (Smallwood 31.21; Figure 1: K MA(I)IS/ANTONIA DIEM SUUM OBIT ["Antonia died on May 1"]), less than a month and a half after Caligula's accession, hardly sufficient time, one would think, to be driven to death, and, more importantly, during the phase when the new emperor was on his very best behaviour. At *Cal.* 15.2 Suetonius seems to contradict the idea that Caligula disrespected Antonia and says that Caligula piled up (*congessit*) honours on her, granting her all those that had been conferred on Livia. Among these honours she seems to have received Livia's title of Augusta, although she does not appear to have used it during her lifetime. Suet. *Claud.* 11.2 claims that Antonia refused the title when offered it by Caligula and that Claudius conferred it on her. But she is called Augusta when sacrifices are recorded in the Arval record on her birthday in 38 and also possibly in 39 (Smallwood 3.2, 8.2). Perhaps Caligula did in fact confer it and Claudius reaffirmed the award on his accession after Caligula's measures had been annulled.

[16] The location of the dining room is not specified, hence it is difficult to assess the plausibility of the story.

[17] Jos. *AJ* 19.204.   [18] Eutropius 7.12.3.

and attributed this moral failing to her being sexually corrupted earlier in her life. Significantly, however, Tacitus does not say that this earlier corruption involved a sexual relationship with her brother, but rather came about through her affairs with Lepidus, the widower of her late sister Drusilla, and with the freedman Pallas, and the marriage to her uncle Claudius, clearly far less scandalous than incest with a brother.[19] This suggests very strongly that Tacitus made no claim of incest between the sisters and Caligula in the part of the *Annals* now lost. The story about Gaius Sallustius Passienus Crispus recorded below (2.8) suggests that the reports of incest may have originated from Caligula's perverse sense of humour, designed to amuse, and also to shock.

2.6 Suet. *Cal.* 24.1 With all his sisters he would have sex on a regular basis, and at a full banquet would have each of them placed in turn below him, with his wife reclining above.[20] Of these, it is believed that he deflowered Drusilla when she was still a virgin and he still a boy, and that he was even caught having sex with her by their grandmother Antonia, in whose house they were being raised together.[21]

2.7 Dio 59.22.6 (...and he put to death) the notorious Lepidus, that lover and beloved of his, husband of Drusilla, the man together with whom he had sex with his other sisters Agrippina and Julia Livilla...[22]

2.8 Suet. *Life of Passienus Crispus*[23] He tried to win the good will of all the emperors, but especially of Gaius Caesar, whom he accompanied on foot when he travelled. When, in no one's hearing,[24] he was asked by Caesar[25] if, like himself, he was having sex with his sister, he answered "not so far"—such an appropriate and prudent reply, since he would neither be criticizing him by saying no nor discrediting himself with lying by saying yes.

---

[19] Tac. *Ann.* 14.2.4.
[20] Caligula would have occupied the host's location at the banquet, on the top position of the lowest couch. The wife would traditionally accompany the host below him on the same couch, but in Caligula's case the sisters took turns occupying the wife's position, while his wife took the last place on the middle couch, the one normally assigned to an honoured guest.
[21] It is to be noted that Suetonius does not vouch for the story ("it is believed").
[22] In late AD 39, a tense period of conspiracies, the imperial house was supposedly involved in a plot by both surviving sisters and their lover Lepidus, the widower of the dead sister Drusilla. The incident is covered in detail in Chapter 4.
[23] Gaius Sallustius Passienus Crispus was a wealthy courtier, twice consul, related to the historian Sallust and noted for his sharp wit. Married first to Domitia, sister-in-law of Caligula's sister, the younger Agrippina, he subsequently divorced her, then married Agrippina herself, and on his death left her a rich woman.
[24] It is important to note that the conversation was private (*nullo audiente*), but we are meant to believe that Suetonius apparently had access to it.
[25] The manuscripts read "Nero" but that cannot be correct. Nero did not have a sister, and Passienus was long dead by the time Nero became emperor. The later stories of Nero's incest with his *mother* may have caused the scribal confusion.

Caligula on Capri

Livia and Antonia may well have been able to offer Caligula some degree of temporary protection, but a far more serious step in shielding him from potential danger was taken in the first part of AD 31, when he was summoned, at the age of eighteen, to join Tiberius in his self-imposed exile, mainly on the island of Capri.

Was Caligula under a real threat during these years in Rome? Tiberius seems to have claimed later that he was, since just before his death he wrote a short autobiography, seen by Suetonius (presumably in the imperial archives), in which, according to Suetonius, Tiberius explained that he brought down Sejanus because the prefect had waged a campaign against "the children of his (sc. Tiberius') son, Germanicus." Tiberius does not specify which of the children he means but it is striking that despite his claim that he was trying to protect those very children, one of them, Drusus, also by then in detention, was not released after the fall of Sejanus (Nero might possibly have been dead by that time). This seems to suggest that despite his use of the plural "children" (*liberos*) Tiberius had only Caligula in mind as a supposedly potential victim (there is no suggestion that Germanicus' daughters were in any sort of danger). On Capri Caligula found himself uprooted from family and familiar surroundings, to spend the next six years in the company of an elderly grandfather on a small island. He was by now old enough to be aware of what was happening to his brothers and mother, and to appreciate how precarious his own position was. This may have encouraged him to exercise total discretion and to keep his own counsel. He may have later encouraged stories of the type that he himself reported (2.17), that he wanted to take his revenge on Tiberius but was restrained by moral scruples. His demeanour on Capri is portrayed by both Tacitus and Suetonius as an exercise in dissimulation. They presumably were using a common source, which apparently was able to read Caligula's mind!

2.9 Suet. *Cal.* 10.1 ... he was in his nineteenth year summoned to Capri by Tiberius, and on that same day he put on the toga of manhood and shaved his beard—but without any such pomp as had attended his brothers' coming of age.[26]

2.10 Suet. *Tib.* 61.1 Tiberius soon exploded into all kinds of brutality, an opportunity for which was never lacking since he could torment first the friends and then even simple acquaintances of his mother, then those of his grandsons, and finally those of Sejanus, after whose death his cruellest phase appeared. From this it was very clear indeed that it was less a case of being usually egged on by

---

[26] Caligula might have expected to receive the toga of manhood in AD 26, when he was fourteen. The ceremony may have been postponed to 29 to help shield him from political intrigues.

Sejanus than of Sejanus having supplied him with opportunities he wanted; and yet in the journal in which he presented his own highly condensed biography[27] he had the effrontery to write that he had punished Sejanus because he found him venting his anger against his son Germanicus' children (one of whom he himself put to death when Sejanus was already under suspicion, and the other after Sejanus finally fell).

2.11 Tac. Ann. 6.3.4 In the same letter Tiberius struck down Sextius Paconianus, much to the delight of the senators; for Paconianus was a head-strong and evil man who ferreted out everybody's secrets and had been chosen by Sejanus to help with the destruction of Gaius Caesar.[28] When this came to light, long-simmering hatreds erupted, and only his willingness to denounce others saved him from the death penalty that was being passed on him.

The Fate of Caligula's Family

While Caligula was in Capri action continued against Agrippina and her oldest son, Nero. The events are difficult to disentangle. There are gaps in the narratives of Tacitus and Dio, and Suetonius does not provide a straight chronological sequence. It seems that they were banished to small islands northwest of the bay of Naples, Agrippina to Pandateria (Ventotene) and Nero to Pontia (Ponza). At some point Nero committed suicide or was executed. Caligula's other brother Drusus had allowed himself to be drawn into the campaign against his mother and Nero, and perhaps felt that he was secure. If so, he was naïve. In AD 30 he was escorted "back to Rome." Dio reports this, without saying from where he was escorted, but Capri is a reasonable assumption.[29] He was imprisoned in a cell deep in the Palatine.

Sejanus was toppled on October 18, AD 31. The loyalty of the Praetorian guard towards their prefect was a cause of concern and the key role in the venture was assigned to Quintus Naevius Cordus Sutorius Macro, at the time prefect of the Vigiles (the fire service created by Augustus). Macro carried out his mission flawlessly, and was rewarded by promotion to the prefecture of the guard, which he exercised solely, without a colleague. He was to play a key role in Caligula's accession and the early phase of his reign. Sejanus was put to death, but his passing

---

[27] Otherwise unknown. It seems to be different from Tiberius' *commentarii* and *acta*, reputedly the later emperor Domitian's sole reading matter (Suet. *Dom.* 20).

[28] Sextius Paconianus was exposed by Tiberius in AD 32 (this correct form of the name is not reported as such in the manuscripts, perhaps not surprisingly, since copyists often get unfamiliar proper names wrong). He was in AD 35 strangled to death in prison for writing verses damaging to Tiberius (Tac. *Ann.* 6.39.1). Presumably the events summarized here were covered in more detail in Tacitus' lost Caligula chapters.

[29] Dio 58.3.8.

would lead neither to Agrippina's nor to Drusus' release. Drusus died a horrific death in that same year.

2.12 Suet *Tib.* 54.2 And after that, by opening up about what he really thought, Tiberius laid the boys open to all manner of allegations, and he provoked them by various tricks so they would be roused to utter reproaches against him and then be betrayed for it; whereupon he levelled the most bitter charges against them in a letter, piling on abusive comments, and once they were declared enemies of the state he had them starved to death,[30] Nero on the island of Pontia and Drusus in the bowels of the Palatium. They think that Nero was forced into suicide when an executioner, purportedly sent on senatorial authority, showed him the noose and hooks, while Drusus was so deprived of food that he tried to eat the stuffing from his mattress, and that the ashes of both were so scattered that they could only with difficulty be gathered together.

2.13 Tac. *Ann.* 6.23.2 Drusus' death came next;[31] he had kept himself alive for eight days on a wretched diet, eating the stuffing from his bed. Some have recorded that in the event of an armed uprising being attempted by Sejanus Macro had been ordered to take the young man out of detention—he was being held in the Palatium—and set him up as the people's leader.[32] Presently, as a rumour spread of the emperor's forthcoming reconciliation with his daughter-in-law and grandson, he chose brutality over a change of heart.

2.14 Tac. *Ann.* 6.24.1 Tiberius went further and cast slurs on the dead man, charging him with sexual perversions and planning murder within his family and treason towards the state. He also ordered the daily record that had been kept of Drusus' actions and words to be read out, and that seemed the cruellest stroke of all. That men had been at Drusus' side for so many years to take note of his expression, his sighs, and even a suppressed murmur, and that his grandfather could have heard all this, read it, and made it public—it simply beggared belief. But it was borne out by letters of the centurion Attius and the freedman Didymus, which gave the names of all the slaves who had beaten and terrorized Drusus whenever he tried to leave his bedroom. 2 The centurion had even added, as though it were to his credit, his own remarks at the time, full of

---

[30] Suetonius seems inconsistent here. He first says that both were starved to death, but then goes on to say that Nero was deceived into committing suicide. Perhaps Nero had already been deprived of food for some time before the trick was played.

[31] Tacitus would presumably have outlined Drusus' fall in the missing chapters of *Annals* 5. Dio 58.3.8 reports that Sejanus, who had previously seduced the wife of Drusus, son of Tiberius, persuaded the wife of this Drusus, brother of Caligula, to make false charges against her husband.

[32] On the surface the story seems bizarre. It is hard to reconcile with the fact that Drusus was kept in custody after Sejanus' fall. Much use is made here of "some" unspecified authorities, as well as of "rumour."

savagery, along with Drusus' dying words. At first Drusus had begun to aim some maledictions against Tiberius, apparently in a fit of madness, but when he then lost hope of remaining alive his curses became studied and carefully worded. Just as Tiberius had murdered his daughter-in-law, his brother's son, and his grandchildren,[33] and had filled his entire house with carnage, so, Drusus prayed, may he also pay the penalty to their ancestors' name and family line, and to posterity.

Death of Agrippina

Agrippina died in AD 33, on the anniversary of Sejanus' death, October 18. The details are unclear but it seems that at the end she demonstrated a courage to match her pride and ambition, and starved herself to death.

2.15 Tac. *Ann.* 6.25.1 That painful episode had not yet faded when news came of Agrippina.[34] After Sejanus' death I think she had lived on buoyed by hope, and then after there was no let-up in Tiberius' savagery she took her own life— unless perhaps she was refused food to produce a death that could be taken for suicide. **2** Tiberius, it is true, flared up with the foulest reproaches against her, charging her with moral turpitude, with Asinius Gallus as her lover, and claiming that it was his death that had made her tired of life.[35] (But Agrippina, intolerant of equality and yearning for power, had in fact thrown off female weaknesses and developed masculine ambitions). **3** Tiberius added that she had died the same day on which Sejanus had paid his penalty two years earlier, and that this was something that should be recorded. He also congratulated himself on the fact that she had not been strangled and thrown on the Gemonian Steps.[36] Official thanks were given to him for that and a decree was passed authorizing the consecration of an offering to Jupiter every year on October 18, the anniversary of the two deaths.

---

[33] Agrippina, wife of Germanicus, Tiberius' adopted son; Germanicus himself; Nero; and, it is presumably anticipated, Drusus himself. Of course at this point Agrippina was still alive; we are perhaps meant to assume that her death had been falsely reported to him.

[34] The "painful episode" refers to the death by starvation of Agrippina's son, Drusus. Clearly there must have been substantial concern that Agrippina was indeed involved in plotting at some level against Tiberius. Tacitus perhaps hints at this when he goes on to assign "masculine ambitions" to her.

[35] In AD 26 Agrippina had sought permission from Tiberius to remarry (Tac. *Ann.* 4.53). Her intended husband at that time was almost certainly Asinius Gallus, whose name was later associated with hers. Asinius came of a distinguished family but would have been viewed with disfavour by Tiberius, since he had married Tiberius' former wife Vipsania after Tiberius had divorced her, for purely dynastic motives, despite holding her in great affection. Asinius was later implicated in Agrippina's supposed machinations and died of starvation in prison.

[36] The Gemonian Stairs seem to have led from the Capitoline to the Roman Forum. Certain condemned prisoners were strangled and hurled down the stairs and left exposed there, although there is no evidence that this custom predated Tiberius. It was the fate suffered by Sejanus.

2.16 Dio 58.22.4 Tiberius thus brought disgrace on himself because of his cruelty in the deaths of Drusus and Agrippina; for people had assumed that everything earlier done to them had been done by Sejanus and they were hoping that they would now be saved; so on learning that they had also been killed, they were extremely distressed, both over the act itself and also because he had not just failed to inter their bones in the imperial burial chamber but had even ordered them hidden somewhere underground for them never to be found.[37]

Life on Capri

The impact of the death of his mother and brothers on Caligula is difficult to determine. Apart from one unconvincing story (2.17), there is no suggestion that he expressed or even felt any disquiet at the time. But this is hardly surprising—he was very isolated on Capri, and it is unlikely that his inner thoughts would have been recorded. In any case he would no doubt have appreciated that it was very much in his interest to keep his own counsel if he was to survive.

Suetonius paints lurid pictures of Tiberius' sex life on Capri and suggests that Caligula lived up to the example that Tiberius set. Yet the individuals whose presence is recorded on the island, mainly rather elderly, suggest a monastic rather than bohemian way of life there, and Tiberius was known to be a devotee of scholarly discourse. Moreover neither Seneca nor Philo, both contemporaries with strong convictions of moral rectitude, assign any riotous living to Caligula, and indeed Philo (3.53) insists that while under Tiberius' tutelage Caligula lived a life of restraint and abstinence.

2.17 Suet. *Cal.* 12.3 And this is not far from the truth, since some authors claim that he himself later declared he had once at least considered murder even if he had not gone through with it;[38] for, these say, when he was talking about his own devotion to his family, he always boasted of how he had gone into Tiberius' bedroom with a dagger when he was asleep to avenge his mother's and his brothers' killings, and how, when overtaken by pity, he had thrown down the weapon and left; and how, although he had been aware of it, Tiberius had never dared ask him about it or taken any action.[39]

---

[37] Caligula will make a particular point of recovering what remains could be found (3.26, 27).

[38] Suetonius cites "a number of authors" but the story is extant in no other literary source. After his accession Caligula's earlier relations with the murderer of his mother and brothers would have created an awkward situation. It would have been in his interest to give such a story currency, depicting him as both driven to avenge his family yet also a person of compassion.

[39] The author of the story was apparently capable also of reading Tiberius' mind.

2.18 Tac. *Ann*. 6.20.1 Gaius concealed a monstrous personality beneath a deceitful veneer of moderation, and had uttered not a word at his mother's condemnation or his brothers' ruin. Whatever Tiberius' mood for the day seemed to be he would adopt the same, using language little different from his. Hence the ingenious comment of the orator Passienus, which gained currency later on, that never had there been a better slave or a worse master.[40]

2.19 Suet. *Cal*. 10.2 Here (sc. Capri) all sorts of tricks were used by people trying to induce or force him into complaining[41] but he gave them no satisfaction, as though forgetting his family's fate as if it had never happened, and also passing over with incredible dissimulation what he was now being subjected to himself; and so deferential was he towards his grandfather and his courtiers that it was not unfairly said of him that there had never been either a better slave or a worse master.[42]

2.20 Suet. *Cal*. 11.1 However, his cruel and wayward nature he could not even then suppress,[43] to the point even of taking very keen interest in punishments and penalties of those surrendered for torture; and hidden under a wig and long robe[44] he would prowl around at night on gluttonous and lecherous escapades and looking for singing and dancing performances (with Tiberius quite readily accepting it, hoping that his wild character might possibly be curbed by such things). This the perceptive old man had clearly discerned, to the point where he would occasionally declare that for Gaius to go on living would spell death for him and for everybody else,[45] and that he was nurturing a viper for the Roman people and a Phaethon for the world.[46]

---

[40] On Passienus, see 2.8. The precise point of the witticism (reported also by Suetonius) is ambiguous, depending on when it was first made. If it belongs to the period when Caligula became princeps (perhaps suggested by *mox* "later on"), it would mean that Caligula combined in his person the attributes of both slave and master; but if it was coined first during the Capri phase, which both Tacitus and Suetonius seem to imply, then it would mean that Tiberius was the dreadful master.

[41] Two possible groups might be seen here. For the first few months Sejanus might have continued to campaign against Caligula. After Sejanus' fall the supporters of Tiberius' natural grandson Gemellus would have had an interest in Caligula's fall from grace.

[42] Clearly a tag celebrated for its association with Caligula. Tacitus is the only source to ascribe it to Passienus Crispus.

[43] Suetonius is here relating events at Capri. His account is clearly based on unverified, probably unverifiable, gossip about goings-on there.

[44] The motif of young men donning disguise to commit mischief was a common one. Nero would supposedly wear a cap and wig and range through the taverns, going so far as to beat people up and throw them into the sewers and break into shops, which led to copycat gangs imitating him in creating mayhem (Suet. *Ner*. 26.1; Tac. *Ann*. 13.25.1–2). What scope Capri would have offered Caligula for such wild licence is far from clear.

[45] In the *Caligula* Suetonius reports the tradition that saw Tiberius murdered by Caligula (2.32).

[46] Phaethon was the son of Helios. Allowed to drive his father's chariot for one day he went too near to the earth and caused mass destruction. The notion of destructive power was attached to both Caligula and Nero: Pliny *NH* 7.45 claimed that both Agrippinas (mother and daughter) gave birth to

Macro and Herod Agrippa

On Capri Caligula came within the orbit of two individuals who were to play a seminal role in his succession and later reign. Through the ouster of Sejanus, Macro had no doubt learned how military strength could be the ultimate determinant in settling political questions and recognized that Caligula, as the only surviving son of the revered Germanicus, was also a highly promising candidate for the principate. According to Philo he spared no effort to promote Caligula's case, even seeking to put Tiberius' mind at rest by claiming that Caligula was so devoted to Gemellus that he would in time step aside for him (2.21). Of course these events predated Philo's visit to Rome by several years and he would have been relying on unverifiable gossip, but the general picture that he paints is certainly consistent with Macro's conduct immediately after Tiberius' death.

Caligula's second close acquaintance on the island is beyond question one of the most colourful characters of the period, Julius Agrippa (generally known as "Herod" Agrippa). He was the grandson of Herod the Great of Judaea, and a man possessed by an apparently incompatible combination of wild recklessness and a sharp instinct for surviving and prospering. Agrippa's later career certainly demonstrates that he enjoyed the favour of Caligula and of his successor Claudius. But we must be very cautious in assessing his influence on events in Rome. Most of our information on him comes from Josephus' *Antiquities* and it has been speculated that it may originate from a highly romanticized lost *Life of Agrippa*. It is worth noting that Suetonius never mentions him and Tacitus refers to him only briefly and casually.[47]

Agrippa was born in 10 BC and was thus more than twenty years older than Caligula. His father Aristobulus was executed by his own father Herod the Great in 7 BC. Subsequently, Agrippa was taken to Rome where, like Caligula later, he stayed with Antonia, and made the acquaintance of the children of the imperial family, including the future emperor Claudius. Recklessly extravagant, he went on to live in various parts of the empire, usually seeking to evade his debtors, and was eventually invited by Tiberius to Capri, where he faced disaster when his debts were revealed. He was rescued by Antonia, who clearly had much affection for him and who paid off what he owed. His charm and tact worked wonders, and he was reputedly asked by Tiberius to take the emperor's grandson Gemellus under his wing. If this did happen, Agrippa seems to have sensed that the future lay elsewhere, and he directed his attention to Caligula, using some of the money he had received from Antonia to win his favour. Agrippa's influence may

---

firebrands (Caligula and Nero) to destroy the human race. Seneca writing in the Claudian period reports in characteristically flattering terms that Caligula bequeathed a world that was scorched and utterly wrecked, which Claudius was in the process of restoring (Sen. *Cons. Polyb.* 17.3).

[47] Tac. *Ann.* 12.23.1.

not always have been the most positive—he was hardly a model of restraint and responsibility—but the relationship endured and he may well have been Caligula's only truly close friend throughout his reign.

It seems that on some occasion Agrippa supposedly displayed his reckless, almost self-destructive, streak by raising with Caligula the possibility of his becoming Tiberius' successor. We can probably rule out plotting as such; more likely he was using his smooth and flattering tongue to promote his own position. But there was an eavesdropper, and Tiberius was apprised of the incident. Agrippa was placed in custody, made more bearable by the comforts that Antonia reputedly arranged for him with the connivance of Macro.[48]

2.21 Philo *Leg.* 35 Macro made every effort to remedy these faults (sc. Caligula's shortcomings), dispelling the suspicions of Tiberius and the issues over which his mind seemed to be tormented through never-ending fear for his grandson Gemellus. **36** Macro represented Gaius as affable and obedient, so utterly devoted to his cousin that from affection he would be willing to remove himself from the succession in favour of Gemellus as the sole candidate.[49]

2.22 Jos. *Ant.* 18.166 The emperor Tiberius Caesar then commended his grandson Gemellus to Agrippa, saying that he should always accompany him on his travels. After being received in friendship by Antonia, Agrippa paid respects to her grandson Gaius, who was in high repute through people's goodwill towards his father. **167** There was also a Samaritan freedman of Caesar, Thallus. Agrippa borrowed a million drachmae from him and repaid his debt to Antonia, and through spending the rest in paying court to Gaius he gained great influence with him.

168 While the friendship of Agrippa with Gaius was at its height and they were in a chariot together, some words about Tiberius on one occasion passed between them. Agrippa prayed (for they were in private) that Tiberius might soon leave the stage and pass the leadership to Gaius, who was in every respect more worthy of it.

First Wife

While on Capri, Caligula married his first wife. During the course of his relatively short life he would marry four times in all. The information that we have on the four wives, and on their marriages, is often confused and contradictory.

---

[48] Jos. *Ant.* 18.203–4.

[49] Philo seems to suggest here that Macro knew the contents of Tiberius' will, in which Caligula and Gemellus had been made co-heirs to Tiberius' estate.

The first, Junia Claudia, belonged to a very prominent family, the Junii Silani, and her father, Marcus Junius Silanus, enjoyed considerable status under Tiberius. He was consul in AD 15, and subsequently made the sycophantic proposal to date the Roman year from the accession of the emperor, rather than from the names of the consuls. By the time of Tiberius' death, he had precedence in casting his vote in the senate, and Tiberius refused to try any case arising on appeal from Silanus' decision.[50] This first marriage should therefore be seen as a "good" one, a sign of Tiberius' favour. The sources provide slightly different details. Suetonius gives Junia the name Claudilla, rather than Claudia, and dates the marriage to AD 31. Tacitus dates it to AD 33, as generally do modern scholars. Dio lists it among the events of AD 35, adding the location, Antium, and most interestingly mentions the attendance of Tiberius, who was by this time living more or less permanently on Capri. It seems that this might have been one of the rare occasions when Tiberius was willing to travel to the mainland, probably to the imperial villa at Antium. Presumably Junia joined Caligula on Capri after the marriage but there is no explicit evidence of her being there.

2.23 Tac. *Ann*. 6.20.1 About this same time Gaius Caesar, who had attended his grandfather when he left for Capri, married Marcus Silanus' daughter Claudia.

2.24 Dio 58.25.2 After that Gaius Gallus and Marcus Servilius were consuls, and Tiberius celebrated Gaius Caligula's marriage at Antium, because he was unwilling to enter Rome even for that occasion.

2.25 Suet. *Cal*. 12.1 Not much later he married Junia Claudilla, daughter of the very high-ranking Marcus Silanus. He was then designated augur to replace his brother Drusus, but before the inauguration he was promoted to the office of pontiff, with outstanding testimony provided to his piety and good character; with Sejanus soon suspected of treason and brought down, and with the court deserted and bereft of its other supports, he was gradually being nudged toward hopes of succession.[51]

2 ... he lost Junia in childbirth ...

2.26 Dio 59.8.5 For Tiberius had had such respect for Marcus Silanus that he was never willing to judge a case on appeal from him but always sent such cases

---

[50] Tac. *Ann*. 3.57.2; Dio 59.8.5–6.

[51] Suetonius places the marriage "not much later" than Caligula's move to Capri, at some point in AD 31, and before the fall of Sejanus (in October of that year). Confusingly Suetonius says that Caligula replaced his brother Drusus as augur. This could have happened only after Drusus' death, which is dated to AD 33, two years after the fall of Sejanus. Suetonius may have confused Drusus here with Caligula's other brother, Nero, who did in fact die before Sejanus was brought down.

back to him again. Gaius, however, kept vilifying him, although his regard for him was great enough for him to call him the "golden sheep,"[52] 6 and so that Marcus should no longer have the first vote—a privilege he was granted by all the consuls both for his age and his reputation—Gaius abandoned the convention that some of the ex-consuls should vote first or second according to the wishes of those putting the question and instead determined that these should also vote in the order in which they had held office. 7 He also divorced Silanus' daughter and married Cornelia Orestilla.[53]

The Succession

As old age crept up on him Tiberius would have become increasingly aware that the issue of the succession would need to be resolved. He did in AD 35 make his two grandsons joint heirs to his personal estate (3.3), a fairly conventional arrangement, but seems to have been willing essentially to leave the matter of who would succeed as princeps in the hands of the senate. But the literary sources needed no encouragement to speculate, and to reveal in considerable detail the private thoughts supposedly going through Tiberius' mind. The anecdotes recorded by Dio are particularly telling, and a useful reminder that we should be very cautious about placing faith in literary speculation. The comment attributed to Tiberius about the earth catching fire under Caligula (2.27) recurs in the context of Nero and the Great Fire of AD 64, where Suetonius claims that when someone quoted the familiar "Let the earth catch fire after I die" Nero wittily retorted, partly in Latin, partly in Greek: "No, while I'm alive."[54] But in Nero's case the incident has nothing to do with succession, it is meant to offer an insight into Nero's motivation for burning down Rome in AD 64. The anecdote about Priam outliving all his kin (2.27) is also recycled. Dio, in the context, again, of Nero's plans to destroy Rome, has Nero declare that Priam was lucky to have been able to see the ending both of his regime and of his country.[55] These motifs have the appearance of clichéd stock phrases, to be trundled out to suit any given context. It all amounts essentially to speculation, of highly dubious plausibility, about what might have been going on in Tiberius' head.

---

[52] Dio seems to have got this Silanus, the "golden sheep," confused with Marcus Junius Silanus, consul of AD 46 and proconsul in Asia in 54, supposedly murdered by Agrippina the Younger at the beginning of Nero's reign. Tacitus (*Ann.* 13.1.1) explicitly says that the later Marcus Silanus was called the "golden sheep" by Caligula.

[53] On Cornelia Orestilla, see 4.9, 10. Dio claims that Caligula divorced Junia after his accession, whereas Suetonius has Junia die in childbirth and the widowed Caligula conduct an affair with Macro's wife well before his accession.

[54] Suet. *Ner.* 38.1.   [55] Dio 62.16.1–2.

2.27 Dio 58.23.1 Such were his actions, and he also appointed Gaius quaestor, not among the first,[56] but with a promise to promote him to other offices five years earlier than the norm (and this despite having asked the senate not to promote him with many premature honours in case he ran amok).

Now he also had a grandson called Gemellus, **2** but he passed over him because of his age (he was still a young child) and also from some suspicion he had of him (for it was not known whether or not he was Drusus' son),[57] and so he leaned toward Gaius as the next ruler, especially since he clearly knew that Gemellus would live only a short time and be murdered by Gaius himself. **3** For there was nothing about Gaius that he did not know; and once when the young man was arguing with him, he even said to him: "you will kill him and others will kill you." Having no one else so closely related to him, however, and aware, they say, that he was going to be an absolutely vile person, **4** he passed the rule to him so his own record would be obscured by Gaius' outrageous behaviour and the majority and best of what remained of the senate would perish with him. At all events, he is said to have often voiced that old saying "When I die let the earth be consumed in flames," and often also that Priam was blessed by being completely destroyed together with both his country and his kingdom.

2.28 Suet. *Tib.* 62.3 Had death not pre-empted him and Thrasyllus not persuaded him (on purpose, so they say) to defer some things in the hope of living longer, he was going to kill more people; and it is thought he was not even going to spare the rest of his grandchildren,[58] as he both harboured suspicions about Gaius and also felt contempt for Gemellus since he was conceived through adultery. Nor is this far from the truth; for time and again he would declare Priam a happy man for having survived all his relatives.

2.29 Tac. *Ann.* 6.46.1 This[59] was known to the emperor, and it made him hesitate over the transfer of the empire, wavering in the first instance between his grandchildren: Drusus' son was closer to him in blood and in affection but had not yet entered puberty.[60] Germanicus' son had a young man's vigour and

---

[56] Dio states that he held the office "not among the first." This may suggest not a lower order of quaestorship but rather that he was not designated to hold office in the succeeding year but in the one that followed it.

[57] If Tacitus is correct (1.22), Gemellus would have been seventeen years old when Tiberius died in AD 37 (hence probably slightly older than Nero when he succeeded Claudius in AD 54). Tiberius is supposed to doubt Gemellus' paternity because of the reputed affair between his mother Livilla and Sejanus.

[58] The sources speculate much on Tiberius' wavering intentions about the succession, but this is the only claim, surely absurd, that he planned to murder *both* Caligula and Gemellus.

[59] "This" refers to the machinations of Macro, Ennia, and Caligula.

[60] Dio (2.27) suggests that Tiberius doubted Gemellus' paternity, a point on which Tacitus remains silent. Gemellus would presumably have been well beyond puberty by the mid-30s.

the enthusiastic support of the people, which was for his grandfather grounds for hatred. He even considered Claudius, because he was at a settled age, and had a keen interest in the liberal arts, but his diminished mental capacity stood in the way. **2** If a successor were sought outside the family, however, he feared that the memory of Augustus and the name of the Caesars would be open to ridicule and insult—for Tiberius was less concerned with the present popularity than the approval of posterity. **3** Soon indecision and failing health left to fate the choice he could not make himself, although he had thrown out some remarks for it to be seen that he had some insight into the future. **4** His reproach to Macro that he was leaving a setting sun to look at one that was rising was no abstruse riddle.[61] And when Gaius Caesar mocked Lucius Sulla in some casual conversation, he made the prediction that he would have all Sulla's vices and none of his virtues.[62] On the same occasion he embraced the younger of his grandsons with floods of tears, and seeing the other's grim expression said: "You will kill him, and another will kill you."

The Death of Tiberius

Some time in early March 37, Tiberius began to feel unwell. He was not on Capri at the time, having earlier crossed over to Campania. He tried to keep up an appearance of business as usual, but he grew worse. He ended up in his fine villa at Misenum, where he eventually took to his bed. His doctor Charicles reputedly behaved like Macro's agent, alerting him that Tiberius had only two more days to live. Macro showed the superb finesse he had displayed during Sejanus' ouster, and played a major role in ensuring Caligula's accession. He gave instructions to the key people on the spot (primarily, it is to be assumed, to members of the Praetorian guard) and dispatched messengers to legionary commanders and to the governors of provinces.

Tiberius died on March 16, at the age of seventy-eight (*EJ* p. 43). The accounts of his actual death illustrate perfectly the difficulty of reconstructing events where Caligula might have played some sort of role. Clearly there was much speculation about the final hours. Dio claims that Caligula put on a show of making Tiberius more comfortable, and then suffocated him, with some help from Macro. Tacitus describes a macabre farce, in which Tiberius had apparently died, but, while

---

[61] The image of the setting/rising sun seems to have been something of a trope, repeated by Dio (4.18). Pompey is said to have used the same image, calling Sulla a setting sun when he refused Pompey a Triumph (Plut. *Pomp.* 14.3).

[62] During the chaotic period of the early first century BC Sulla had seized control of Rome in a military coup and assumed the office of dictator. He instituted a number of reforms and retired after holding his second consulship. He died in 78 BC.

Caligula was being hailed as his successor, unexpectedly showed signs of revival. He was then finished off. In this version Tacitus has Macro do the suffocating.

Suetonius presents a smorgasbord of theories, from which we are essentially invited to take our pick. Caligula poisoned Tiberius, or he starved him, or he smothered him, or he strangled him. A version to suit every taste. But in the *Tiberius* (not the *Caligula*) Suetonius casts a pall over the whole idea of a sensational demise. He informs us that in some work (not identified) Seneca (it is not clear whether this is the famous philosopher or his namesake father) suggested that the death was perfectly natural—Tiberius simply stood up, his strength failed him, he swooned, he then fell dead near the couch.

The wild speculations by all sources, balanced by the sober version of the contemporaneous Seneca, cast serious doubt on the idea that Tiberius was murdered at all. It is to be noted that Tacitus observes that Tiberius had indulged himself up to his final days, putting on a pretence of robust health and ridiculing the idea of consulting physicians. He may well simply have paid the price for excessive self-confidence.

2.30 Tac. *Ann.* 6.46.5 However, though his health was declining, Tiberius did not at all relax his debauchery, faking good health in his suffering; and he constantly ridiculed the physicians' skills and those people who, after the thirtieth year of their life, needed a stranger's advice in distinguishing what was good from what was harmful for their own bodies.

2.31 Tac. *Ann.* 6.50.1 By now Tiberius' body and strength were failing him, though not yet his dissimulation. His inflexible will was unaltered; and, firmly controlling his conversation and appearance, he would sometimes try to conceal his evident decline with contrived affability. After numerous changes of residence he finally settled in a villa that Lucius Lucullus had once owned on the promontory of Misenum.[63] There it was discovered that he was nearing the end, in the following way. 2 There was a doctor called Charicles, a man well known for his skill, who, while not regularly employed in treating the emperor's illnesses, did make himself available to him for consultation.[64] When leaving, ostensibly to conduct some private business, he grasped Tiberius' hand as a mark of respect and felt his pulse, but did not fool him in doing so. 3 For Tiberius, possibly offended and so concealing his anger all the more, ordered

[63] Lucius Lucullus was an outstanding general during the first half of the final century BC, but he is remembered primarily for his extravagance, especially for the splendour of his table, hence the term "Lucullan." There is a possibility that the villa may have been owned originally by the famous republican general Marius. According to tradition it would eventually be converted to a church and house the bones of St Severinus.
[64] Charicles is mentioned as Tiberius' physician by Suet. *Tib.* 72.3. He was significant enough to be cited by the distinguished physician Galen.

the banquet to be renewed and reclined at the table longer than usual, as if to honour his departing friend. Charicles, however, assured Macro that Tiberius' breathing was failing and he would last no more than two days. All arrangements were then accelerated, with discussions amongst those present, and messages sent to legates and armies. 4 When on March 16 his breathing failed, he was thought to have ended his mortal existence; and Gaius Caesar, surrounded by a large crowd of well-wishers, was going out to initiate his reign when word suddenly came that Tiberius' voice and vision were returning and people were being called to bring food to revive him after his fainting spell. 5 Then there was total panic and they all fled in various directions, everyone feigning grief or ignorance; but Gaius, frozen in silence, was now after the highest hopes anticipating the worst. Undaunted, Macro ordered the old man to be smothered with bedclothes piled on him, and for people to leave the doorway. Thus, in the seventy-eighth year of his life, Tiberius met his end.[65]

2.32 Suet. *Cal.* 12.2 Caligula poisoned Tiberius, so some believe, and ordered his ring taken from him while he was still breathing; and then, because he seemed to be holding on to it, he ordered a pillow to be put over his face and actually strangled him with his own hand, a freedman who cried out at the horrible deed being swiftly sent off for crucifixion.[66]

2.33 Dio 58.28.1 He died at Misenum before he knew anything of these matters. For he was ill over a long period, but since he was expecting to remain alive because of Thrasyllus' prophecy he would not consult his doctors or change his regimen;[67] 2 however, advanced in years and suffering an illness that was not debilitating, he would often waste away gradually and almost expire but then recover. And by this he brought great pleasure to everyone, Gaius as well, when they thought he would die, and also great fear when they thought he would live. 3 So fearing that he might indeed recover, Gaius would give him nothing to eat when he asked for it, claiming that it would actually do him harm, and he heaped many thick articles of clothing on him, saying that he needed warmth, and in this way he smothered him, Macro also lending a helping hand.

---

[65] Tiberius was born November 16, 42 BC.

[66] The anecdote must be treated with much caution. Crucifixion was a highly unusual punishment except for slaves and foreigners, and in any case Caligula cultivated an image of benevolence and moderation in the early months of his reign.

[67] The astrologer Thrasyllus was a scholar of some standing. He had met Tiberius when the latter was in self-imposed exile in Rhodes, and predicted that Tiberius would be recalled to Rome and designated as Augustus' successor. He remained one of the closest confidants of the emperor until his own death in AD 36.

Macro had secured the conviction of a number of his enemies on the supposedly false charge of plotting against Tiberius. To encourage Tiberius to take his time with the death sentences, even though he knew that the emperor's death was imminent, Thrasyllus made a false prediction that the emperor would live another ten years (2.28; Dio 58.27.3).

2.34 Suet. *Tib*. 73.2 There are some who think Tiberius had been given a slow-acting, emaciating poison by Gaius, others that he was denied food that he asked for while recovering from a fever he happened to have; some think a pillow was set over his face when he came to and asked for a ring that had been removed from him while in a faint. Seneca writes that, being aware of his failing state, he took the ring from his finger as if to pass it to someone but then held onto it for a moment, and resetting it on his finger and lying immobile for quite some time clenching his left hand, he suddenly called his attendants. Then, receiving no reply, he got up and, his strength giving out, fell not far from his bed.

Further Reading

Bird, H. W. 1969. "L. Aelius Sejanus and His Political Influence." *Latomus* 28: 61–98.

Deline, T. 2015. "The Criminal Charges against Agrippina the Elder in AD 29." *CQ* 65: 766–72.

Levick, B. 1999. *Tiberius the Politician*. 2nd edition. London: Routledge.

Rogers, R. S. 1931. "The Conspiracy of Agrippina." *Transactions and Proceedings of the American Philological Association* 62: 141–68.

Seager, R. 2005. *Tiberius*. Oxford: Blackwell.

Woods, D. 2007. "Tiberius on Caligula the Snake and Other Contextual Problems." *Arctos* 41: 117–27.

3

Accession

When word of Tiberius' death reached Rome, people at first found it hard to believe the news, some even suspecting it was all some sort of a trick to test their loyalty. Once the truth had sunk in, many would likely have felt a more sober concern, about who would now replace him. Once again, as he had during the earlier Sejanus crisis (see Chapter 2), Macro rose to the occasion. Even before Tiberius had actually died he had sent instructions to the provincial legates informing them of the change of regime (2.31). Instantly after the death he set out on the roughly 150-mile journey from Misenum to Rome, which he reached within two days, on March 18. We are told by Josephus that Macro carried two letters. One was intended for the prefect of the city, with instructions to move Herod Agrippa from his jail into more comfortable quarters. The other was far more significant, since it constituted the official report to the senate of Tiberius' passing. More significantly, it also supposedly contained what Josephus describes as Caligula's "own succession to sovereignty," which in that strict formulation is hardly conceivable, and surely Josephus' own conjecture about what the letter in fact *signified*, rather than what it actually said. In the long run, of course, Josephus was proved essentially right, since the communication to the senate marked the first step in a delicate manoeuvre initiated by Macro to ensure Caligula's smooth progression to the principate.

The First Steps

The first issue to be confronted was Tiberius' will. He had identified Caligula and Gemellus as joint heirs to his estate, and both Dio and Philo understand this to mean that he had conferred on them the joint rule of the empire (3.4, 5; implied by Phil. *Flacc.* 10). This is surely unjustified: the constitutionally scrupulous Tiberius could hardly have presumed simply to pass down the principate, let alone a shared principate, to a successor. This is not to say that the will was not politically significant. Since neither of Tiberius' grandchildren had held an office important enough to mark him out unmistakably as the next emperor, their only quasi-legal and very tenuous claim was that they were heirs to the estate of the previous emperor. As such, neither case was technically stronger than the other, beyond the fact that Caligula was older and had assumed the toga of manhood, a rather tenuous basis for elevation to the position of emperor. Macro had a simple

The Emperor Caligula in the Ancient Sources. Anthony A. Barrett and J. C. Yardley, Oxford University Press.
© Anthony A. Barrett and J. C. Yardley 2023. DOI: 10.1093/oso/9780198854562.003.0004

solution. He had quiet words with the consuls and others beforehand and ensured that the senate would declare the will null and void, on the grounds that Tiberius had not been *compos mentis*, according to Dio (3.4). In the event Caligula did in fact inherit the entirety of Tiberius' estate but seems to have done so by virtue not of a will, but by a principle that on succession the new emperor not only acquired the constitutional powers of his predecessor, he also acquired his property, not through the regular process of inheritance but by virtue of his being the next emperor. Later emperors generally simply gave up writing wills, and henceforth the regular laws of inheritance did not seem to apply in imperial succession.

3.1 Jos. *Ant.* 18.224 After appointing Gaius successor to the realm,[1] Tiberius died, living on for only a few days and having himself held power for five months and three days over the twenty-two years.[2] Gaius was the fourth emperor.[3] **225** Romans received the tidings of Tiberius' death, and while they rejoiced at the good news they did not have the confidence to believe it...

3.2 Jos. *Ant.* 18.234 Reports grew through the city the following day, with more assurance that Tiberius was dead; men had the confidence to talk openly about it and some were even offering sacrifices; and letters arrived from Gaius, one to the senate with confirmation of Tiberius' death and his own succession to sovereignty, **235** and the other to Piso, prefect of the city, reporting the same thing and ordering that Agrippa be moved from the prison to the house where he had resided before being detained.

3.3 Suet. *Tib.* 76.1 He had made a will in duplicate two years earlier, one in his own handwriting and one in a freedman's (though with the same provisions), and he had had them signed and sealed by very lowly witnesses. In that will he left as joint heirs Germanicus' son Gaius (sc. Caligula), and Drusus' son Tiberius (sc. Gemellus).[4]

---

[1] This contradicts Suetonius' claim (3.3) that Tiberius had made his will two years before his death, and had named both male grandchildren joint heirs.

[2] Tiberius was born on November 16, 42 BC.

[3] Josephus' term is *autokrator*; he clearly includes Julius Caesar (followed by Augustus and Tiberius) in the list.

[4] Either the official will or a copy would probably have been stored in the imperial archives, where Suetonius presumably gained access to the details described here. It is possible that the will in Tiberius' own hand had earlier been deposited with the Vestal Virgins, following the precedent of Augustus (Suet. *Aug.* 101.1) and that the copy was retained by Tiberius, to avoid any later chicanery; it is not clear which copy was read out to the senate by Macro (3.4). The reference to the lowly status of the witnesses (3.3) might possibly reflect the arguments made to invalidate the will. It is to be noted that despite the reports of Tiberius' dithering in his final years he had apparently already made his determination about Caligula and Gemellus two years before his own death.

3.4 Dio 59.1.1 Such then is what has been transmitted about Tiberius, and he was succeeded by Gaius, the son of Germanicus and Agrippina whom, as I have said, they used to call both "Germanicus" and "Caligula." He also left the empire jointly to his own grandson Gemellus; **2** but with Macro as intermediary Gaius sent his will to the senate and had it annulled by the consuls and others that he had earlier primed, on the grounds that Tiberius was not *compos mentis* since he had entrusted authority over them to a boy not yet allowed entry to the senate. **3** Caligula thus abruptly cut Gemellus off from power, and after doing so had him put to death (and this although Tiberius had often expressed his wishes in his will, anticipating that through it they would have some force, and although it was then read out in full in the senate by Macro).

3.5 Philo *Leg.* 23 For he executed his cousin, who had also been left as co-heir to the principate together with him and was closer to the succession since he was grandson of Tiberius by birth, while Gaius himself was so only by adoption. He claimed it was for conspiracy, not taking account of his age in that charge (for the poor lad had barely left boyhood for puberty).

3.6 Philo *Leg.* 87 You steel-hearted, pitiless wretch, you savagely murdered a brother, who was also your joint heir, in the bloom of his youth.

Imperial Powers

In the absence of a will, and in the absence of someone previously groomed as successor by the sitting princeps and who in that position had shared many of the princeps's offices (true of Tiberius on the death of Augustus), and in the absence of any formal constitutional mechanism for selecting a new princeps, it seems that the basis for Caligula's accession rested upon a fundamental principle that had been very dear to Augustus, that of *consensus*, namely, that Caligula was the choice of all three ranks of the Roman state, the ordinary people, the equestrians, and the senators. Macro, of course, as noted, had already sent out instructions to the provincial legates in command of the armies, and he himself commanded the Praetorian guard, the branch of the army present in Rome and Italy, so it might be said that the senators who confirmed the process of succession with the consensus of the other orders had a figurative gun to their heads. Yet they do seem to have yielded to Macro's *fait accompli* with considerable enthusiasm. Perhaps they felt demoralized after what many would have seen as the repressive terror of the Sejanian/Tiberian years. Moreover, they may well have hoped that a son of Germanicus would herald a new and liberal age, and if into the bargain he was relatively young and almost totally inexperienced that might mean that he could be controlled by them. It perhaps seems remarkably naïve, but also hardly surprising—the very same senators, or at least that majority still alive some seventeen years later, would repeat the exact same mistake when they eagerly welcomed Caligula's nephew, the even younger and, if anything, less experienced Nero, as their new emperor.

By the time that Augustus died in AD 14, Tiberius had already been invested with considerable constitutional power, and his succession, though unprecedented, progressed almost by its own momentum. In Caligula's case the mechanism had to be created and had to be cranked into motion. There can surely be little doubt that it was Macro who did the cranking and who engineered the important process of formal senatorial acknowledgment. Things happened quickly. The Arval record (3.7) shows that already by March 18, two days after Tiberius' death, the senate had acknowledged Caligula as *Imperator* (3.7: the relevant section of the inscription is in fact missing for AD 37, but it is extant for the next two years, when the anniversary of the acclamation is recorded). *Imperator* was a very old Roman term. After a major victory a commander in the field might be acclaimed as *Imperator* by his troops. The commander could then assume the title *Imperator* at the end of his nomenclature, for the remainder of his term of office, although Caesar and others retained it after their term had expired, and it became part of the regular nomenclature of Octavian, who assumed it as a praenomen, thus at the beginning of his list of names. By Tiberius' time the term seems to convey little more than the notion of princeps, a process that Tiberius felt was regrettable, causing him to insist that he would remain *Imperator* only to his troops.[5] It is probably safe to assume that, on the death of Tiberius on March 16, Macro would have ensured that the praetorians in attendance at Misenum acclaimed Caligula as *Imperator* (we have no explicit evidence). In that case, the senate followed suit two days later, on March 18.

3.7 Acts of the Arvals (Smallwood 3.10: March 18, AD 38; 8.14: March 18, AD 39)

(*sacrifices were carried out*) because on this day he was acclaimed *Imperator* by the senate.[6]

3.8 RIC² 1.32. Brass sestertius. April AD 37–April 38, reissued 39–41 (Figure 3)

Obverse: laureate head of Caligula, facing left: CAESAR AVG(ustus) GERMANICVS PON(tifex) M(aximus) TR(ibunicia) POT(estate) "Caesar Augustus Germanicus, Chief Priest, endowed with Tribunician Authority"

[5] Dio 57.8.1.
[6] According to Suetonius (Suet. *Cal.* 8.12), Caligula ruled three years, ten months, and eight days, which seems to date his accession from this senatorial acclamation. Dio (59.8.13) says that he ruled three years, nine months, and twenty-eight days, thus presumably dating the accession from the senate meeting held ten days later, after Caligula's arrival in Rome.

Figure 3 Brass sestertius. Yale University Art Gallery.

Reverse: on the right, the emperor standing on a platform, facing left, right arm raised, haranguing five soldiers facing right, holding standards: ADLOCUT(io) COH(ortis/ortium) "The addressing of the cohort(s)"

The grant of tribunician authority, awarded to emperors at the beginning of their reigns through a law passed by a popular assembly, was renewed on each anniversary, and when reference is made to that tribunician authority in the official record the year of renewal is systematically recorded. Where no number is indicated (as here) the reference is by default to the very first year of tenure, that is, to the first year of a given reign. Hence this coin was minted between April 37 and April 38.

This is a strikingly innovative issue, the first to depict an emperor addressing his troops. Dio observes (3.17) that Caligula carried out a review of the guard with the senators and handed out to them the legacy bequeathed by Tiberius and matched that with funds from his own pocket. It has been suggested that this coin may have been one of those distributed on that occasion. But it could hardly have been minted in time, and in any case we might expect that a donative of the size recorded for the Praetorians would be made mainly in silver denarii. This coin perhaps more likely commemorates the acclamation of Caligula as *Imperator*, probably made in the first instance by the Praetorians.

Arrival in Rome

Caligula in the meantime had accompanied Tiberius' body in spectacular fashion from Misenum to Rome, greeted with rapturous enthusiasm in every town he passed through, no doubt at least in part because of advance preparation by

Macro. He reached Rome on March 28, ten days after his acclamation by the senate as *Imperator* (above), and on that, or the following, day he went before the august body. This was a hugely significant meeting. It was attended not only by senators but also by equestrians and even by the common people, no doubt deliberately to emphasize that the formal transmission of powers was occurring with the consensus of all three orders.[7] Perhaps even more remarkably, at that same meeting Caligula was granted what Suetonius calls "supreme authority." Augustus had acquired his authority gradually and almost imperceptibly. This was less true of Tiberius, but Tiberius' position was still to a degree nuanced. It seems that Caligula's powers were granted to him by a "law of imperial rule," a *lex imperii*, approved in a single piece of block legislation at one sitting of the senate (to be formally confirmed afterwards by the popular assembly). It was a truly momentous event. In one stroke Caligula made the transition from relatively obscure low-level magistrate to all-powerful princeps. There could no longer be the fiction that the princeps was merely a first citizen whose power rested on an undefined authority and prestige, exercised with discretion, a position that Augustus handled with finesse and one that seems to have been a constant source of angst for Tiberius. By this one piece of legislation Caligula became emperor, with autocratic powers, and he would very soon return the favour by acting like an emperor with autocratic powers. But for the moment he conducted himself with admirable restraint, and his accession was greeted with jubilation, both in Rome and, to judge from the reaction in Alexandria (5.48:356), throughout the empire as a whole.

3.9 Suet. *Cal.* 14.1 On entering the city he was immediately granted supreme authority with the full agreement of the senate and the crowd that had pushed its way into the senate house, and this contradicted the wishes of Tiberius, who had made his other grandson coheir with him in his will when the boy still wore the praetexta,[8] and this brought such great joy to the people that over the next three months—and not even that—more than 160,000 animals are said to have been sacrificed.[9]

3.10 Dio 59.6.1 Now in the year that Tiberius died and Caligula came to power, he was at first very flattering towards the senators on the occasion when there were a number of equites and ordinary people present in the senate, and he committed to sharing power with them and doing everything to their

---

[7] In his *Res Gestae*, Augustus declares that "exercising power in all things through consensus I transferred the state from my authority to the jurisdiction of the senate and Roman people" (*RG* 34).

[8] See "toga" in the glossary.

[9] The figure presumably comes from the imperial archives, but we do not know if it applies specifically to Rome or to the empire as a whole.

satisfaction, saying he was their son and their charge. 2 He was five months and four days short of being twenty-five years old at the time.

3.11 Dio 59.3.1 He followed just the same pattern in almost everything else. At first appearing supremely democratic, to the point of writing nothing either to the senate or the common people or having anything to do with imperial nomenclature, he then became an absolute ruler, **2** going so far as to accept in a single day all the things that Augustus had barely accepted one at a time when they were voted to him over the period of such a long reign, and some that Tiberius had downright refused. For apart from the designation "Father" he put off acceptance of no other title; and even that one he took after no long wait.[10]

Honours for Tiberius

In the delicate matter of divine honours for Tiberius, Caligula, perhaps under the firm guidance of Macro, demonstrated an appropriate balance between *pietas* in showing respect to the memory of his late grandfather, and deference to the senate, who had little enthusiasm for the late emperor. Caligula had clearly requested such honours in the letter that he sent to that body through Macro, but the senators perhaps could read through the lines and appreciate that this was not an issue close to the new emperor's heart. They therefore procrastinated and the matter appears not to have been pursued further. Dio seems to suggest that Caligula treated Tiberius with disrespect, sneaking the body into the city and holding the funeral early the next day. This is yet another episode that illustrates the value of being able to check the literary authorities against the epigraphic evidence. The Fasti of Ostia show that in fact Tiberius' body reached Rome on March 19 and that the funeral took place six days later, not a hurried affair at all. Moreover Suetonius says that the funeral was elaborate (3.26) and Josephus refers to an extravagant event.[11]

3.12 Dio 59.3.7 He asserted that Tiberius himself, whom he referred to as "grandfather," should receive the same honours from the senate as had Augustus. Then, when these were not immediately voted (for the senators, who, though not inclined to respect Tiberius had not dared to disrespect him either, were still unaware of the young man's character and were deferring everything until he arrived) the respect he showed for the man went no further than a state funeral in which he had the corpse brought into the city at night and put on view at dawn. **8** He did indeed say some words over him, not so

---

[10] It was customary to postpone acceptance of the title of *Pater Patriae* ("Father of the Nation"). See the discussion on 3.50, 51.

[11] Jos. *Ant.* 18.236.

much praising him as reminding the people about Augustus and then putting himself in their hands.

3.13 Fasti Ostienses (Smallwood 31.16, Figure 1). Ostia. AD 37
Four days before the Kalends of April (March 29) the body was brought into the city by the soldiers. Three days before the Nones of April (April 3) he was seen off in a public funeral.

3.14 Philo *Leg.* 12 Certainly, all that you could see in the cities were altars, sacred offerings, sacrificial victims, cheerful people dressed in white and wearing garlands, beaming goodwill from happy countenances, festivals, gatherings, musical contests, horse races, revelry, all-night feasts with the music of flutes and cithara, jollity, abandonment, holidays, every imaginable pleasure appealing to every one of the senses.

Legacies

One particular gesture of Caligula's would have made his accession very welcome—the payment of Tiberius' legacies. As Suetonius indicates (3.16), with the abrogation of Tiberius' will the legacies would become null and void. But it would be politically astute to ensure that they were paid anyhow. The chief beneficiary of his generosity was the Praetorian guard, and Caligula was in effect the first claimant to reward them for their assistance in his accession, establishing a precedent for his successors (including his immediate successor, his uncle Claudius, who paid them 15,000 each!). Of course it could be argued that his father Germanicus had set a sort of precedent when he used cash to attempt to buy the acquiescence of the mutinous legions after Augustus' death (Tac. *Ann.* 1.37).

The Fasti of Ostia also record the distribution in June and July of 150 sestertii in all to each of the people as largesses. (See Figure 1 ll. 9–10: K IVN CONG D X LXXV XIIII [K]/AVG ALTERI X LXXV.) These are presumably separate from the sums paid out from legacies.

3.15 Suet. *Tib.* 76.1 He also left legacies to several people, including the Vestal Virgins, but also to all the soldiers, every member of the Roman people, and even, as a separate bequest, to the magistrates of the city wards.[12]

3.16 Suet. *Cal.* 16.3 Although the will of Tiberius had been set aside, he forthwith paid out the legacies in that will faithfully and without quibbling,

---

[12] Rome was organized by *vici* (wards). There were 265 in the time of Pliny the Elder (died AD 79). They were under the direction of local magistrates, *vicomagistri*, who could be either free-born Romans or freedmen. They wore official dress and were accompanied by two lictors (essentially bodyguards).

and in addition he paid in full the legacies in Julia Augusta's will, which Tiberius had suppressed.[13]

3.17 Dio 59.2.1 Moreover, by granting all of Tiberius' bequests as if they came from him personally, he gained something of a reputation for generosity among the common people. Then, after a review of the Praetorian guard that he conducted together with the senate, he distributed among them the thousand sestertii per person that had been left to them, and added a further amount equal to it. **2** To the people he also paid out forty five million (such was the amount left to them) and also added the 240 sestertii per person that they had not received at the time of his adoption of the toga virilis, plus a further 60 sestertii in interest. **3** He paid out bequests to the Urban Cohorts,[14] to the Vigiles,[15] to the legionary troops on active service outside Italy, as well as to such citizen elements as were serving in the smaller forts,[16] as follows: to the Urban Cohorts 500 sestertii each, to all the others 300.

4 He also did the very same thing in seeing to the disposition of Livia's bequests; for he distributed all of them. And had he spent the rest of the money in a magnanimous way he would have been thought a great-minded and magnificent man. He actually took such steps from fear of the people and the troops, but generally it was a matter of conscience, since he released to the general public as well as to individuals bequests that came not just from Tiberius but also from his great-grandmother.

3.18 Fasti Ostienses (Smallwood 31.21). Ostia. AD 37
Kalends of June (June 1). Largesse distributed, 75 (sestertii). 14 days before the Kalends of August (July 19), 75 (sestertii).

---

[13] The invalidation of Tiberius' will at the beginning of the reign technically absolved Caligula of the obligations to honour its provisions. Tiberius had already declined to honour his mother's will (Tac. *Ann.* 5.1.4; Suet. *Tib.* 51.2, *Galb.* 5.2; Dio 58.23ª). The political pressure on Caligula to honour Livia's will would not have been as powerful as in the case of Tiberius'. Caligula's gesture might reflect his affection for his great-grandmother, or his appreciation, perhaps at the prompting of Macro, that it would be a good public relations gesture to pay the bequests anyhow.

[14] The Urban Cohorts were formed by Augustus some time before AD 5 (they are included by Dio 55.24.6 in his survey of Rome's military forces in that year). Initially made up of three cohorts, they were based in Rome under the command of the prefect of the city, with the task of maintaining public order. On Caligula's assassination the Praetorians supported Claudius, while the Urban Cohorts were loyal to the senate.

[15] The Vigiles ("watchmen") were formed by Augustus in AD 6, primarily to fight fires, although their remit gradually became much wider, to cover looting, fraud, burglary, and runaway slaves. They were less politically significant than the Praetorians but under Macro's command they were used in AD 31 to bring down Sejanus, when the loyalty of the Praetorians to their prefect no doubt was a cause for concern.

[16] The Roman frontier army at this time consisted of two basic groups, legionaries, generally stationed in large garrison fortresses, and auxiliaries, housed in much smaller forts, although considerable flexibility is observed in these arrangements. Legionary troops were Roman citizens, while auxiliaries were usually recruited from among non-citizens in the provinces, but citizens are also found serving in the auxilia, both as officers and also as private soldiers.

Maiestas

The action that would have brought the greatest sense of relief to the upper levels of society would surely have been Caligula's declared intention to abolish *maiestas* (loosely "treason") trials, a source of enormous fear and distress under Tiberius, when harsh sentences had become common, and when many of the trials seem to have been motivated by political enmity rather than the need to punish criminal wrongdoing. Caligula dismissed all the current cases, allowing those previously convicted to return from exile (two years later he reintroduced such processes). As a further grand gesture he declared that he bore no grievance against those who had attacked his family, and made a big show of burning the papers from their cases—copies, quite clearly, since he would not hesitate later to make use of the originals (4.36, 38).

3.19 Suet. *Cal.* 15.4 Similar populist measures were: recalling people condemned and exiled; granting amnesty for all charges pending from earlier days; having documents pertaining to cases of his mother and brothers brought into the forum and burned (after loudly praying to the gods to bear witness that he had not read or touched any of them); and refusing to accept a note brought to him about his personal safety, claiming that he had done nothing to make anybody hate him and that he did not listen to informers.[17]

3.20 Dio 59.6.2 He then freed those who were in prison, including Quintus Pomponius, who had been kept in jail for all of seven years after his consulship and been badly manhandled there;[18] and he put an end to charges of *lèse-majesté*, which he saw as being detainees' greatest scourge, **3** and, gathering together the relevant documents that Tiberius had left, he burned them, or so he claimed. "This I have done," he said, "so that no matter how much resentment I may feel for someone over my mother and over my brothers,[19] I shall not be able to punish him."

---

[17] Aurelius Victor (*Caes.* 3.8), who records this action, claims that it followed the exposure of a conspiracy. But it would be unsafe to assume a conspiracy so early in the reign. Victor may have been influenced by Suetonius' claim (*Jul.* 81.4) that Julius Caesar was handed a similar note just before his assassination. Suetonius uses identical words for the "note" (*libellus*) in both cases.

[18] Pomponius was a man of some significance. He was a successful playwright, and considered a great orator. He was also the subject of a biography by the elder Pliny. Tainted by an indirect connection with Sejanus, he was imprisoned, and on release showed his gratitude to Caligula by hosting an expensive banquet. He later enjoyed a consulship and military command under the next emperor, Claudius.

[19] The precise nature of the papers relating to Agrippina and Nero is not clear. Dusus seems to have been tried formally, presumably before the senate, if Dio reports events correctly (Dio 59.3.8). Despite their supposed destruction, the papers reappeared later in Caligula's reign. Claudius eventually destroyed them (Dio 60.4.5).

Reaction of the Empire

Macro's prompt action in informing the provincial governors of Caligula's accession bore fruit. This is demonstrated by the actions of Vitellius, legate of the key province of Syria. Vitellius was in Jerusalem for the Passover (in AD 37 it fell on April 20), on the verge of a campaign against King Aretas of Nabatea, when Macro's communication reached him. On learning of Tiberius' death, Vitellius immediately administered an oath of loyalty to Caligula and acknowledged his authority by calling a halt to his planned military operation, since it had not yet been authorized by the new emperor (see Chapter 7, n.1).

> **3.21 Jos.** *Ant.* **18.124** When a letter reached Vitellius on the fourth day reporting Tiberius' death, he made the masses swear an oath of allegiance to Gaius. He also recalled the troops to their various winter quarters since he was no longer able to initiate the war because of the transfer of authority to Gaius.

From the western part of the empire we have a piece of contemporary and concrete evidence for the routine procedure following the accession of a new emperor. It comes in the form of an inscription from the province of Lusitania where, on May 11, the legate of the province, Gaius Ummidius Durmius Quadratus, is seen administering the oath of loyalty to the new emperor in the city of Aritium (modern Alvega, Portugal).

> **3.22 *ILS* 190 (Smallwood 32). Aritium, Lusitania, May 11, AD 37**
> Gaius Ummidius Durmius Quadratus, propraetorian legate of Gaius Caesar Germanicus Imperator.[20]
> The oath of the citizens of Aritium:
> I swear in my heart that I will be the enemy of those I discover to be the enemies of Gaius Caesar Germanicus and I shall not cease to pursue in armed warfare by land and sea anyone who brings or might bring danger upon him and his welfare until that person has been punished, and I shall not consider myself or my children more precious than his welfare, and those who have been of hostile intent towards him I shall consider to be my enemies. If I deliberately belie my declaration now or in the future, then may Jupiter

---

[20] Caligula has the title of *Imperator*, perhaps through an acclamation from the troops in Lusitania, or perhaps reflecting the decree of the senate recognizing him as such on March 18. He is not "Augustus," a title that technically only the senate could confer, which would not happen until his first meeting with that body (3.11).

Optimus Maximus and the deified Augustus and all the other immortal gods remove from me my country, my security, and all my future prospects.

May 11 in Aritium Vetus, in the consulship of Gnaeus Acerronius Proculus and Gaius Petronius Pontius Nigrinus, in the magistracy of Vegetus, son of Tallicus...

Family

Caligula went out of his way to show his dedication to his family, a gesture that would have struck a chord with most Romans, given the huge emphasis that they placed on family loyalty (an important element of the much-admired concept of *pietas*).

Germanicus

Caligula's father Germanicus was singled out for particular distinction. While there is no reason to doubt that Caligula felt a genuine affection for his late father, his action is reminiscent in some ways of the great efforts made by Octavian/ Augustus to honour his adoptive father Julius Caesar, in that there were distinct political benefits in reminding Romans of a distinguished and admired ante- cedent. Coins were issued bearing Germanicus' image, and even more remarkably, the month of September was renamed after him. There were precedents for this last measure: Quinctilis had been renamed after Julius Caesar (it was the month of his birth), and Sextilis had been renamed after Augustus. These two earlier changes were long-lasting and have survived to today. Caligula's reform proved ephemeral.

3.23 Suet. *Cal.* 15.2 Now to commemorate his father he renamed the month of September "Germanicus" after him.

Precious metal coins were issued honouring Germanicus, identifying him as Caligula's father (see also the issues for Agrippina [3.29, 30]).

3.24 *RIC*² 1.18. Silver denarius. AD 37 (Figure 4)
Obverse: laureate head of Caligula, facing right: C(aius) CAESAR AVG(ustus) GERM(anicus) P(ontifex) M(aximus) TR(ibunicia) POT(estate) "Gaius Caesar Augustus Germanicus, Chief Priest, endowed with Tribunician Authority"
Reverse: head of Germanicus, facing right: GERMANICVS CAES(ar) P(ater) C (aii) CAES(aris) AVG(usti) GERM(anici) "Germanicus Caesar, Father of Gaius Caesar Augustus Germanicus"
On *tribunicia potestas*, see 3.8.

Figure 4 Silver denarius. Münzkabinett, Staatliche Museen zu Berlin. Photographs by Dirk Sonnenwald.

Figure 5 Copper as. Yale University Art Gallery.

3.25 *RIC²* 1.35. **Copper as.** AD 37 (Figure 5)
Obverse: Head of Germanicus, facing left: GERMANICUS CAESAR TI(berii) AUGUST(i) F(ilius) DIVI AUG(usti) N(epos) "Germanicus Caesar, son of Tiberius Augustus, grandson of deified Augustus"
Reverse: C(aius) CAESAR AVG(ustus) GERMANICVS PON(tifex) M(aximus) TR(ibunicia) POT(estate), around large S(enatus)C(onsulto) "Gaius Caesar Augustus Germanicus, Chief Priest, endowed with Tribunician Authority" "By a decree of the senate")

This coin was issued only in AD 37 (Caligula's tribunican authority carries no numeration and must be the first award [3.8]), clearly in connection with the honours that were voted then for Germanicus. The reverse is identical to that used on the special issue of his brothers Nero and Drusus (3.33), the identical type possibly conveying the sense of unity of the family.

The legend SC (Senatus Consulto, "by a decree of the senate") is generally (though not totally) limited to base metal coinage, and the traditional view was long that from Augustus on the emperor controlled gold and silver coinage, and left the minting of the low-value issues to the senate, which accordingly indicated its authority with this legend. There is in fact no direct evidence for such a shared responsibility and more recently other explanations have been offered, for instance that it distinguished official coinage from local issues and thus suggested its greater authority and reliability. It may be that over time the abbreviation became something of a traditional motif, with little administrative or constitutional significance.

Mother and Brothers

Because the fates of Agrippina and of her two oldest sons were similar, and because to some degree the honours paid to them were also similar, it will be convenient to consider both topics together. After his accession Caligula publicly exploited to the full the tragedy of his mother and two brothers, displaying himself as a devoted son and brother. He went to the islands of Pontia and Pandateria where Agrippina and Nero had died and recovered their ashes, which in Nero's case at least must have been difficult since they had been dispersed in order precisely to prevent their recovery. The journey was not an easy one, since the seas were rough, which would have made his dutiful piety all the more striking. Their ashes joined those of Caligula's father Germanicus in the mausoleum of Augustus. Inscriptions that accompanied the funerary urns have survived (3.28, 3.31, a copy in the case of Nero). Nero is there identified as the son of Germanicus, great-grandson of Augustus; the name of Tiberius (technically his grandfather) is omitted, possibly because Tiberius was seen as causing his death, and Caligula may have wished to avoid stirring up public resentment. Moreover, by omitting Tiberius' name, the inscription as it stands serves to emphasize his brother's Augustan genealogy. Drusus' remains could not be recovered and cenotaphs were built to honour him (3.32). Statues for the two dead brothers were ordered; Claudius was responsible for arranging them, and bungled the task.[21]

3.26 Suet. Cal. 15.1 He also personally tried to arouse people's enthusiasm with all kinds of popularity-seeking measures. After praising Tiberius with

---

[21] Suet. *Claud.* 9.1.

floods of tears at an assembly and giving him a most elaborate funeral, he immediately hurried off to Pandateria and the Pontian islands to bring back the ashes of his mother and brother,[22] doing so in a violent storm for his family loyalty to be evident; and he approached them respectfully and set them in their urns himself.[23] With no less melodrama he had them conveyed to Ostia with a banner on the stern of his bireme, and from there up the Tiber to Rome, where he had them brought on two stretchers into the Mausoleum by the most distinguished members of the equestrian order in a crowded middle of the day;[24] and he also established funeral rites to be offered every year at public expense, as well as circus games in his mother's honour, with a wheeled carriage for her to be carried in effigy in the procession.[25]

3.27 Dio 59.3.5 Sailing over in person, he gathered and brought back the bones of his mother and dead brothers[26] with his own hands, and dressed in the purple-fringed toga and with an entourage of lictors as at a Triumph laid them in the mausoleum of Augustus.

3.28 Smallwood 84a. Rome. AD 37 The bones of Agrippina, daughter of Marcus Agrippa, granddaughter of Deified Augustus, wife of Germanicus Caesar, mother of Gaius Caesar Augustus Germanicus, Princeps.
A silver denarius was issued to honour his mother, Agrippina, matching the issue honouring his father (3.25).

3.29 *RIC*² 1.55. Silver denarius. AD 37 (Figure 6)
Obverse: laureate head of Caligula, facing right: C(aius) CAESAR AVG(ustus) GERM(anicus) P(ontifex) M(aximus) TR(ibunicia) POT(estate) "Gaius Caesar Augustus Germanicus, Chief Priest, endowed with Tribunician Authority"
Reverse: draped bust of Agrippina, facing right, hair in plait behind AGRIPPINA MAT(er) C(aii) CAES(aris) AVG(usti) "Agrippina, mother of Gaius Caesar Augustus Germanicus"
On *tribunicia potestas*, see 3.8.

---

[22] Modern Ponza and Ventotene. These islands were at this period places of exile for the Roman upper crust; Agrippina was sent to Pandateria, Nero to Pontia (as, in more recent years, was Mussolini, following his dismissal in 1943).
[23] Tiberius' funeral was held on April 3 (3.13), and Caligula apparently departed immediately afterwards. This means that he travelled when the seas were considered dangerous for shipping (traditionally until May 27), which would make his *pietas* seem all the greater.
[24] The ship could in fact have deposited the urns right at the actual Mausoleum of Augustus since there seems to have been access by boat: Calpurnius Piso, the rival of Germanicus, caused offence by landing his own boat there after returning from Syria (Tac. *Ann.* 3.9.3). Caligula seems however to have landed some distance away, no doubt deliberately, so as to stage a procession at a time of day when the neighbourhood was at its busiest.
[25] The *carpentum* was a two-wheeled carriage (see 3.30).
[26] Dio is particularly casual here. The remains of Drusus were not recovered.

Figure 6 Silver denarius. Yale University Art Gallery.

Figure 7 Brass sestertius. Yale University Art Gallery.

Germanicus and Agrippina were commemorated in matching issues of precious metal coins. In addition each was honoured by a distinctive base metal issue (3.25 for Germanicus). The Agrippina coin is undated but was probably issued initially in the first year of the reign, and also probably continued throughout.

3.30 *RIC*² 1.55 (Smallwood 84b). Brass sestertius. Undated (Figure 7)
Obverse: draped bust of Agrippina, looking right: AGRIPPINA M(arci) F(ilia) MAT(er) C(aii) CAESARIS AUGUSTI "Agrippina, daughter of Marcus, mother of Caius Caesar Augustus"
Reverse: *carpentum* drawn by mules, moving left: S(enatus)P(opulus)Q(ue) R(omanus) MEMORIAE AGRIPINNAE "Senate and Roman people, to the memory of Agrippina"

The *carpentum* was a two-wheeled, covered, mule-drawn carriage, used by women and associated in particular with women of the imperial family. On this coin the window curtains are raised, to display the image mentioned by Suetonius (3.26).

3.31 Smallwood 85a. Rome. AD 37 The bones of Nero Caesar son of Germanicus Caesar, grandson of the Deified Augustus, Flamen of Augustus,[27] quaestor.

3.32 *ILS* 187 Bergamo. AD 37(?) To the shades of Drusus Caesar [son of] Germanicus.

The very public act of family piety towards his brothers was emphasized by the issue of a dupondius (worth half a sestertius) depicting Nero and Drusus, minted initially in the first year of the reign. It shows them on horseback, with their cloaks flying behind them.

3.33 *RIC*² 1.34,42,49 (Smallwood 85b). Brass dupondius. Minted with slight variants in each subsequent year of the reign
Obverse: Nero and Drusus on horseback galloping to the right, with flowing cloaks: NERO ET DRVSVS CAESARES "Nero Caesar and Drusus Caesar"
Reverse: identical to reverse of Figure 4.

The memory of Nero and Drusus (like that of Caligula's youngest sister, Drusilla) remained untarnished, and unlike the two surviving sisters, they did not sully their reputations by involvement in plots against their brother; Caligula honoured them with this coin throughout his reign.

Sisters

Striking honours were granted to Caligula's three sisters. Apart from receiving the privileges of the Vestal Virgins they were included also in the traditional formula used by the consuls when putting motions before the senate, to wish success to the emperor. They were also named in the annual vows taken for his safety. Tiberius had taken vigorous exception to the inclusion of Caligula's brothers Nero and Drusus in such vows in AD 24.[28] Even more remarkably the sisters were included also in the annual vows of allegiance taken to the emperor.

3.34 Suet. *Cal.* 15.3 In the case of his sisters, he ensured that their names were included in all oaths ("Nor shall I hold myself and my children more dear than

---

[27] A flamen was a priest assigned the worship of a particular god. Flamines were appointed to the worship of deified emperors in Rome and in the provinces.
[28] Tac. *Ann.* 4.17.1; Suet. *Tib.* 54.1.

Figure 8 Brass sestertius. Yale University Art Gallery.

Gaius and his sisters")[29] as well as in the consuls' motions ("may it turn out well for Gaius Caesar and his sisters").[30]

3.35 Dio 59.3.4 He also gave his sisters the privileges granted to Vestal Virgins, together with the right to watch the horse races in the same front seats as he, to be included in prayers made annually by magistrates and priests for his and the common welfare, and in the oaths of allegiance sworn to his sovereignty.

3.36 *RIC*² 1.33 (Smallwood 86). Brass sestertius. April 37–April 38 (Figure 8).
Obverse: bust of the emperor: C(aius) CAESAR AUG(ustus) GERMANICUS PO(ntifex) M(aximus) TR(ibunicia) POT(estate) "Gaius Caesar Augustus Germanicus, Chief Priest, endowed with Tribunician Authority"
Reverse: Caligula's sisters: AGRIPPINA, DRUSILLA, IULIA. S(enatus) C(onsulto) "By a decree of the senate"
This is a remarkably innovative coin, a powerful piece of contemporary physical evidence for the high regard in which Caligula held all three sisters, Agrippina, Drusilla, and Julia Livilla, during the initial phase of his reign. This issue is also sadly ironic, since Drusilla died some time in AD 38, and Agrippina and Livilla became involved in AD 39 in a conspiracy against Caligula, resulting in their exile.

---

[29] In the oath taken by Ummidius, governor of Lusitania (3.22), the sisters are not mentioned, presumably because Ummidius reacted to the instructions of Macro before the formal accession and the formal inclusion of the sisters in the vows.

[30] When proposals were presented to the senate by the consuls they normally began with an invocation to the emperor, which could include a broad reference to the imperial house. When the senate approved the conferring of the title of "Father of the Country" on Augustus they prefaced their proposal with "May fortune and favour attend you and your house, Caesar Augustus" (Suet. *Aug.* 58.2). In Caligula's case the invocation itself was fairly conventional; what was unprecedented was the specific mention of the sisters.

To the extent that this coin image might have a political purpose (as opposed to reflecting genuine personal and sentimental feelings, a motive not to be discounted), it is doubtless meant to enhance the prestige of the imperial family and thus of Caligula himself. There is no justification for reading into it any suggestion that Caligula planned to give his sisters any kind of partnership in the exercise of actual power.

On tribunician authority, see 3.8; on the letters SC, see 3.25.

Marcus Agrippa

There was even provision for the honouring of Caligula's grandfather, Marcus Agrippa, the loyal lieutenant then later son-in-law of Augustus.

3.37 Suet. *Cal.* 23.1 He did not wish to be either considered or referred to as Agrippa's grandson because of the man's poor pedigree, and would fly into a rage if anyone slipped him in among the ancestors of the Caesars either in an oration or in poetry. He even used to claim that his own mother was born through incest committed by Augustus with his daughter Julia.[31]

3.38 Philo *Leg.* 290 This temple, Lord Gaius, has from the start accepted no man-made image because it is the abode of the true god... **291** Your grandfather Agrippa held the temple in honour when he went there, and so did Augustus.[32]

3.39 *RIC*² 1.58 (Smallwood 82b). Copper as. Undated (Figure 9).
Obverse: head of Agrippa, facing left: M(arcus) AGRIPPA L(ucii) F(ilius) CO(n)S(ul) III "Marcus Agrippa, son of Lucius, three times consul"
Reverse: standing Neptune facing left, holding a dolphin in the right hand and a trident in the left. S(enatus) C(onsulto) "By a decree of the senate"
The figure of Neptune celebrates Agrippa's role as a great naval commander.
The date of this coin, generally known as the "Agrippa as," is unknown. It is broadly agreed that it was issued by Caligula, and as such it would be the commonest Caligulan issue, possibly minted in the provinces as well as in Rome. It was imitated in local coins of Caesaraugusta (Zaragoza), seemingly the most active of the local mints of Spain, and is found with greatest frequency

---

[31] On this topic, see Introduction: The Problem.
[32] This passage comes from a supposed conversation between Herod Agrippa and Caligula on the advisability of demanding that the emperor's image be erected in the Temple at Jerusalem. Philo claims that Agrippa persuaded Caligula to change his policy, but his role as described there is almost certainly much exaggerated. In any case Caligula supposedly changed his mind once again.

Figure 9 Copper as. Yale University Art Gallery.

on the Rhine frontier. The minting may well have continued under Claudius, and some have also argued that it began under Tiberius.

On the letters SC, see 3.25; on the numbering of the consulship, see 4.24.

Gemellus

One particularly thorny issue for Caligula and the new regime was the status of Gemellus. There does not seem to have been a distinct or organized pro-Gemellus party as such, but his disinheritance through the annulment of Tiberius' will might have raised embarrassing questions, and Caligula, probably under Macro's guidance, tried to allay the concerns. He awarded Gemellus a number of honours, and, most important symbolically, adopted him as his son on the very day when Gemellus assumed the toga of manhood. This could be represented as a declaration of his intention to be succeeded by him, but Caligula was clearly young enough to expect male offspring and events were to show that any implied promise was of little value. The adoption could have taken one of two possible forms. *Adoptio* was used in the case of someone whose paterfamilias (male head of household) was still alive. With the death of Tiberius this does not seem to have applied to Gemellus. *Adrogatio* involved the adoption of someone who was no longer subject to someone else's jurisdiction. While Gemellus was still a minor, not yet having received the toga of manhood, he was not eligible for *adrogatio*. This may explain the apparent sequence of the ceremony of manhood followed by adoption. Complicating the issue is the fact that after his death Gemellus is not identified on his funerary inscription as Caligula's son (4.1): he is described as the son of his late natural father Drusus (the son of Tiberius). And in the Arval record he is similarly described as the son of Drusus (Smallwood 3.34 Dru[*si f*...]). Does this mean that the adoption was abrogated after his death? Is it even possible that he was not in fact adopted? Philo, who admittedly seems at times to use his imagination as a historical source (and he does, surely wrongly, place the adoption *after* Caligula's illness), seems quite specific on this matter. He tells of Caligula speaking to "people in authority" and of inscribing himself (*grapho*) as his father.[33] If Caligula's paternity was simply dropped from official inscriptions after Gemellus' death it would be an act of breathtaking arrogance.

> **3.40 Suet. Cal. 15.2** Caligula adopted his brother Gemellus on the day that he assumed the gown of manhood, and gave him the title of Princeps Iuventutis.
>
> **3.41 Dio 59.8.1** Falling ill after that (sc. the end of his consulship) he did not die himself, but he did get rid of Gemellus, although the boy had assumed the toga virilis, and been made Princeps Iuventutis and finally adopted.

Claudius

During the first six months or so of his reign Caligula's conduct seems to have been beyond reproach, and in one sphere that conduct garners particular admiration—the treatment of his uncle Claudius. Because Claudius suffered from a speech impediment and from difficulties in walking, he had faced insurmountable barriers to any real progress in public life. Nor was it just a matter of prejudice on the part of the broader population. His own family felt that he was mentally and physically defective and something of a public embarrassment.[34] Thus there can have been little general enthusiasm for promoting Claudius to office, despite Suetonius' claim that Caligula's efforts in this direction were aimed at courting popularity. It does seem that in this particular sphere Caligula was in some ways ahead of his time. He selected his uncle as colleague, in consulships that were the first for both men, assumed on July 1 and held for two months (Smallwood 31.15). Claudius was now forty-six years old, and the office gave him access to the senate for the very first time. This was an astonishingly enlightened gesture, as was the decision to entrust him with the task of arranging the statues in honour of Caligula's late brothers.

This good will was not to last. Claudius mishandled the statue commission,[35] and there seems to have been no further effort by Caligula to advance his uncle's career. There is no indication that Caligula at any point felt actually betrayed by Claudius, but by the end of AD 37 he reputedly considered him a laughing stock

---

[33] Philo *Leg.* 27.   [34] Suet. *Claud.* 3–4.   [35] Suet. *Claud.* 9.1.

(although this claim, by Suetonius,[36] may be totally speculative) and he did not take kindly to Claudius leading a delegation of senators to congratulate him on his escape from the conspiracy (or conspiracies) of Gaetulicus and Lepidus in late AD 39 (see 4.57, 5.12). In the end it was of course Claudius who enjoyed the last laugh. After he succeeded Caligula he seems to have shown little gratitude for his nephew's earlier kindness, and he went out of his way to sully his memory (6.8, 7.28).

3.42 Tac. Ann. 6.46 Tiberius even considered Claudius (sc. as his successor) because he was at a settled age and had a keen interest in the liberal arts, but his diminished mental capacity stood in the way.

3.43 Suet. Cal. 15.1 He himself would try to win people's favour with all sorts of popular measures...**2** he took his uncle Claudius, until then a Roman eques, as his colleague in the consulship.

Augustus

One of the distinctive features of the first phase of Caligula's reign was his persistent effort to identify himself with his great-grandfather Augustus. An excellent opportunity to provide a very concrete and very public demonstration of this connection occurred at the end of August 37 when Caligula, on his birthday, August 31, dedicated the Temple of Divus Augustus. This structure had in fact been decreed very soon after Augustus' death in AD 14,[37] and it was more or less completed, though not yet dedicated, when Tiberius died in March, 37. As a further reinforcement of the association between Caligula and Augustus, sacrifices were carried out successively in AD 38, 39, and possibly also 40 (the Arval record for 40 is missing) at the temple on the anniversary of Caligula's acclamation by the senate as *Imperator* on March 18 (3.44, 48). The Temple of Divus Augustus has since disappeared, but is generally thought to have been located in the depression between the Capitoline and Palatine hills. Suetonius (6.27) provides a useful topographical clue in his bizarre account of Caligula erecting a bridge that passed over this temple and connected those two hills. After the dedication Caligula was able to step down from his consulship, along with his uncle Claudius, on a very high note, allowing those candidates who had been designated prior to his succession to take office, on September 1 (Smallwood 31.15).

[36] *Cal.* 23.3.   [37] Dio 56.46.3.

3.44 Arval record (Smallwood 3.15). March 18, AD 38, see also 3.48 (Smallwood 8.10) On the 15th day before the Kalends of April Taurus Statilius Corvinus, promagister, in the name of the college of the Arval Brothers, sacrificed three major victims to Jupiter, Juno, and Minerva on the Capitol and to the Deified Augustus before the new temple, because on this day[38] Gaius Caesar was acclaimed Imperator by the senate.

3.45 Suet. *Cal.* 21 Those projects left half-complete by Tiberius he finished off[39]—the Temple of Augustus and the theatre of Pompey.[40]

3.46 Dio 59.7.1 After that, wearing triumphal dress, he dedicated the temple to Augustus.[41] Boys of the highest-born families with both parents still alive sang the hymn, together with girls in the same situation, and senators feasted together with their wives, as did the common people; and there were all kinds of shows. 2 There were musical performances as well as horse races over a two-day period, twenty on the first and forty on the second (that one, since it was the last day of August, which was his birthday).[42]

3.47 *RIC*² 1.36. Brass sestertius. April 37–April 38 (Figure 10)
Obverse: Pietas seated left, holding a patera (flat dish) and resting her left arm on a columnar figure: C(aius) CAESAR AUG(ustus) GERMANICUS PO (ntifex) M(aximus) TR(ibunicia) POT(estate) "Gaius Caesar Augustus Germanicus, Chief Priest, endowed with Tribunician Authority"
Reverse: Caligula facing left, veiled and wearing toga, holding a patera, sacrificing at an altar before a six-columned Temple of Deified Augustus, with two attendants behind holding the sacrificial bull: DIVO AVG(usto) S(enatus) C(onsulto) "To the Deified Augustus. By a decree of the senate"

There is a close link between the obverse and reverse of this coin. Pietas was a powerful concept for the Romans, denoting the principle of family duty and here emphasizing Caligula's loyalty to his famous great-grandfather, manifested

---

[38] The previous year, AD 37.
[39] In fact Tiberius must previously have made considerable progress on the temple, since Pliny says that he dedicated several pictures in it, including a Hyacinthus by Nikias (Plin. *NH* 35.28.13).
[40] The theatre, built by Pompey in 52 BC, was famous as the first permanent stone theatre built in Rome. It was destroyed by fire in AD 22 and Tacitus suggests that its repair was completed by Tiberius, while Dio claims that Tiberius' repairs were actually completed by Claudius (Tac. *Ann.* 3.72.2; Dio 60.6.8–9). Only Suetonius suggests that the repair was made by Caligula. Suetonius tends to look kindly on Caligula's building programme, and he may provide a more reliable account of this specific topic than do other sources.
[41] It is noteworthy that Caligula wore the embroidered purple cloak that draped Jupiter's statue on the Capitoline, a privilege of generals celebrating a Triumph, in a phase when he was going out of his way to stress moderation.
[42] Caligula placed great store by his birthday, Augustus 31, and in AD 40 he would delay the celebration of his Ovation until that day. In the case of the dedication of the Temple the coincidence would have emphasized his direct blood link with Augustus (in contrast to Tiberius, who was not directly connected to his predecessor).

Figure 10 Brass sestertius. Yale University Art Gallery.

by his dedication of his temple early in the reign. The type was reissued each year of the reign.

On tribunician authority, see 3.8; on the letters SC, see 3.25.

Honeymoon Period

Few emperors illustrate so effectively Tacitus' famous adage *optimus est post malum principem dies primus* ("after a bad emperor, the first day is the best").[43] The first six months or so of Caligula's reign seemed to confirm the expectations of those who had looked forward to a new golden age after the grim experiences of the Tiberian regime. Suetonius provides a catalogue of what he considers his statesmanlike measures.

3.48 Dio 59.9.4 Gaius' decent and praiseworthy acts are these: The accounts of state funds not released while Tiberius was away[44] he published in full, as had Augustus. After extinguishing some fire with the assistance of the soldiers he also helped people who were damaged by it.[45]

---

[43] Tac. *Hist.* 4.42.5.

[44] Augustus is recorded as publishing the accounts of public funds on only two occasions, when he fell ill, in 23 BC (Suet. *Aug.* 28.1; Dio 53.30.2), and in his will (Tac. *Ann.* 1.11.4; Suet. *Aug.* 101.4; Dio 56.33.2), but Suetonius' "generally" may be borne out by Dio 59.9.4, who says that it was a customary practice of Augustus, abandoned by Tiberius.

[45] Both Dio and Suetonius (3.49.3) record that Caligula paid compensation for fire losses; Dio also speaks of his involvement in fighting a specific fire. Imperial involvement in fire fighting, and generosity to the victims afterwards, were features of the Julio-Claudian rulers. The fire noted by Dio was most likely one that destroyed part of the Aemiliana district on October 21, AD 38, recorded in the Fasti of Ostia (Smallwood 31.30, Figure 0.1): XII K NOV AEMILIANA ARSER[unt] "twelve days before the

3.49 Suet. *Cal.* 16.1 "Spintriae," men of frightful sexual behaviour, he drove from the city[46] and was only with difficulty persuaded from drowning them in the sea.[47] The works of Titus Labienus, Cremutius Cordus, and Cassius Severus, banned by senatorial decree, he permitted to be sought out, handled, and generally perused since, he said, it mattered to him that everything be transmitted to future generations.[48] He had the imperial accounts, generally released by Augustus but suppressed by Tiberius, made public.

2 To the magistrates he permitted unrestricted jurisdiction without having to refer to him.[49] The Roman knights he reviewed carefully and punctiliously but also with moderation, quite openly removing his horse from anyone guilty of some vicious or infamous misdeed, but simply passing over the names of people held responsible for any minor offence.[50] To make the work of jurors less arduous he added a fifth panel to the four earlier in place.[51]

3 Although Tiberius' will had been set aside, he forthwith paid out legacies within it quite faithfully and without quibbling, and in addition he paid out those in Julia Augusta's will, which Tiberius had suppressed. He dropped the half-per cent auction-sale tax;[52] he compensated many for losses from fires; and to any to whom he restored kingdoms he also granted all the tax income and

Kalends of November (= October 21) the Aemiliana district burned down"). Dio may be using "soldiers" loosely to refer to the Vigiles, the fire-fighting service established by Augustus, but he could be referring to the Praetorians, who did on occasion help in the extinguishing of fires.

[46] *Spintriae* was a recently coined name for a class of sodomites, particularly associated with Tiberius' stay in Capri (Tac. *Ann.* 6.1.2); it was a nickname of the later emperor Vitellius, who spent some time on the island (Suet. *Vit.* 3.2). Caligula will later gain a reputation for all manner of sexual excess; his behaviour on this occasion was if anything prudish, and perhaps meant to draw a contrast between him and Tiberius.

[47] The ancient method of execution was to place the accused in a sack with an ape, a dog, a snake, and a cock and throw him into the sea.

[48] Titus Labienus was an Augustan orator. His ferocious texts on those who met with his disapproval (there were many of them) earned him the nickname Rabienus ("rabid"). His works were ordered burnt and Labienus immured himself in the family tomb, refusing to outlive his own writings. Cassius Severus wrote vicious diatribes against prominent members of society and was charged with *maiestas* under Augustus and exiled on the desolate island of Seriphus, where he died in 32. Cremutius Cordus was the subject of the most celebrated case for libel under Tiberius, accused in AD 25 of writing in praise of Caesar's murderers of and calling Cassius, who played a key role in the murder, the last of the Romans. But at the heart of the case against him was the enmity of Sejanus. Cremutius avoided condemnation by suicide. His books were burnt but his daughter Marcia preserved some, to be published under Caligula.

[49] The right of the emperor, through his *tribunicia potestas*, to hear appeals against the decisions of the courts was regularly exercised by Tiberius (Dio 59.8.5; Tac. *Ann.* 3.18.1, 70.2). Caligula professed a more enlightened policy but he did in fact at times interfere in court actions, writing speeches either for the prosecution or for the defence (Suet. *Cal.* 53.2; Dio 59.18.2).

[50] The formal review of the knights involved an actual parade. It was a tradition much observed by Augustus. Members could be removed from the list by the emperor's staying silent when the names were called.

[51] Augustus added a fourth panel of jurors to the three that existed by the time of Julius Caesar's death, to ease the burden on those who served. Caligula added a fifth and there was an unsuccessful attempt to add a sixth under Galba (Suet. *Galb.* 14.3).

[52] See 4.22, 23.

revenue accrued in the intervening period (such as the 100 million sestertii accrued in the treasury allowed to Antiochus of Commagene).[53]

4 To make it clear that there was no good case he did not support, he gave a freedwoman 800,000 sestertii for remaining silent about her patron's guilt despite having been subjected to the severest tortures.[54] Among various honours decreed to him for such acts was a golden shield, which the priestly colleges were to carry to the Capitol every year on an appointed day, with the senate in attendance and boys and girls of noble families praising his virtues in harmonious song. It was also decreed that the day that he took power be designated the Parilia, as though suggesting a second founding of the city.[55]

3.50 (see also 3.11) Dio 59.3.2 Apart from the designation "father" he put off acceptance of no other title; and that one, too, he took after no long wait.

Father of the Country

These last passages of Suetonius and Dio offer an excellent opportunity to demonstrate how the combination of literary texts, inscriptions, and coins can at times produce invaluable information. Dio mentions that in March AD 37 Caligula accepted in a single transaction the titles that Augustus had amassed over a lifetime, with the single exception of that of *Pater Patriae* ("Father of the Country"), which he assumed a short while later. A significant fragment of the Arval record, discovered in 1978, has enabled us to vindicate Dio here. It records a ritual performed on September 21, 38 to mark the anniversary of Caligula's receiving that title of *Pater Patriae*, offered with the consensus of the senate in the previous year, AD 37 (the record for AD 37 itself is missing).

Cicero was the first recipient of this title, to mark his handling of the Catilinarian conspiracy. Along with it, the senate voted to grant Cicero the oak wreath (*corona civica*), a distinction awarded to a soldier who saved the life of a comrade in battle. The title was awarded to Julius Caesar, also, in 45 BC, and appears on his coins in the following year. The oak crown was granted to Augustus

---

[53] In AD 18 Commagene was incorporated into the empire by Germanicus on the death of its king, Antiochus III. In 37 Caligula restored the kingdom to his son, Antiochus IV, along with the coastal area of Cilicia.

[54] Dio 59.26.4 recounts the same event, giving the name Pomponius, and claiming that he was suspected of plotting against Caligula. Jos. *Ant.* 19.33 gives the name as "Pompedius" and identifies the woman as Quintilia, claiming that she was tortured under the supervision of Cassius Chaerea, chief assassin of Caligula. The compensation of 800,000 sestertii seems extraordinarily high.

[55] The Parilia was an ancient festival, originally associated with shepherds, but eventually linked with the day of Rome's founding, April 21, perhaps on the same day, or close to it, when the senatorial decree of a Lex Imperii conferring powers on Caligula was passed by the popular assembly.

by the senate in 27 BC. He also received a golden shield, inscribed with his virtues, to be displayed in the senate house, and in the record that he composed of his achievements he lists the shield immediately next to the award of the crown. He postponed acceptance of the award of the honorific "Father of the Country" until 2 BC, regarding that award as an event of great significance, when he tearfully declared that he hoped that he would strive to retain the consensus of the senate. The oak wreath, the title of *Pater Patriae*, and the shield were prominently displayed on his coins.[56]

Hence it is probably safe to assume that the "appointed day" mentioned by Suetonius (3.49.4), on which the shield was to be carried to the Capitol, was September 21, especially since the new Arval fragment shows that sacrifices were carried out on the Capitol in association with the grant of the title of *Pater Patriae* to Caligula. The shield would clearly be meant to recall the famous shield awarded to Augustus in 27 BC. It is also fair to assume from his coins that Caligula received the *corona civica* at the same time (3.52). Certainly he is said to have worn one on the occasion of the crossing of the bay of Naples (4.40, 41), and Suetonius does note that the shield was granted "among various honours."

3.51 Fragment of the Arval record (Smallwood, p. 10.5.1; J. Scheid and H. Broise 1980, pp. 224–5). September 21, AD 38

On the 11th day before the Kalends of October (= September 21), because on this day Gaius Caesar Augustus Germanicus accepted the title of "Father of his Country" that was offered to him with the consensus of the senate, the vice-president Taurus Statilius Corvinus, in the name of the college of the Arval Brethren, sacrificed three major victims to Jupiter, Juno, and Minerva on the Capitoline and sacrificed one to the Deified Augustus at the New Temple.

The event is almost certainly commemorated in a coin of AD 37, where Caligula is identified as *Pater Patriae* in a legend that appears within an oak crown and carries the usual reference to the saving of the citizens.

3.52 *RIC*[2] 1.28. Silver denarius. AD 37, probably after September, continued through reign. A very similar type appears on a Sestertius issue (*RIC*[2] 1.37) (Figure 11)

Obverse: Caligula, laureate head right: C(aius) CAESAR AVG(ustus) PON(tifex) M(aximus) TR(ibunicia) POT(estate) CO(n)S(ul) "Gaius Caesar Augustus Germanicus, Chief Priest, endowed with tribunician authority. Consul"
Reverse: S(senatus)P(opulus)Q(ue)R(omanus) P(ater?) P(atriae) OB C(ives) S(ervatos), within oak wreath "The senate and the Roman people. Father (*the*

---

[56] Cicero: Cic. *Pis.* 3.6; Plut. *Cic.* 23.6; Gellius 5.6.12–15; Caesar: Appian *BC* 2.106, 144; Augustus: *RG* 34.2; Suet. *Aug.* 58.2.

Figure 11 Silver denarius. Yale University Art Gallery.

intended grammatical case of this word in the abbreviated Latin original can not be determined) of his country. For saving the citizens"
On tribunician authority, see 3.8.

Illness

The euphoria that marked the first phase of Caligula's reign came to an alarming close when towards the end of the year he fell seriously ill. Philo provides fairly precise information on the date, placing the setback in the eighth month of his reign (October 18–November 18, or thereabouts, depending on how Philo defined the beginning of his reign), just before the traditional close of the sailing season (November 11). Dio seems to suggest that the illness followed Caligula's consulship, held until the end of August, but Dio's "after this" is far from precise. We know that Caligula received the title of *Pater Patriae* on September 21 amidst much ceremony, and he was therefore almost certainly in good health at that time. Perhaps Philo and Dio can best be reconciled by supposing that Caligula fell ill late in September and that his condition became serious in mid-October. Nor do we have any good indication of how long the illness lasted. He was supposedly asked to provide a name for Nero, the future emperor, born December 15, and for the story to be plausible (though not necessarily true, of course) he would have had to be recovered by then, but of course the recovery might have happened considerably earlier.

The illness was clearly a major one, given the panic that it caused, and one can extrapolate from Dio's account that there was a fear that he would die. There has been much speculation about its nature. Because there was a clear change in the tone of the regime after his recovery it has been suggested that he suffered some sort of mental decline, perhaps caused by a disease like encephalitis. But he was clearly capable of making rational decisions after late 37, and the serious breakdown in his dealings with the senate does not occur until 39. Philo might be close to the mark in suggesting that the accession had marked a major change in Caligula's lifestyle; even if we put aside the scenario of drunken orgies that Philo paints there can be little doubt that the pace of life, both political and personal, would have been transformed dramatically by the accession and that some kind of nervous breakdown would not be implausible.

3.53 Philo *Leg.* 14 But in the eighth month a serious disease overtook Gaius (he had changed his way of life a little earlier, when Tiberius was still alive, one that was simpler and thus healthier...)

15 So when news spread that he was ill while it was still sailing weather—for it was the start of late autumn, the final sailing period for sailors...

3.54 Suet. *Cal.* 14.2 Now when he fell ill and everyone started spending entire nights around the Palatium, there was no shortage of people swearing that they would fight with weapons to save the patient's life, or declaring on a placard that they would give their own lives for it.[57]

3.55 (see also 3.40) Dio 59.8.1 Falling ill after that (sc. giving up his consulship), he did not die himself, but he did get rid of Tiberius Gemellus...

Further Reading

Benediktson, D. T. 1992. "Caligula's Phobias and Philias: Fear of Seizure." *CJ* 87: 159–63.

Brunt, P. A. 1977. "Lex de Imperio Vespasiani." *JRS* 67: 95–116.

Fishwick, D. 1992. "On the Temple of Divus Augustus." *Phoenix* 46: 232–55.

Hammond, M. 1956. "The Transmission of the Powers of the Roman Emperor." *MAAR* 24: 61–133.

Scheid, J., and H. Broise. 1980. "Deux nouveaux fragments des Actes des Frères Arvales de l'année 38 ap. J.C." *MEFR* 92: 215–48.

Sidwell, B. 2010. "Gaius Caligula's Mental Illness." *CW* 103: 183–206.

---

[57] Presumably Suetonius alludes here to placards carried in some sort of procession. He refers to the practice elsewhere, saying that people in the time of Augustus put a clause in their wills that after their death there should be sacrificial offerings taken to the Capitol to celebrate their being survived by the emperor, with the information displayed on placards (Suet. *Aug.* 59).

4

Tensions

The serious illness that brought down Caligula towards the end of AD 37 seems to have been followed by a dramatic change in the tone of the regime. Whether or not there was any actual cause and effect cannot be determined, but there can be little doubt that when he eventually recovered Caligula felt that his honeymoon period had come to a disquieting end. The most glaring symptom of this change was a series of high-profile deaths in the months that followed. Their chronology is far from certain but they began, it seems, with the forced suicides both of Gemellus and of Caligula's father-in-law, Marcus Silanus, followed by the even more astonishing demise of the once all-powerful Macro.

Frustratingly, the sources provide few coherent details, and we are very much in the dark about when the deaths occurred, and if they were interconnected. Philo and Dio place Gemellus first in their lists of named victims, although perhaps we should not necessarily read too much into this reported sequence. Dio includes the death among the events of AD 37, and it certainly does seem plausible that Gemellus was dead before the end of the year. At any rate he was not included with Caligula's sisters in the vows taken by the consul on January 1, 38 (3.34; see also Smallwood 1.17). Dio gives as the grounds of Gemellus' forced suicide that he had supposedly anticipated Caligula's death. Philo records the pretext that he was involved in a conspiracy, and adds the touching story of Gemellus' last moments. Suetonius relates an unconvincing anecdote about a misinterpreted cough. Gemellus' funerary inscription was found near the mausoleum of Augustus, and he may well have been buried there (4.1).

What might have happened to change the mood in the imperial circle so profoundly? During the most severe stage of Caligula's illness the routine of government would have needed to continue, and the titular authority of government may well have devolved on Gemellus, as the son of the princeps. We simply do not know, but that situation might explain the deep suspicion that Caligula seems to have entertained after his recovery about Gemellus' ambitions, and, to judge from a comment of Dio (4.6), also about the loyalty of others, who died in the post-illness phase.

Gemellus and Silanus

We can do no more than speculate about any connection that there might have been between the ends of Gemellus and Silanus, since the sources are at their most

The Emperor Caligula in the Ancient Sources. Anthony A. Barrett and J. C. Yardley, Oxford University Press.
© Anthony A. Barrett and J. C. Yardley 2023. DOI: 10.1093/oso/9780198854562.003.0005

anecdotal in their treatment of the latter. Silanus was clearly an ambitious man, and if there were indeed fears that Caligula was not likely to survive the illness, then he might well have made a show of loyalty to Gemellus. Gemellus would have been eighteen by now (the later emperor Nero was sixteen when he succeeded), and circumstances may well have placed him at the centre of what might later have been interpreted as an embryonic plot, involving himself and Silanus. Others might also have been found themselves drawn into the aftermath: Tacitus records that Julius Graecinus, father of the famous commander Agricola (Tacitus' father-in-law), was obliged to commit suicide because he had been unwilling to prosecute a "Marcus Silanus" (4.8), which may be connected with these events.

4.1 *ILS* 172 (Smallwood 88) Rome, mausoleum of Augustus AD 37 or 38
Here lies Tiberius Caesar, son of Drusus.[1]

4.2 Phil. *Leg.* 23 For he executed his cousin, who had also been left joint partner in the rule and was a more rightful successor than he (since the one was Tiberius' grandson by adoption, the other by birth), with the treacherous pretext of a plot, though even his age would not countenance such a charge; for the poor boy was just passing from childhood to puberty.[2]

4.3 Phil. *Leg.* 30 It is said that Gemellus was even ordered to kill himself by his own hand...

31 Taking the sword himself, he was told when he asked (for he had no knowledge or experience) where the most appropriate spot was for cutting short his unhappy life with a well-aimed thrust. And, experts in villainy, they gave him his instructions and pointed to the part where he must thrust the sword. Learning what was his first lesson and his last, the poor boy became his own murderer.

4.4 Phil. *Leg.* 65 Thus, supposing this man (sc. Marcus Silanus) also to be a nuisance, one who would arrest the impulse of his sexual needs, he bade many farewells to the shades of his departed wife and treacherously murdered the man who was *her* father and *his* father-in-law.

4.5 Suet. *Cal.* 23.3 When his brother Gemellus[3] was off-guard he had him murdered by a tribune that he suddenly sent to him, and his father-in-law Silanus he also forced to commit suicide by slashing his throat with a razor.[4] In the two cases his justification was that Silanus had not accompanied him when he

---

[1] Note that in the funerary inscription that would have accompanied his urn (4.1) Gemellus is not identified as the son of the emperor.

[2] The delayed toga of manhood (in his seventeenth or eighteenth year, rather than the traditional fourteenth), along with the pathetic account of his death, reinforce the possibility that Gemellus may have been very immature for his years (see Chapter 1, n. 49).

[3] Gemellus was in fact Caligula's cousin (and adopted son).

[4] The identification of Silanus as his father-in-law suggests that this happened before Caligula's remarriage (4.9, 10), but this may not be the case: the term may be intended to emphasize the heinousness of the act.

had set out on a rather rough sea but had remained behind, hoping to take over the city if anything happened to him in the stormy weather; and that Gemellus had wreaked of antidote, which was taken as if to protect himself against being poisoned by him. Now Silanus had actually been trying to avoid sea sickness and the ennui of sailing, and Gemellus had taken a remedy for a constant and worsening cough.

4.6 Dio 59.8.1 Falling ill after that (sc. giving up his consulship), he did not die himself but he managed to get rid of Gemellus, although he had assumed the toga virilis and been made Princeps Iuventutis, and had finally been adopted, the charge against him being that he was praying for his death and expecting it. On the same pretext he also put many others to death...3 So it was that Gemellus was destroyed, ostensibly for brooding over Caligula's illness.

4.7 Dio 59.8.4 And for these men that was the reason for their death. Now his father-in-law Marcus Silanus had made no promise or taken any oath, but as he was a nuisance to him both because of his integrity and their family connection and was treated with contempt by him, he took his own life.

4.8 Tac. *Ag.* 4.1 His (sc. Agricola's) father Julius Graecinus, who was a man of senatorial rank and well known for his eloquence and sagacity, earned Gaius Caesar's anger by those very virtues. Ordered to arraign Marcus Silanus he refused and was put to death.

Second Marriage

The illness, and possibly concerns about the ambitions of Gemellus and others close to the centre of power, may well have served to focus Caligula's mind on the issue of the succession. In any case, before the end of AD 37 he remarried. There is considerable uncertainty about the name of his new bride, Livia or Cornelia, followed by Orestilla or Orestina, as well as about the circumstances of the marriage. One obvious, although in the event not very formidable, obstacle was that she was already married, to Gaius Calpurnius Piso. His family was a politically prominent one, which apparently did not suffer seriously from the supposed earlier involvement of their kinsman, Gnaeus Calpurnius Piso, in the death of Germanicus. Gaius, the husband, would himself later gain notoriety as the lacklustre leader of the poorly executed "Pisonian Conspiracy" against Nero in AD 65. Clearly, a divorce was needed (not a complicated process in Rome at that time).

Suetonius claims that Caligula boasted that he followed in the footsteps of Augustus and Romulus, both of whom had "seized" their wives from their husbands (Livia in the case of Augustus, Hersilia in that of Romulus). This seems like a fairly typical piece of Caligulan humour (see Chapter 5), although we should not rule out the possibility that the two great historical figures were formally cited as precedents. The new marriage as reported is a curious one, as is the claim that Caligula divorced Livia/Cornelia after a few days, hardly time for him to doubt her capability of becoming pregnant.

4.9 Suet. *Cal.* 25.1 As for marriages, whether he was more disreputable in contracting them or annulling them is not easy to see. When Livia Orestilla was marrying Piso, he actually attended the ceremony in person, then ordered her taken to his house, divorced her within a few days, and two years later banished her on suspicion of having again taken up with her husband in the meantime. Others record that when invited to the matrimonial feast he sent a message to Piso, who was reclining opposite him, saying, "Don't fuck my wife!" and immediately took her with him from the feast and declared the next day that he had found a wife for himself, just like Romulus and Augustus.[5]

4.10 Dio 59.8.7 Divorcing Marcus Silanus' daughter, he married Cornelia Orestilla, whom he carried off right in the middle of the wedding festival that she was celebrating with her betrothed, Gaius Calpurnius Piso. Before two months passed he exiled the two of them for actually having sex with each other. 8 He allowed Piso to take ten slaves, and then when he asked for more, he allowed him to have as many as he wanted, adding, "You'll have the same number of soldiers with you."

Fall of Macro

During the first part of the following year, AD 38, a political bombshell fell. This time the focus of attention shifted to Caligula's most stalwart supporter, Macro. He was forced to commit suicide, and his wife, Ennia, suffered the same fate. The exact date when these events unfurled is unknown, but they did follow Macro's appointment to the powerful prefecture of Egypt, which he was not able to take up. Dio puts the death early in 38, and this accords with Philo's information that Flaccus, prefect of Egypt, received news of it in the first part of that year (Philo *Flacc.* 16).

Macro's fall from grace is particularly difficult to understand. Philo sees the situation simplistically, that he did his best to make Caligula behave like a respectable princeps, and that Caligula resented his tutelage. Philo makes no hint of any personal aspirations on Macro's part, but of course Philo's aim was to portray Caligula as arbitrary, if not mentally unbalanced. One can merely speculate. It is possible that, along with Silanus, Macro, who had given plenty of

---

[5] The passage illustrates well the dilemma faced by the historian. The comment about Augustus suits well the possibility that Caligula's second wife was called Livia, the name given by Suetonius (4.9). But the comment may on the other hand have encouraged a careless source to assume that the wife's name was Livia, rather than Cornelia. The notice may well be derived ultimately from a formal edict from Caligula, although the content could well be much garbled here.

evidence already of his ambitions, saw Gemellus as the next hope during the darkest time of Caligula's illness. If there was indeed a gap between his fall and that of the two others (and the chronology is very obscure) it could be that his elimination would have needed more delicate handling, and that the promise of the prefecture of Egypt was a feint to distract him from guessing the truth. Sejanus similarly had anticipated high honours before he was eliminated in AD 31 (with Macro playing a major role in his downfall).

The issue of Macro's death is complicated by a supposed earlier affair between Caligula and Macro's wife Ennia Thrasylla. There is much speculation about their relationship in the sources, and, hardly surprisingly, little precise information. Suetonius alone assigns the initiative in the affair to Caligula. Tacitus, followed by Dio, suggests that Macro played the pander and persuaded Ennia to seduce Caligula and win his favour. Philo blames Ennia entirely, insisting that Macro was deceived. But he also usefully concedes that there is no consensus about Ennia's role, and that he is dependent on hearsay. It is to be remembered that it was common in this period to obfuscate female disloyalty within the court by means of claims of sexual misbehaviour, in order to avoid revealing the potential weakness of the princeps (the scandal of Augustus's daughter Julia is a case in point). The story might then have been a deliberate ploy to avoid making public just how precarious Caligula's position had been. Tacitus claims that Caligula had promised to marry Ennia, and Suetonius at least implies that he had actually seen a marriage contract.

Macro and Ennia killed themselves, presumably to pre-empt a trial and thereby protect their estate, a traditional tactic at the time. Macro was able to leave sufficient funds to provide an amphitheatre in his hometown of Alba Fucens, as recorded in an inscription there (*AE* 1957.250).

Confusing further an already confused picture, Dio claims that a number of other Romans were brought down following the death of Macro (4.36). He unfortunately does not give concrete examples, and it is possible that he transposed to AD 38 measures taken by Caligula against his opponents in AD 39 and 40.

4.11 Tac. *Ann.* 6.45.3 For not long afterwards, the last consuls of Tiberius' reign, Gnaeus Acerronius and Gaius Pontius, came to office,[6] at a time when Macro was now excessively powerful, a man who had never neglected Gaius Caesar's favour but was now courting it more enthusiastically every day. In fact, after the death of Claudia (whose marriage to Gaius I have mentioned),[7] Macro had pushed his own wife Ennia into leading on the young man by feigning love for him and then binding him to a promise of marriage. And Gaius would refuse nothing as long as he could gain power; for despite a mercurial temper he had nevertheless learned the arts of dissimulation in his grandfather's lap.

---

[6] They are the *consules ordinarii* of AD 37.
[7] Caligula's first wife; Suetonius records her name as Junia Claudilla (2.25).

4.12 Philo Leg. 39 For the most part, whatever one could say in praise of one's brothers or legitimate sons Macro said even more fulsomely to Tiberius in Gaius Caligula's case. The reason, most say, was not only that Macro was also being fawned on by Caligula for his great, and even total, influence in the matter of the succession, but also because Macro's wife (for some reason that was kept secret) was daily urging and steeling her husband to withhold no support or effort on the young man's behalf. It is a frightful power that a woman has in distracting and altering a man's judgement, especially if she is wanton, for being a co-conspirator she becomes more of a flatterer.

4.13 Philo Leg. 61 For it is said that the unfortunate man was forced to kill himself by his own hand, and that his wife met the same fate despite being thought to have once had a sexual relationship with him.[8]

4.14 Philo Flacc. 14 The ill-starred man suffered the most grievous punishments for his extraordinary kindness: with all his house he was destroyed with his wife and children for being too grievous a burden and a nuisance.[9]

4.15 Suet. Cal. 12.2 To feel more secure in this (sc. his ambitions for the succession), after his loss of Junia in childbirth he seduced Ennia Naevia,[10] wife of Macro, the man then in command of the Praetorian guard, even promising her marriage to him if he gained the imperial power; and on that he took the precaution of a written oath of contract.[11]

4.16 Suet Cal. 26.1 It would be uninteresting and tedious to append how he treated his relatives and friends, King Juba's son Ptolemy, his cousin (for he was Mark Antony's grandson by Antony's daughter Selene),[12] and especially Macro himself and Ennia herself, both assistants in his accession to power; for whether it was for their family ties or for loyal service they all were rewarded with a bloody death.

4.17 Dio 59.10.6... and (sc. he was also blamed) for forcing Macro into suicide along with Ennia, with no thought for her love or his benefactions through which, among other things, he helped him gain imperial power, and although

---

[8] Philo's testimony is often useful, since he was in Rome shortly afterwards, and can be said at least to reflect views that were then current, if not necessarily accurate.

[9] Philo is the only source to suggest that Macro's children were also put to death and his testimony must be treated with the greatest caution. It is possible that this detail is a doublet of the fate of Macro's predecessor as Praetorian prefect, Sejanus.

[10] Tacitus and Dio both suggest that Ennia, at her husband's bidding, took the initiative. Suetonius is alone in suggesting here that Caligula actively sought Ennia's favours.

[11] The notion of the marriage contract seems implausible. The whole uncertainty about the Ennia–Caligula relationship makes it highly unlikely. It may be an elaboration by those who argued that Ennia had taken the initiative, since it would almost certainly have meant that Macro was to be out of the picture.

[12] Ptolemy, son of Cleopatra Selene, the daughter of Mark Antony, was indeed Antony's grandson, but Caligula, son of Germanicus, the son of Antonia, the daughter of Mark Antony, was his *great*-grandson, hence they were not strictly cousins.

he had put him in charge of Egypt he also exposed him to dishonour for which he was himself most responsible (for he brought against him, among other things, a charge of pandering).

4.18 Dio 58.28.4 For when Tiberius was already seriously ill Macro was paying a lot of attention to the young man, especially since he had induced him into a love affair with his own wife Ennia Thrasylla.[13] Suspecting this, Tiberius even once remarked: "Yes, you are doing well in abandoning the setting sun for the one rising."[14]

Popular Measures

In this period of growing stress and tensions there are signs that Caligula was keen to maintain the broad support of the masses. One of the measures that he undertook was a change in the election procedure, another was the abolition of the sales tax.

Election Procedures

During the republic, candidates for office were elected by the popular assemblies (*comitia*). Julius Caesar had reduced their role and personally nominated half the candidates, except those for the consulship. Augustus went back to the old republican system in 27 BC, but in practice maintained considerable control over it. Tiberius took an important step in assigning elections to the senate, with the assemblies limited to ratifying formally the candidates who were already determined. The precise form of Tiberius' reform has been much discussed, but in any case it met with little opposition. Caligula restored the elections to the people, although it is more than likely that he would have taken steps to ensure that in practice the choice of candidates met with his favour, and the reform may well have been to a great extent in name only. There was little taste for competing for office and apparently the number of candidates usually equalled the number of vacancies. The people showed little interest in reasserting an authority that was largely notional, and Caligula eventually went back to the Tiberian system and restored the privileges of the senate. Domitius Afer (4.46) is the only consul identified as elected under the Caligulan reform.

4.19 Suet. *Cal.* **16.2** He also tried to restore voting to the people by bringing back the practice of elections.

---

[13] Dio is the only source to provide her full name, Ennia Thrasylla. Little is known about her, but it has been speculated that she was the granddaughter of Thrasyllus, the famous astrologer associated with Tiberius.

[14] For the expression, see 2.29.

4.20 Dio 59.9.6 When he restored election of magistrates to the people, however, cancelling whatever Tiberius had decided about them, and then annulled the 1 per cent tax, and threw tickets around after staging some gymnastic contest and passed gifts around to people who had caught the most, he delighted the rabble; but to right-thinking people he brought only distress since they understood that if the magistracies again fell into the hands of the rabble, if current resources were exhausted, and if private resources dried up, the outcome would be disastrous.

4.21 Dio 59.20.3 He had indeed brought elections back to the people, 4 but they had now become quite indolent from not doing as free people any of the things that lay within their authority; and in general there were no more seeking office than actually needed to be chosen, and if there *were* more candidates than were required they simply settled the matter among themselves and so maintained a façade of democracy when there really was no such thing. 5 The result was that elections were once again abolished by Gaius himself. Everything else then continued as under Tiberius, except that in the case of the praetors sometimes fifteen were selected but sometimes more and sometimes fewer, just as chance would have it.

Taxation Reform

One measure aimed unequivocally at garnering popularity was the abolition of the sales tax. In this period provinces paid direct taxes to Rome, in the form of tribute, except where exemptions had been granted. In Italy, by contrast, tribute was not levied, and residents paid only indirect taxes. The most significant of these was the 1 per cent tax on sales at auction, used to provide revenues for the military treasury. There is some uncertainty about that 1 per cent rate. It seems that Tiberius had early in his reign reduced the level to 0.5 per cent (Tac. *Ann.* 2.42.6), but under financial pressure was obliged to restore the original 1 per cent in 31 (Dio 58.16.2), and Dio claims that when Caligula removed the tax completely it did indeed stand at 1 per cent; Suetonius, however, puts it at 0.5 per cent at that time (4.22). If that figure of 0.5 per cent is correct, either Caligula or Tiberius must have reduced the tax previously in an unrecorded act, or possibly Tiberius had not in fact restored the 1 per cent rate in 31. This is yet another insoluble historical problem that the inconsistent sources have created for us.

Whatever rate it stood at, the removal of the hated sales tax would have been a highly popular measure, and that measure is thought by some to be reflected in a small but intriguing coin issue that appeared in 39.

4.22 (see also 3.49) Suet. *Cal.* 16.3 He dropped the half per cent auction-sale tax.

Figure 12 Copper quadrans. Yale University Art Gallery.

4.23 Dio 59.9.6 (Caligula) annulled the 1 per cent tax.

4.24 *RIC²* **1.52 Copper quadrans.** AD 40 (Figure 12)

Obverse: *pileus*, between S(enatus) C(onsulto), encircled by C(aius) CAESAR DIVI AVG(usti) PRON(epos) AVG(ustus) "By a decree of the senate. Gaius Caesar, great grandson of the deified Augustus"

Reverse: RCC, surrounded by CO(n)S(ul) TERT(ius) PON(tifex) M(aximus) TR(ibunicia) P(otestate) IIII P(ater) P(atriae) "RCC(?) Consul for the third time, Chief Priest, endowed with Tribunician Authority for the fourth time, Father of the Country"

For SC see 3.25.

A reference to *tribunicia potestas* on a coin among the attributes of an emperor (on which see 3.8) can provide very useful dating information, since it means that the coin was issued during the term of that award, renewed annually. The same principle does not apply to the numbering of consulships. Caligula was consul for the third time in AD 40, standing down at the end of January. But the designation as Consul III does not necessarily mean that the coin was issued in that January, but rather that that the emission occurred at any time between the first day of that third consulship and the first day of the fourth, even if the fourth had not occurred until several years later (in fact in Caligula's case on January 1 of the following year, AD 41). The reference to the fourth tenure of *tribunicia potestas* on the coin illustrated here enables us to be more precise, since that fell in the period April 40–February 41 (his death). Hence the example of the coin illustrated here was minted in AD 40, some time after April. The copper quadrans was valued at one quarter of an as (hence one sixteenth of a sestertius). It was used for small change in low-value transactions. This is the only quadrans issue of Caligula's reign.

This small unassuming coin is perhaps the most intriguing of all Caligulan emissions. The images on quadrantes tend to have a commercial theme, and the

RCC on the reverse has generally been taken to stand for *remissa ducentessima* ("on the remission of the 200th part"), a reference to a removal of the sales tax of 0.5 per cent. There are some difficulties with this notion. This coin series began in AD 39, and on the first issue Caligula is identified as consul designate for the following year, hence it can be placed late in 39. But the sales tax was remitted in AD 38. Also, it is far from certain that the tax stood at 0.5 per cent, rather than at 1 per cent.

The cap of liberty (*pileus*) on the obverse is taken to refer to the restoration of the elections to the popular assemblies. But, again, the elections were restored to the people in 38, in the year before the coin was first issued. We in fact have no way of knowing what the letters RCC signify (it is an unparalleled combination) or what the cap of liberty was meant to convey. It is possible that the cap has some association with the suppression of the major conspiracies in late 39, the date of the first issue.

Death of Drusilla

The political problems that beset Caligula during the course of AD 38 were accompanied by a great personal tragedy, when on June 10 of that year (the date recorded in the Fasti of Ostia, 4.25, Figure 1), his sister Drusilla died. The sources depict her as the favourite of his three sisters, but of course unlike the other two she did not live long enough to betray him, and due allowance must be given to that circumstance. But there is no reason to doubt that he was deeply attached to her and was devastated by her death. She was granted a public funeral, which Caligula was too grief-stricken to attend, and he sought distraction by travelling through Italy and Sicily. A *iustitium* (a period of public mourning) was proclaimed, and business was halted. This clearly happened throughout the empire—Philo, for instance, notes that in Alexandria Jews closed their shops (7.25). Special honours were bestowed on her. We know that after Livia's death mourning for the women was decreed, as well as a memorial arch, and Dio suggests that Drusilla was granted the same honours, quite remarkable for a person who, unlike Livia, had apparently played little or no role in the public arena. But more was to come. Tiberius, a man of restraint, had vetoed divine honours for his mother, Livia. Caligula felt no such compunction, and the senate decreed that Drusilla was to be deified, the first woman whose worship as a goddess was established within the city of Rome. This was unprecedented, but perhaps not as remarkable as seems at first sight. Although Tiberius had refused such honours for Livia, a sizable group in the senate must clearly have been prepared to grant them. Livia was in fact eventually deified, in AD 42, under Claudius, as later were Nero's daughter Claudia and his wife Poppaea.

The consecration seems to have fallen on September 23, the birthday of Augustus (Smallwood 5.5–12, as restored), preceded by an eyewitness account of the soul on the way to heaven, a phenomenon witnessed also for Augustus' ascent—on that earlier occasion the sharp-eyed Numerius Atticus claimed to have seen the late emperor's soul ascend, for which he was rewarded with a million sestertii. Effigies of Drusilla were planned for the senate house, as well as for the Temple of Venus in the forum.

It is perhaps telling that after his initial frenzied bout of grief Caligula became more restrained. Drusilla's birthday was initially to be celebrated in the most extravagant form. By early 40, as we see from Dio, this flamboyant gesture fell into abeyance; henceforth she would receive the same honours, still considerable of course, as Augustus and Tiberius.

4.25 Fasti Ostienses AD 38 (Smallwood 31.30, Figure 1)

IIII IDVS IVN DRVSILLA EXCESSI[T]. Four days before the Ides of June (June 10) Drusilla died.

4.26 Suet. *Cal.* **24.1** Later on when Drusilla was married to Lucius Cassius Longinus,[15] Caligula took her away from him and kept her as if she were his own legitimate wife; and when he fell ill he also named her heir to his property and throne.[16] **2** On her death he declared a *iustitium* (period of public mourning),[17] during which laughing, bathing, and dining with one's parents or wife or children were deemed a capital offence. And, overcome with grief, he suddenly fled the city at night, crossed Campania, and headed for Syracuse, returning swiftly from there with beard and hair uncut; and never after that did he swear an oath on any matter, however important, either before an assembly of the people or among his soldiers, except by Drusilla's divine spirit. **3** His other sisters he did not love with such passion and esteem.

4.27 Dio 59.11.1 Marcus Lepidus was married to Drusilla, though he was also Gaius' homosexual companion and lover, but Gaius would also have sexual relations with her; and when she died at this time her husband gave the eulogy and her brother deemed her worthy of a state funeral. **2** The Praetorian guards, with their commander and the equestrian order separately . . . (lacuna) . . . and well-born boys rode their horses in the Troy manoeuvre around her tomb,[18]

---

[15] Drusilla had been married first to Lucius Cassius Longinus in AD 33 at the same time as her sister Livilla was married (to Marcus Vinicius) (Tac. *Ann.* 6.15.1; Dio 5.21.1). Longinus had been consul in AD 30 and little beyond that is known about him; Drusilla was divorced from him later to marry Marcus Aemilius Lepidus.

[16] Suetonius seems here to acknowledge the principle that a new emperor would inherit the estate of his predecessor by virtue of his office. He is the only source to say that Caligula intended to be succeeded as princeps by Drusilla, which is on the face of it a ludicrous notion. According to Dio (4.56), Caligula had determined on her husband Lepidus as successor and Suetonius may have confused the prospects of husband and wife in this context.

[17] The *iustitium* presumably lasted from the date of her death (June 10) to the date of her deification, possibly September 23.

[18] On the "Game of Troy," see glossary.

and whatever honours had been given to Livia were also voted to her. It was also decreed that she be deified, that a gold monument of her be set up in the senate house, and that in the Temple of Aphrodite in the forum a statue of her be erected of the same size as that of the goddess and worshipped with the same rites. 3 A personal shrine was also to be set up, and there would be twenty priests, not only men but women too, and whenever they gave testimony they were to swear on her name. And on her birthday there would be a festival celebrated like that of the Megalesia and the senate and equites were to be given a feast.[19] So at that time she received the name Panthea and was deemed worthy of divine honours throughout all the cities;[20] 4 and one Livius Geminius, a senator, swore on oath—invoking curses on himself and his children if he were lying—that he had seen her rise to heaven and intermingle with the gods, and he called on the other gods and the lady herself as witnesses, and for that he received one million sestertii.

5 In such ways did Gaius honour her, and he would also not allow festivals then falling due to be held either at the appointed time (unless they were prescribed by religion) or even later. Everybody faced some censure, whether they were objecting to something from distress or behaving as if they were pleased; for they faced accusation if they failed to mourn for her as a human or lament her as a goddess. From just one incident everything then happening can be put in perspective: he executed a hot-water seller on a charge of treason.

4.28 Dio 59.13.8 And returning after this to commemorate Drusilla's birthday, he had her statue brought into the Circus on a carriage drawn by elephants and put on a free show for the people lasting two days. On the first day, in addition to the horse races, five hundred bears were killed, and on the next the same number of Libyan beasts met their end,[21] and pankratiasts competed simultaneously in many places.[22] The common people were given a feast and senators and their wives given presents...

4.29 Dio 59.24.7 And included among the votes was one that Tiberius' and Drusilla's birthdays should be held in the same manner as that of Augustus.

4.30 Sen. *Polyb.* 17.4 On the death of Drusilla, Gaius Caesar, one who could no more demonstrate his grief than he could his joy as a princeps should, avoided seeing and talking to his fellow citizens and did not attend his sister's funeral or arrange appropriate tributes; rather he kept trying to alleviate his distress over

[19] The Megalesia was a two-day festival celebrated on April 4 and 5. It marked the arrival of the goddess Cybele in Rome.
[20] It is not clear why she received the title of Panthea ("all-embracing deity"). It is a relatively common epithet, applied to both male and female divinities.
[21] Libya was famous in antiquity for its lions.
[22] The *pancration* was a Greek sport, a mixture of boxing and wrestling with few restrictions on the range of moves permitted.

her most lamentable death by playing dice in his Alban villa and in the forum, and with other such common pastimes.[23] What a disgrace for the empire! A Roman princeps's solace for his grief over his sister was playing with dice! And that same Gaius, with his crazed impulsiveness, sometimes allowing his beard to grow long, sometimes close-shaving, and wandering all over the coastlines of Italy and Sicily, never quite sure whether he wanted his sister mourned or worshipped, was, during all the time that he was establishing temples and ceremonial couches for her, also inflicting the cruellest of punishments on people who had not grieved enough.

4.31 Sen. *Apoc.* 1 I wish to put on record what happened in heaven on the third day before the Ides of October of the new year at the start of our most happy era. I won't be influenced either by fear or favour ... However, if it will be necessary to produce someone to confirm it, ask the man who saw Drusilla going up to heaven: he too will say he saw Claudius making the journey, with uneven steps![24]

4.32 (see also 7.25) Philo *Flacc.* 56 ... breaking open the Jews' workshops, which were closed through grieving for Drusilla, they carted off whatever they found.[25]

Third Marriage

Caligula married for the third time in the course of AD 38, an event placed by Dio shortly after the death of Drusilla, presumably following her formal consecration and the end of the *iustitium*. His new bride, Lollia Paulina, came from a prestigious family; she was also a beautiful and, more importantly, very wealthy woman. According to Pliny she wore jewellery worth 40 million sestertii and carried the receipts on her person for those who doubted its value.[26] Her previous husband, Publius Memmius Regulus, was consul in AD 31, when he played an important part in toppling Sejanus. He was appointed legate of the province of Macedonia and Achaea in 35 and would remain in that office until 44. We know that Memmius was in Rome in the second half of 38 since he took part in the Arval rituals then.[27] The claim made by Dio about the role of Memmius in the marriage (4.34) is obscure. It is possible that Lollia had technically been Memmius' ward, but Dio's explanation is simply too cryptic to permit a full understanding of what happened. There may be a confused account of a Caligulan joke here about the appropriateness of Memmius participating in the marriage.

---

[23] The manuscripts are very confused here and Seneca's meaning is far from clear.

[24] The *Apocolocyntosis*, a spoof on the deification of Claudius, traditionally assigned to Seneca, ridiculed the notion of the eyewitness accounts. Claudius had a childhood disease which made him drag his foot along the ground "with uneven steps" (*non passibus aequis*), quoted from Vergil's *Aeneid* where it is used of the infant Ascanius trying to keep up with his father Aeneas (*Aen.* 2.724).

[25] On the historical events behind these activities see Chapter 7.   [26] Pliny *NH* 9.117.

[27] Smallwood 5.11.

4.33 Suet. *Cal.* 25.2 Lollia Paulina was married to the ex-consul Gaius Memmius,[28] a former consul in command of armies, and when a remark was made that her grandmother had once been a very beautiful woman Caligula suddenly recalled Lollia from the province and taking her from her husband married her and shortly afterwards divorced her, forbidding her ever to have sex with anyone.[29]

4.34 Dio 59.12.1 Now after an interval of a few days, he married Lollia Paulina,[30] having forced her own husband Memmius Regulus to have her engaged to him so he would not have her unengaged, contrary to law.[31] And he immediately divorced her, too.

Confrontation with the Senate

Josephus claims that Caligula reigned wisely for the first two years of his reign (4.35). This is little more than an expression of opinion, but it may not be far from the mark. Clearly the early euphoria had disappeared even before AD 38 and there had been a number of executions of people within the inner circle of power. But the first manifestation of a ruler who feels himself seriously beleaguered and in conflict with serious and determined opponents is not really discernable until AD 39. At some point in the year, in an astonishing confrontation, Caligula entered the senate house to deliver a savage tirade against the members, initiating what is depicted in the sources as a campaign of unrestrained brutality. Precisely when this happened we cannot tell. The chronology for the year 39 is very confused—it is arguably the murkiest period of Caligula's reign. Dio is the only extant literary source who places the events of the reign in some sort of sequence, and his account is especially confused for this particular year.

At this dramatic meeting Caligula vented his rage against the venerable institution. He charged senators with hypocrisy in criticizing Tiberius and went through the individual cases of the victims of Sejanus, noting that in each instance the responsibility for the conviction had lain not with Tiberius but with the senators themselves. The proof for this, it turned out, came from the very same papers that he had supposedly made a great show of destroying at the outset of the reign (3.19–20). His conclusion was that there was no security for him in seeking to please the senators—the prudent course was to make them fear him. The threat

[28] His name was in fact Publius.
[29] There may be a confused allusion to the injunction against newly divorced women engaging in sex during the period when the paternity of any subsequent pregnancy might be disputed.
[30] The marriage to Lollia took place a few days after the consecration of Drusilla (September 23, AD 38).
[31] The precise meaning of Dio's text, and the reference to legality, has been much discussed, but remains opaque. There were precedents for the role that Memmius seems to have played. Tiberius Claudius, Livia's first husband, gave away his former wife to Octavian.

of widespread use of the *maiestas* trials, the most hated feature of the Tiberian years, had returned with full vigour.

Nothing prepares us for this outburst, and it has led to the suspicion that Caligula had unearthed some sort of senatorial conspiracy. The actions taken against Gemellus, Macro, and Silanus in late 37/early 38 seem too remote to be particularly relevant. There are several high-profile charges of conspiracy later in AD 39, and there may be some connection between them and Caligula's behaviour before the senate, but no such explicit connection is made by the sources. Of course any information relayed to Caligula about individual disloyal senators would have been conveyed in secrecy.

4.35 Jos. *Ant.* 18.256 In his first and second year Gaius conducted business in quite a high-minded manner, and by even-handed conduct he promoted much good will for himself both among the Romans themselves and among the subject peoples.Afterwards, however, he, because of the extent of his power, left the point of thinking as a human and conducted all his affairs in a manner disrespectful of god.

4.36 Dio 59.10.7 After that (sc. the death of Macro) many others were also put to death, some after sentencing, some even before being convicted, the pretext being his parents and also his brothers and the others that had died because of them, but it was really for their possessions—since the treasury was depleted and he never had enough. 8 They were accused on the basis both of people's evidence against them and also from papers that he once said he had burned. And there were others for whom the illness that overtook him the previous year[32] as well as his sister Drusilla's death brought destruction; for, among other things, anyone was punished who had offered entertainment, greeted someone, or even taken a bath during those days.

4.37 Dio 59.13.2 In both those and the following days (sc. first part of AD 39) many of the most prominent men were condemned; for large numbers even of those released from prison were punished for the very same reasons for which they had been feared by Tiberius, and many of the others also died fighting as gladiators.

4.38 Dio 59.16.1 Until now he would not only himself criticize Tiberius, and do it persistently in everybody's presence, but neither did he object to others censuring him either privately or in public, and far from objecting he actually took pleasure in it; but on entering the senate on this occasion he now heaped praise on him, and severely denounced both the senate and the people for unjustly censuring him.

---

[32] These might have included both those individuals who had been foolish enough to pledge their lives in return for the emperor's recovery, but also possibly officials caught up in the administrative ambiguity that the illness might have created.

2 "I as emperor am permitted to do even that," he said, "but *you* are not only doing wrong but are also guilty of treason in taking such an attitude toward your former ruler." And with that he one by one took up the cases of all who had been put to death and showed (or at least appeared to show) that the senators had been responsible for the deaths of most of them, some by denouncing them, others by their testimony, and all by voting against them. **3** And these "facts" (emanating, apparently, from the very papers that he said he had burned) he then had read aloud by the freedmen and added, "Even if Tiberius did you some harm, you should not, good heavens, have shown him respect while he lived and then later changed your minds about things you had often said and voted on. **4** But you treated him capriciously, and Sejanus, too, a man that you put to death after filling him with conceit and ruining him, so that I, too, can expect no fair treatment from you."

5 After some such comments he then brought Tiberius himself into his address as saying, "You have spoken both well and truthfully about all this, so don't be gentle with any of them or spare anyone. They all hate you and are all praying for your death, and they will kill you if they can. **6** So don't even think about what you can do to please them, and don't worry about their chatter; concentrate only on what is nice and safe for you, which is also the best option. This is how you will suffer least harm and enjoy all the sweetest things; and in addition you will be respected by them, whether they like it or not. **7** The other way you will actually gain nothing, earning only a worthless reputation and nothing more, and after facing plots you will die a death without honour. For no man is ruled willingly; rather, as long as he lives in fear, he is obsequious to the stronger man, but on gaining confidence he takes revenge on the weaker one."

The Bridge of Boats

It is probably during this general period of heightened tension between Caligula and the senate that we should place one of the most celebrated events of Caligula's reign, the construction of a temporary bridge of boats across a section of the bay of Naples. The precise location of this famous structure is uncertain. The eastern end was almost certainly at Puteoli (Pozzuoli), the major port for the importation of grain destined for Rome until Ostia was developed under Claudius. Puteoli by Caligula's time was furnished with an enormous mole, a great tourist attraction in Seneca's day, and that mole would be a logical eastern terminus of the bridge.[33] The starting point on the western side is more difficult to locate, but it seems to have been in the general vicinity of Baiae. Nor can we be certain about the date.

---

[33] Sen. *Ep.* 77.1.

Dio puts the bridge among the events of AD 39 and in doing so receives some support from Suetonius, who says that the structure was intended to overawe the Britons and Germans against whom Caligula was planning a campaign (which began in late 39). Most scholars accept that general date.

Dio provides the fullest account of the celebrations, lasting over three days. Caligula supposedly entered the bridge at the Baiae end in spectacular array, and spent the intervening night in Puteoli, returning next day in even more spectacular fashion. Things got rather wild. In the chaotic carousing afterwards people got drunk and the revellers threw one another into the sea, where a number drowned— the casualties might have been higher but happily the seas were unusually calm.

There was much speculation about Caligula's motives, generally described as frivolous, such as the desire to ride a chariot over the sea or a determination to outdo Xerxes. It is noteworthy however that Suetonius does not depict the bridge as a piece of crass irresponsibility—he includes it among the positive achievements of the reign and provides the rational explanation, noted above, that it was to demonstrate Roman power to the Britons and Germans. Also, beneath Josephus' claim that the bridge was a manifestation of madness he seems to be suggesting a practical, if perhaps not well-thought out, scheme for simply improving communications. Suetonius also interestingly relates a quite different claim of his grandfather, who had heard it from a courtier, that Caligula's motive was to refute the prediction of Tiberius' astrologer Thrasyllus that Caligula had as much chance of riding over the sea at Baiae as he did of becoming emperor. But if there ever had been such a prediction in the first place, it had been thoroughly disproved by events, and even if there is something to the story it is very possible that the unnamed courtier might have been relaying a casual and facetious comment made by Caligula after the event. Perhaps the primary motive was simply irresponsible extravagance. Caligula was in 39 engaged in a power play with the senate—what better way to display the magnitude of his unchallengeable power than by constructing an utterly pointless structure like this bridge? He could simply be demonstrating to the world that only he had access to the resources needed for such a grandiose venture.

4.39 Jos. *Ant*. 19.5 The other things he did were also nothing short of madness. He thought it intolerable to complete the crossing by trireme from the city of Dicaearchia, which lies in Campania, to another coastal city, Misenum;[34] **6** and then, thinking that as master of the sea he also had the right to demand of the sea exactly what he demanded of the land, he joined up 30 stades of the sea from one headland to the other,[35] and after thus cutting off the entire bay within

---

[34] Dicaearchia is the Greek colony that preceded Puteoli.
[35] Josephus' distance of 30 stades (3.75 Roman miles) should be treated with caution. At *Ant*. 18.249, he seems to make the absurd claim that Puteoli was 5 stades from Baiae. Numbers in manuscripts are especially prone to errors in transmission.

drove over the bridge in his chariot. He said that for a god to travel like that was quite appropriate.[36]

4.40 Suet. *Cal*. 19.1 He also came up with a new and extraordinary sort of spectacle. For he bridged the space between Baiae and the causeway at Puteoli[37] (some 3,600 paces away) by assembling merchant ships from all around, setting them at anchor in two parallel lines and piling earth on them to match the shape of the Appian Way.[38] **2** He went back and forth over this bridge for two days in succession,[39] on the first day on a horse with trappings and striking a remarkable pose with an oak-leaf crown,[40] a small shield, a sword, and a golden cape, and on the second in charioteer's clothing on a two-horse chariot drawn by a pair of famous horses parading before him a boy named Dareus, one of the Parthian hostages and escorted by a body of Praetorian guards and a cohort of friends in war chariots.[41] **3** I know that many have assumed that a bridge of this sort was devised by Gaius to emulate Xerxes whose bridging of the considerably narrower Hellespont met with admiration,[42] and others that it was to intimidate Germany and Britain with stories of some immense construction.[43] But as a boy I would hear my grandfather say that the reason for its building was given away by Gaius' more intimate courtiers,[44] that when Tiberius was concerned about his successor and was more in favour of his true grandson,[45] the astrologer

[36] Josephus' sequence of thought seems muddled here. He presents the bridge as a practical measure, to avoid a dangerous sea crossing, then characterizes it as a manifestation of megalomania.

[37] The manuscripts seem to be full of errors at this point and Suetonius' precise intentions are far from clear.

[38] A surface had to be placed on the pontoon to allow proper movement of traffic. On a well-constructed road like the Appian Way the crown is raised to allow the rainwater to run off into ditches.

[39] Suetonius' meaning is not totally clear here. He could be saying that the procession went back and forth a number of times over a period of two days, or that it completed a single return trip, each of the stages confined to each of two successive days. The latter makes most sense, and is reasonably close to Dio's version, which envisages a three-day event involving a single journey out, followed by a return trip after a day of rest.

[40] On the *corona civica* (oak wreath) see the discussion preceding 3.51.

[41] Darius was the son of Artabanus III of Parthia. He had been sent to Rome as part of the settlement between Rome and Parthia two years earlier (see 7.1, 3). His presence at the event would offer the bonus of reminding people of an earlier "foreign policy" coup.

[42] The Persian king Xerxes famously crossed the Hellespont in 480 BC. His action was traditionally viewed as a manifestation of arrogance, but here, unusually, it is seen as an impressive achievement, although one bettered by Caligula.

[43] The suggestion is essentially nonsensical: it is hardly likely that tribes in Germany or Britain would have taken the slightest notice of marine activities in the bay of Naples. Yet the information is extremely valuable. For the anecdote to have the remotest plausibility the event must have taken place within a reasonable period before the northern expedition, which seems to have been initiated in September AD 39. This accords well with Dio's including the event, albeit vaguely, under the year AD 39.

[44] The identity of his grandfather is unknown. At *Otho* 10.1 Suetonius explains that his father served as a legionary equestrian tribune under Otho. His grandfather, then, was likely a person of some substance but probably not important enough to be an intimate of the imperial court, and we do not know how he might have become privy to the information reported.

[45] At Suet. *Tib*. 62.3 Tiberius supposedly suspects that Gemellus is the illegitimate offspring of his mother and Sejanus.

Thrasyllus had assured him that Gaius had no more chance of becoming emperor than he had of riding horses over the bay of Baiae.[46]

4.41 Dio 59.17.1 Gaius' preference, however, was certainly not for that kind of triumph—driving a chariot on land was to his thinking no great feat—but he had his heart set on somehow driving through the sea, bridging the distance between Puteoli and Bauli (for this place lies opposite the city of Puteoli, 26 stades away).[47] **2** Some of the ships for the bridge were simply brought together there, but others were built *in situ* because what could be assembled in a short time was insufficient,[48] even though all available vessels were brought together there, precipitating a very severe famine in Italy, especially in Rome.[49] **3** Not only was a sort of passageway built, but resting places and guest chambers were also constructed along it that even provided potable running water.[50]

When everything was ready, he put on what he claimed was Alexander's breastplate[51] and a silk, purple cloak studded with lots of gold and many precious Indian stones, and he hung a sword at his side, took a shield, and set an oak-leaf crown on his head. **4** After that he offered sacrifice to Poseidon and a number of other gods, Phthonos included (so no malice should attend him, he said)[52] and then he stepped onto the bridge from the Bauli end, taking along with him a retinue of crowds of armed horsemen and foot soldiers, and charged into the city (sc. Puteoli) as if chasing an enemy.[53]

5 After spending the next day there, resting after the battle, as it were, he was brought back over the same bridge clad in a gold-embroidered tunic; and he rode in a chariot drawn by superb, prize-winning horses (and among the many "spoils" that went with him was also the Arsacid Darius, one of the Parthians then living as hostages in Rome). **6** His friends and companions attended him in chariots, dressed in flowery clothes, and then came the army and the rest of

---

[46] The prediction is to be assigned presumably to the period between Caligula's summons to Capri in AD 31 and Thrasyllus' death in AD 36; on Thrasyllus, see 2.33.

[47] There is no consensus on where Bauli was located: Pliny *NH* 9.172 seems to place it in the general region of Baiae; Tac. *Ann.* 14.4.3–4 gives Bauli as the name of a villa between Misenum and *Baianus lacus* (Lucrine lake?). Some modern scholars opt for the site of modern Bacoli, about halfway between Misenum and Baiae. Dio uses a ratio of 7.5 stades to the Roman mile; hence 26 stades produces a distance of about 3.45 Roman miles, 3.15 modern miles (5 km). The distance from Puteoli to Bacoli is in fact 2.25 modern miles.

[48] Dio here contradicts Suetonius, who limits the boats used to those already built and ready to be assembled together.

[49] The claim of a famine may be taken from Seneca (4.43).

[50] Dio presents a more elaborate structure than that found in Suetonius, who describes the pontoon as a more practical affair, even admiring its construction techniques, comparable to the engineering of the Appian Way.

[51] Suetonius omits this detail. His account is far more restrained but even so the omission would be surprising if it had appeared in his sources. It may be a much later addition to the story.

[52] Phthonos ("envy") meted out punishment to mortals who had transgressed the boundaries of what was reserved for the divine.

[53] Dio specifies that Caligula began the journey from the Baiae/Bauli end, hence the destination (the "city") must be Puteoli.

his crowd, all wearing whatever they fancied. And naturally, given such a campaign and so great a victory, some speech was also necessary, and he mounted a dais that had itself also been mounted on ships near the centre of the bridge; 7 and there he first flattered himself on his enterprise in accomplishing great feats and then praised the soldiers for having faced both hardship and danger, especially in this instance for crossing the sea on foot. 8 He also awarded them money for this, and after that they spent the rest of the day and all night feasting, he himself on the bridge as if on some island, and they at anchor around him on some other boats, with much light shining on them from the place itself and from the mountains. 9 This was because the area was crescent-shaped and fires were lit all round as in a theatre, so there was no awareness of darkness, for he wanted to turn night into day, I suppose, as he had turned sea into land! When stuffed and full of food and strong drink he hurled many of his companions into the sea from the bridge, 10 and many others he drove underwater as he sailed around in boats fronted with beaks, so that a few even lost their lives, though most were saved despite their inebriated state. The reason for this was that the sea was smooth and calm both when the bridge was being constructed and when everything else was going on. 11 And by this he was certainly elated, declaring that even Poseidon feared him since he had made a total mockery of Darius and Xerxes, having now built a bridge over a much greater expanse of the sea than they had.[54]

4.42 Suet. *Cal.* 32.1 Even when relaxing and resigning himself to recreation and dining, the cruelty of his words and actions remained unchanged. Often important judicial investigations with torture were held in his sight as he had lunch or was drinking, while a soldier who was a master of decapitation would lop off the heads of those brought from prison. At Puteoli, after inviting large numbers of people to come from the shore for the dedication of a bridge that had been devised by him (as I mentioned above), he suddenly threw everyone overboard, and some grabbing the ship's helm he pushed back into the sea with poles and oars.[55]

4.43 Sen. *Brev. Vit.* 18.5 Just recently, within those few days during which Gaius Caesar died, sorely grieved (if the dead have any feelings) to leave the world knowing that the Roman people had survived, they said there was certainly enough food left for seven or eight days. While he was building bridges of boats and amusing himself with the mighty resources of the empire, we were faced with the worst that people under siege can endure, lack of food. His

---

[54] Suetonius limits the comparison to Xerxes. Darius crossed the Bosphorus in about 512 BC.

[55] In his main description of the building of the bridge (4.40), Suetonius includes it among Caligula's meritorious actions. In this different section, which is intended to highlight Caligula's savagery, he includes the deaths during the festivities among Caligula's stereotypical acts of cruelty. This illustrates how Suetonius' interpretation of the historical evidence can be very much influenced by his current task in hand.

copying of a crazy, foreign, inauspiciously overweening king almost included our destruction and starvation as well as the consequences of starvation.[56]

Caligula and the Consuls

The sequence of events during the course of AD 39 is virtually impossible to disentangle, but in the political sphere things seem to have reached a breaking point by the beginning of September, when Caligula summarily dismissed the two consuls (they had presumably assumed office on July 1). We do not know their identity, and his motives are depicted as the familiar mix of the trivial and the substantial. On the one hand he claimed that they had not properly celebrated his birthday, August 31. Much more significantly, he was angry that they had celebrated the victory at Actium (September 2), when Octavian had defeated the combined forces of Mark Antony and Cleopatra in 31 BC, and also Octavian's earlier victory won in 36 BC off Naulochus in Sicily over the naval forces of Sextus Pompeius, the rebellious son of Pompey. Caligula was of course a descendant of Mark Antony, through his grandmother Antonia, Antony's daughter, and may have acquired an admiration for him when he stayed at her house. But it is harder to explain his apparent attachment to Sextus Pompeius. It may well be that, as Suetonius hints, Caligula was ahead of time in seeking a healing of old rifts. But one must be very cautious. One of the consuls apparently committed suicide after his dismissal, which hints at a serious political situation, and perhaps the exposure of active opposition against the emperor.

We might get some insight into the general conditions of the time from the two men who were appointed to replace the dismissed consuls, since they might both be expected to be safe appointments in troubled times. Immediately (Dio: 4.46), or, more precisely, within three days (Suetonius: 4.48), Gnaeus Domitius Afer was appointed one of the replacements. Domitius is a familiar character of the Julio-Claudian period, as someone who perfectly mastered the art of survival. An eloquent and witty man, he had placed his skills in the service of Sejanus and acted against the allies of Caligula's mother Agrippina. He was later supposedly charged because of a flattering inscription placed on a statue of Caligula listing the emperor's achievements, clearly meant to please, but Caligula supposedly saw it as an offensive comment on his youth. Caligula reportedly gave the prosecution speech against Domitius in the resulting proceedings and Domitius shrewdly declared himself too overwhelmed by the emperor's eloquence to try to refute

---

[56] The text of this passage is very uncertain and the translation offered is based on a standard emendation of the manuscripts. Unlike Dio, Seneca is careful not to claim an explicit connection between the bridge and food shortages. He simply says that Caligula indulged in such extravagance at a time when Rome had food supplies for only seven or eight days, and places the event shortly before his death, in AD 41. Seneca may have in mind a famine that occurred under Claudius in AD 42 (Dio 60.11.1; Suet. *Claud.* 18.2).

him. Tellingly, Domitius' case was championed by Callistus, the most powerful of Caligula's freedmen. This garbled account, as transmitted in the sources, seems to point to Domitius as someone willing to go to any lengths for his own advancement, an attractive ally in certain contexts. He continued his successful public life well into the reign of Nero, and reputedly died in grand style, by eating himself to death.

Domitius Afer's colleague is not mentioned by any of the literary sources, and much effort has in the past been devoted to identifying him. Some of the arguments presented have been very persuasive, but all were proved quite wrong by the discovery in the early 1970s of a name that no one had in fact suggested. The evidence was preserved on a *tabula cerata* (wax tablet), where the impression of the writing tools can leave decipherable indentations in the wood. A cache of such tablets was discovered on the outskirts of Pompeii, preserving a number of financial transactions, one of them dated to mid-September, AD 39 (*AE* 1973.138), by the names of two consuls, Domitius Afer and his colleague.

This colleague is identified as Aulus Didius Gallus, a man perhaps not of great intellect or political genius, but hardworking and competent. He was quaestor in AD 19, and worked his way up to the suffect consulship in AD 39, and soon after was appointed water commissioner (curator aquarum), a position he held until AD 49. He accompanied Claudius to Britain in AD 43 and was a legate in Moesia, where he earned triumphal insignia. He was proconsul of Asia between 49 and 52, and from 52 to 57 was legate of Britain, where his term of office was noteworthy mainly because nothing noteworthy happened during it,[57] suggesting the very quality that Caligula might have been seeking in a consul at this time, careerism untainted by any desire for personal aggrandisement. Such careerism is nicely demonstrated by a clever quip of Domitius Afer, preserved by Quintilian. When Didius displayed a spurious reluctance to accept a provincial governorship, Domitius suggested, "Well, then, do it for your country's sake."[58]

4.44 Dio 59.18.1 This was how that bridge ended up, and it also caused many people's deaths; for after bankrupting himself on it he plotted against many more people for their wealth; for he staged trials both on his own account and with the entire senate. **2** Some cases this body could also try on its own, but it did not have final authority and appeals against it became very numerous. The findings of the senate were released as usual, but for sentences given by Gaius names were displayed in public as if he were afraid they might escape notice. **3** These people accordingly received their punishment, some by imprisonment, others being flung down from the Capitoline hill, and still others committing suicide. Nor was there any safeguard even for those who were exiled; many perished either on the journey or during their exile.

---

[57] Tac. *Ag.* 14; *Ann.* 14.29.1.   [58] Quintilian 6.3.68.

4.45 Dio 59.19.1 Among those then on trial was also Domitius Afer, a man who became exposed to a bizarre danger and had an even more extraordinary escape. For Gaius hated him anyway since in Tiberius' reign he had denounced some woman related to his mother Agrippina; **2** and because of that, when Agrippina came face to face with him and realized that he stood back from her out of embarrassment, she said: "Relax, Domitius; it's not you I blame but Agamemnon."[59] Then, when he erected a statue of Gaius and wrote an inscription on it indicating that he was consul for the second time at the age of twenty-seven,[60] **3** Gaius was upset, thinking he was reproaching him for his youth and his lawless conduct, and for that reason—although it was something Domitius expected even to be honoured for—he took him before the senate and delivered a long speech against him. For he generally thought himself superior to all orators, and aware that this man was particularly gifted he was eager to outdo him. He certainly would have executed him if Domitius had actually competed with him in any way. **4** In fact Domitius made no reply and even pretended to admire and be overawed by Gaius' brilliance, and repeating the charge in every detail he praised it as if he were just someone listening to it and not himself on trial; **5** and when given leave to speak, he turned to entreaties and lamentations, and finally dropped to the ground and lying prostrate pleaded with him as if fearing him more as an orator than as the Caesar. And so after seeing and hearing this Gaius melted, actually believing he had bested him with the finesse of his oratory; **6** and because of this and also because of the freedman Callistus (whom he himself held in esteem and whom Domitius fawned on), he ceased to be angry. And when Callistus later reproached him for accusing him in the first place he replied, "I could not keep a speech like that to myself."[61]

4.46 Dio 59.20.1 He also immediately appointed Domitius consul, dismissing the current office holders for not having announced a festival on his birthday even though the praetors had held a horse race that day and killed some animals (something which did occur annually), and because they celebrated the

---

[59] Agrippina places the blame on Tiberius, as leader of the opposition against her and her family, drawing an analogy with Agamemnon, leader of the Greek expedition against Troy. She may be alluding to the claim of Poseidon in the *Iliad* that the recent poor performance of the Greeks in battle could be blamed on Agamemnon's quarrel with Achilles (Hom. *Il.* 13.112).

[60] According to Suetonius (*Cal.* 32.1), Caligula had prohibited the erection of a statue to any living Roman anywhere in the city, with reference presumably both to public places and to private residences. It is not certain that Domitius ran into trouble because of a breach of this rule, which was designed to prevent congestion, and probably did not apply to statues of the emperor. Domitius' sin seems to have been the addition of what was deemed an inappropriate inscription.

[61] Callistus was a key figure in Caligula's regime and there was even a rumour that the emperor had an affair with his daughter Nymphidia, resulting in the birth of Nymphidius Sabinus, who as Praetorian prefect made a short-lived and fatal bid for the principate in AD 68 (Plut. *Galb.* 9.1). Callistus survived Caligula's assassination and went on to become a powerful and enormously wealthy figure in the court of Caligula's successor Claudius (see Chapter 7). He was at one time accused of plotting against Caligula, a claim treated as frivolous (8.4), but he may well have been an early supporter of Claudius and seems to have played a shadowy role in the plot against Caligula (8.8, 10, 11).

customary feast for the victories that Augustus gained over Antony.[62] **2** For in order to have some trumped-up accusation against them, he decided to be seen as a descendant of Antony rather than Augustus. And he did in fact give advance notice to the people with whom he shared his personal information that whatever the consuls did they would be in the wrong, whether they slaughtered oxen for Antony's misadventure or were neglectful over Augustus' victory. **3** Such were his pretexts for peremptorily removing these men from their posts, first smashing their fasces, at which one of them was so mortified that he committed suicide.[63] Domitius was then nominally chosen by the people as his colleague, but it was really Gaius himself who chose him.

4.47 Suet. *Cal.* 23.1 ... and not satisfied with casting this aspersion on Augustus, he forbade celebration of the victories at Actium and in Sicily on their traditional days, claiming they were ill-omened and disastrous for the Roman people.

4.48 (see also 6.1) Suet. *Cal.* 26.3 When the consuls forgot to announce his birthday he revoked their offices, and for three days the state was without its supreme magistrates.

4.49 *AE* 1973: 138 September 15, AD 39. Murecine, suburb of Pompeii
In the consulship of Gnaeus Domitius Ahenobarbus and Aulus Didius Gallus, 17 days before the Kalends of October (September 16), I Novius Eunius have written that I owe 1,250 sestertii to Hesicus ...[64]

Fourth Marriage, Caesonia

After two apparently unsuccessful, at any rate very brief, marriages following the death of his first wife, Caligula seems to have achieved marital success with his fourth union, and to have found a true soulmate. Milonia Caesonia was the

---

[62] Suetonius (4.47) records that Caligula put an end to the celebrations for both the battle of Actium, won on September 2 (31 BC), and the battle of Naulochus, which Marcus Agrippa, on behalf of Octavia, won against Sextus Pompeius on September 3 (36 BC). We do not know if the measure was still in place in the following year (the relevant epigraphic evidence is missing), and Caligula was assassinated early in AD 41. His birthday fell just before September 2 and 3, on August 31, hence any contrast in the level of celebrations would have been evident. Suetonius also refers to the negligence of the consuls on his birthday and their subsequent dismissal (4.48). Their apparent conduct is baffling, but it is to be noted that Caligula had ordered the total cancellation of festivals following the death of Drusilla in June of the previous year, and there is the possibility of crossed wires.

[63] The dismissed consuls are not named. It is tempting to suspect that the one who committed suicide was in some way connected with the conspiracies in this year, perhaps through a link to Lepidus or to Gaetulicus. In a different context Dio indicates under the events of AD 39 that Gnaeus Domitius Corbulo was made consul in gratitude for his assistance in prosecuting corrupt officials responsible for road repairs (Dio 59.15.3–5; see also Tac. *Ann.* 3.31.3; Pliny *NH* 7.39); the only slot available to him among the consuls of Caligula's reign seems to be as one of the dismissed suffects. His is a famous name, associated mainly with the distinguished general who conducted a very effective campaign against Parthia under Nero. The consul of AD 39 is probably the father of the future great commander, but he could conceivably be the commander himself.

[64] A chance discovery, recording an utterly trivial event but indirectly containing through its dating indicator a vital piece of information for the reconstruction of the confused events of AD 39.

daughter of Vistilia, a woman who had in total six husbands and seven children, the latter born in a range of gestation periods between seven and eleven months so varied that they were recorded in Pliny's *Natural History*.[65] Caesonia probably resulted from the sixth marriage; her father is unknown. She was already the mother of three daughters when she married Caligula; nothing is known of her previous husband(s). The existence of the three earlier children (their ultimate fates are unknown) would in a way be seen by Caligula as a commendation, rather than as an obstacle, since they demonstrated that she was fertile. Dio places this last marriage among the final events of AD 39 after Caligula had departed for his northern expedition. But Dio's narrative is very confused at this point and his timing seems to be contradicted by Caligula's presence in Rome on the birth of his daughter, supposedly a month after the marriage. Suetonius claims that the birth occurred on the actual day of the marriage (4.50), although that supposition may have originated from a misunderstood joke (also there is a manuscript problem in Suetonius at this point). It may be that they were married earlier in AD 39 and that Dio did not know the precise date.

4.50 Suet. *Cal.* 25.3 Caesonia was neither particularly attractive nor very young[66] and was already the mother of three daughters by another man, but she was given to high living and depraved sexuality; and he loved her with both more passion and fidelity, to the point of often showing her off to his soldiers riding beside him, decked out with cloak, shield, and helmet, and even displaying her naked to his friends.[67]

He did not grant her the honour of being called his wife until she had given birth, declaring on one and the same day that he was her husband and also the father of the child born from her. 4 The infant, however, named Julia Drusilla, he carried around the temples of all the goddesses and set her in Minerva's bosom[68] and commended her feeding and upbringing to her. And no better evidence did he have for believing that she really was his own seed than the ferocity she showed even then, so great that with her wild fingers she would attack the faces and eyes of infants playing with her.[69]

4.51 Dio 59.28.7 When Caesonia gave birth to a daughter thirty days after their marriage, he made out that this was itself a miracle, priding himself on having

---

[65] Pliny *NH* 7.39.

[66] Caesonia might have been born about AD 5, and would thus have been Caligula's senior by some seven years.

[67] The allusion to nudity may be a misrepresentation of information that she was not carrying weapons when depicted in military garb.

[68] The text here reads *gremium*, which can refer to either the lap or the bosom. The latter seems preferable, given the reference in 4.51 to Minerva's being entrusted with the nursing.

[69] The child was named after Caligula's late sister. The reference to proof of paternity should not be seen as an indication of uncertainty about her legitimacy but another example of Caligulan humour.

become both husband and father within days of each other; and naming her Drusilla he took her up to the Capitol, set her on Jupiter's knees as though she were actually his child, and put her in Minerva's charge for nursing.[70]

4.52 Dio 59.23.7 Then, divorcing Paulina with the excuse that she had produced no child (but in fact because he had tired of her), he married Milonia Caesonia, a woman with whom he had earlier been having an affair and now wanted also to marry so that, since she was pregnant, she could bear him a child thirty days later...

9 Meanwhile they were also badly affected by a heat wave; so oppressive was it that awnings were stretched over the forum.[71] Among those exiled at that time was also Ofonius Tigellinus, expelled for having sex with no less than Agrippina.[72]

Conspirators

The most serious threat to Caligula in this period may well have been posed by a man who seems to dominate events in the latter part of AD 39, Cornelius Lentulus Gaetulicus. The son of a brilliant military commander, if less than brilliant senator (the father was fond of alcohol and regularly fell asleep during senate speeches, needing to be carried home), Gaetulicus had been a close ally of Sejanus, and his colleague in the consulship in AD 26. It was very possibly through Sejanus' influence that he became legate of Upper Germany in AD 29, a powerful position in itself, but rendered even more powerful by his father-in-law being legate of Lower Germany. Tacitus suggests that Gaetulicus had *de facto* control in both zones,[73] thus in a sense having at his disposal eight legions, nearly one third of the whole of Rome's total legionary forces. As a mark of his high status his daughter had been betrothed to Sejanus' son, and he was the only close associate of the

---

[70] The nature of the dedication, whether to Jupiter or, as suggested by Suetonius, to Minerva, is obscure. There have been suggestions that the action was in imitation of Egyptian or Etruscan rites, but the evidence for the parallels is not convincing. The activity described may be in keeping with Roman practice: Quintus Catulus reportedly dreamt that he saw the infant Augustus in the lap of Jupiter Capitolinus (Suet. *Aug.* 94.8). The Temple of Jupiter Capitolinus contained a statue to Minerva (Athene).

[71] This might be taken to indicate that Caesonia's marriage and delivery took place in the middle of the summer. But it is possible that Dio simply relegated the marriage and the detail about the heat of the summer to the closing section of AD 39, where he grouped a number of events that he could not date precisely within the year.

[72] Tigellinus Ophonius is familiar as the sinister prefect of the Praetorian guard under Nero, one of the emperor's special favourites. He was an ambitious man and could well have been distantly involved in the dynastic intrigue occurring in late 39. The claim of the affair with Agrippina might have been the usual smokescreen to cover the political intrigues of the imperial women. We are told by a scholiast on the poet Juvenal (on Juv. *Sat.* 1.55) that Tigellinus was a close associate of Gnaeus Domitius Ahenobarbus, Agrippina's husband, father of the emperor Nero, but it is not clear what role Tigellinus might have played in any conspiracy, nor is there any hint that Domitius Ahenobarbus was involved—he was estranged from Agrippina soon after Nero's birth and in very poor health in AD 39.

[73] Tac. *Ann.* 6.30.

hated prefect to survive his downfall. Tacitus reports that Gaetulicus supposedly wrote to Tiberius from Germany to point out that his association with Sejanus had met with Tiberius' blessing, and that his failure of judgement was no worse than Tiberius' own. He asserted that he remained loyal to the emperor, suggesting that Tiberius should remain princeps, and he, Gaetulicus, should remain legate. Tacitus admits that the story seems incredible. But it does at the very least serve to confirm Gaetulicus' reputation as a powerful and ambitious political figure.

Gaetulicus may well have been an adept political schemer. His competence as a military legate is more open to question. There had been problems in the frontier area of Germany, in both the Upper and Lower zone, for a number of years, and Gaetulicus' lax discipline does not seem to have helped matters. At some point late in Tiberius' reign he was unable to prevent a serious incursion of German tribes, which broke over the Rhine and caused major devastation in Gaul.[74] The incursion had still not been fully checked by late AD 39, when he was replaced by Galba (7.17).

It would not have been surprising had Caligula decided to replace Gaetulicus. But he went much further. He put him to death, and the circumstances of that death are shrouded in mystery. Caligula left Rome and travelled north in AD 39 to launch his military expeditions against Britain and Germany. At some point before October 27 it was reported in Rome that Gaetulicus had been executed because of "wicked plots" (4.53). We cannot be certain where Caligula was when the execution was carried out. The emperor was apparently still in Rome in early September, when he dismissed the consuls (see above 4.46, 48), and we are told that when he made his departure he did so very hastily. We do not know whether he was present at the execution. Nor do we know *why* Gaetulicus was executed. He might have resisted relinquishing his command, or he might indeed have been actively plotting against Caligula. The issue has provoked much scholarly speculation.

4.53 Arval record (Smallwood 9.18–20) October 27, AD 39 Six days before the Kalends of November (*sacrifices were conducted*) to mark the exposure of the wicked plots of Gnaeus Lentulus Gaetulicus against Gaius Germanicus.

4.54 Dio 59.22.5 I have no need to list by name most of the others (sc. victims of Caligula), but I shall put on record those of whom history needs a record. There was Lentulus Gaetulicus, a man with a fine overall reputation and also the governor of Germany for ten years; he executed him because he was popular with his soldiers.[75]

---

[74] Suet. *Tib.* 41.
[75] Dio puts Gaetulicus' name first in a short list of those put to death and sees Gaetulicus' popularity with the soldiers as a positive feature of the man. Suetonius (7.17) simply records that Galba imposed strict military discipline on the armies when he replaced Gaetulicus in the German command.

The actions undertaken by Caligula against Gaetulicus may reflect a nervousness about powerful provincial legates who had command over several legions. Another victim in this year was Calvisius Sabinus, former legate of the province of Pannonia. It is perhaps noteworthy that Sabinus' colleague in the consulship for AD 26 had been Gaetulicus. Also, Cornelia, Sabinus' wife, may well have been Cornelia Gaetulica, the sister of Gaetulicus.

> **4.55 Dio 59.18.3** There is no need to bother readers with petty details of the other cases; 4 Calvisius Sabinus, however, was one of the leading men in the senate at the time and on returning from his province of Pannonia he and his wife Cornelia were arraigned on charges (she was accused of having inspected sentries and watching soldiers at their drill); they did not wait for their trial but did away with themselves ahead of time.[76] Titus Rufus also did the very same thing when indicted for declaring that the senate held one opinion but voted for another.[77]

The Net Widens: Marcus Lepidus and Caligula's Sisters

In his list of named victims in this year, AD 39, Dio places Gaetulicus first. Then, without explicitly stating any connection, he next identifies Marcus Lepidus, widowed husband of Caligula's sister, Drusilla, and, reputedly, also Caligula's lover. After the death of Gemellus, Lepidus had apparently been marked out by the emperor as his successor (4.56). As concrete evidence of his status his statue stood in the Sebasteion, a shrine dedicated to the imperial cult, in Aphrodisias, in the province of Asia.[78] Dio offers no explanation for Lepidus' demise, but his narrative suggests that his downfall was somehow connected to affairs with both of Caligula's surviving sisters. Suetonius is far more explicit and states that Lepidus conspired with the sisters and that at his trial Caligula released the damning correspondence between them. Lepidus was put to death, and in what seems almost a parody of her mother's return to Rome with her father Germanicus' ashes, the younger Agrippina was obliged to carry Lepidus' bones in an urn back to the city. Both sisters were then deported.

---

[76] Calvisius Sabinus was a member of an established noble family. His father was consul in 4 BC and he was himself consul in AD 26. He was one of a group of leading senators targeted by Macro with charges of treason in AD 32, after the fall of Sejanus. There may have been a suspicion at that time that they had been acting against the interests of Caligula. He survived this and went on to be appointed legate of Pannonia some time after AD 36. He was charged on his return to Rome in 39, along with his wife. The precise accusation is not specified but we are given some details about his wife's behaviour. To judge from Dio's comments she seems to have provoked the traditional Roman animosity towards women who involved themselves in military matters. Tacitus adds another traditional element, sexual misconduct used as a cover for political improprieties. She reportedly went around the camp dressed as a soldier, having sex with the guards, and was caught "in the headquarters building" with a Titus Vinius (Tac. *Hist.* 1.48.2–3; Plut. *Galb.* 12). Whatever the truth lurking inside this bizarre episode, the case was serious enough for both of them to commit suicide.
[77] Nothing further is known of this incident.   [78] *SEG* 30.1251.

The events surrounding Lepidus' death are a mystery. It is generally assumed that he and the two sisters accompanied Caligula north to Gaul/Germany. None of the ancient sources explicitly claims this but it seems to be implied. Dio states that Caligula gave a written report to the senate about the sexual misbehaviour of Lepidus and the sisters, which makes it very likely that the condemnation occurred when the emperor was not in Rome. The story that Agrippina was obliged to carry Lepidus' remains back to Rome shows that his death occurred some distance from the city, but it does not tell us where. Certainly, none of this means that Lepidus died in Gaul or in Germany. Caligula departed for his expedition not directly from Rome but after a sojourn in Mevania, some 60 miles north of the city (7.18) and this provides a good context for the exposure of their misdeeds. It would hardly make sense for Caligula to take a group of would-be conspirators all the way to Gaul or Germany.

Lepidus' supposed motives are also a mystery. Caligula clearly believed that Lepidus had made an attempt on his life. Was he acting alone? The claims of adultery between Lepidus and the sisters might well reflect the traditional Roman approach to concealing female political misbehaviour behind a screen of sexual misbehaviour. But if there was some sort of intrigue involving Lepidus and the two sisters then it must presumably have been designed to further their interests. Caligula's marriage to Caesonia and the birth of their child might have been the stimulus to action, as there would have been every reason to assume that Caesonia would eventually bear the emperor a son. Lepidus might have felt that his chance of achieving the principate would be much strengthened by a link to one of the imperial sisters, as is reflected much later in the words of the early fifth-century poet Namatianus (4.61). Agrippina, the older of the two, was ruthlessly ambitious for her son Nero, and Tacitus in looking back at Agrippina's affair with Lepidus says she became involved with him "because of her lust for power" (4.64). Her husband Gnaeus Domitius Ahenobarbus was already dying in late 39. The other sister Livilla's possible motives are less evident and her role may be exaggerated or misrepresented by the sources. It is to be noted that only Agrippina was reputedly obliged to carry the ashes of Lepidus back to Rome.

4.56 Dio 59.22.6 Furthermore there was Lepidus, his homosexual lover and Drusilla's husband, who, together with him, had been having sex with his other sisters Agrippina and Julia Livilla; to this man he granted the right to stand for office five years before the legal time, 7 and he also declared he would leave him as his successor to the throne and then killed him! And he gave the soldiers money to mark that event as though he had overcome some enemies and sent three daggers to Mars the Avenger in Rome.[79] 8 The sisters he sent off to the

---

[79] The Temple of Mars Ultor had been built by Augustus to mark the assassination of Julius Caesar. After the suppression of the Pisonian conspiracy in AD 65 Nero dedicated the dagger intended to kill him in the Capitol (Tac. *Ann.* 15.74.2). Similarly Vitellius sent the dagger that Otho used to kill himself to Cologne, to be dedicated to Mars (Suet. *Vit.* 10.3).

Pontian Islands for having sexual relations with Lepidus, first writing to the senate about their many unholy, licentious activities. And to Agrippina he presented the man's bones in an urn, telling her to carry it back to Rome holding it to her bosom all the way.

4.57 Dio 59.23.1 Then as if he had avoided some great plot he sent off a report on this; for he was in any case always pretending to be in danger and living a stressful life. When they learned of it, the senators, among other things, voted him an Ovation and for it they sent ambassadors, a number of them chosen by lot, but with Claudius quite deliberately selected; and that so annoyed him that he again disallowed any praise or honour to be accorded his relatives, and felt that he had not been shown the respect he deserved.

4.58 Dio 59.23.8 Those in Rome were shaken by this (sc. marriage to Caesonia) and shaken, too, by the fact that many cases were being brought against them over their friendship with his sisters and with people who had been put to death; and even a number of aediles and praetors were forced to abandon their posts and face trial.[80]

4.59 Suet. Cal. 24.3 His other sisters (i.e. other than Drusilla) he did not feel so passionately for or treat with such respect but would often prostitute them to his old sexual partners, which made it easier for him to condemn them at Aemilius Lepidus' trial as adulterous and involved in conspiracies against him. And not only did he release documents in all of their handwriting, which he obtained through deception and sexual blackmail, but he also consecrated to Mars Ultor three swords (with an inscription added) that had been prepared for ending his own life.

4.60 Sen. *Ep.* 4.7 Gaius Caesar ordered Lepidus to offer his neck to the tribune Dexter; Gaius Caesar himself offered his neck to Chaerea.[81]

4.61 Namatianus 1.303 while Lepidus desired to insinuate himself into the realm of the Caesars he paid the penalty for foul adultery…[82]

4.62 Phil. *Leg.* 87 You later banished your sisters; did not even they generate fear in you of losing your power?

4.63 Suet. *Vesp.* 2.3 When Vespasian was a praetor and Gaius was feuding with the senate, he did not want to lose any opportunity to please him and so demanded special games for his German victory and recommended as a further penalty for the conspirators that they should be thrown out without burial. He

---

[80] Dio here suggests that a number of Roman magistrates who lost their lives could be identified as specific allies of the conspirators, but frustratingly he omits to provide any actual names.

[81] Seneca here looks forward to Caligula's assassination, when he will be stabbed by the tribune Cassius Chaerea (8.12, 13).

[82] Namatianus was a fifth-century poet from Roman Gaul.

also gave him wholehearted thanks before that most distinguished order for having honoured him with a dinner invitation.[83]

4.64 Tac. *Ann.* **14.2.5. AD 59** Agrippina...had, after all, had illicit intercourse with Marcus Lepidus in her young years because of her lust for power.

Lepidus and Gaetulicus

Perhaps the most intriguing element of the mystery of Lepidus is an almost casual comment in Suetonius' *Life of Claudius*, where we learn that Claudius was despatched to Germany to offer congratulations to Caligula for the exposure of what is tantalizingly called the "the conspiracy of Lepidus and Gaetulicus" (4.65). This is the only hint in any literary source of any joint action between these two men. We can do little more than speculate. Suetonius' focus in this *Life* is on Claudius, and he may of course simply have casually bundled two quite separate, unconnected actions under one convenient heading. But collaboration between Lepidus and Gaetulicus would have made sense. Lepidus might have felt that some military backing would have been essential for his otherwise purely political campaign. And Gaetulicus may have felt that he faced dismissal from his command in Germany and exposure as an old henchman of Sejanus, and could therefore have seen in Lepidus the best possible chance to maintain his career (and perhaps even to stay alive). But balancing that plausible scenario is the silence of the other sources. Dio in his list of victims makes no formal connection between Lepidus and Gaetulicus, nor does Suetonius in the *Life of Caligula*, and in fact there Suetonius speaks pointedly of the conspiracy of Lepidus only. Lepidus' name does not appear in the Arval account of celebratory rites that marked the detection of Gaetulicus' conspiracy on October 27 (nor does there seem to be space in the missing section for his name to be recorded). According to Dio and Suetonius only three daggers, symbolizing Lepidus, Agrippina, and Livilla, were sent to the Temple of Mars Ultor. Unless Gaetulicus was simply overlooked, which is hardly likely, this seems to suggest that his conspiracy was a separate event. The mystery must for the moment remain unresolved.

4.65 Suet. *Claud.* **9.1** When the conspiracy of Lepidus and Gaetulicus was brought to light...

---

[83] Vespasian was presumably praetor in AD 39 or 40 when word of Caligula's achievements in Germany was despatched to Rome. Unfortunately Suetonius omits to identify the executed conspirators. There is a chronological problem here—the German victories presumably belong to AD 40 but Gaetulicus certainly and Lepidus almost certainly died in AD 39. The reference may be to the unnamed individuals mentioned by Dio as those brought down after the exposure of Lepidus and the sisters (4.58).

Seneca

The difficulties faced by one other individual in this period should be noted, since he is one of our sources for the reign, none other than the philosopher Seneca. Dio informs us that Seneca's only crime was to plead a case well in the presence of Caligula, and that he was spared because he was in an advanced state of consumption and would die soon anyhow. The story of Seneca's deliverance should be treated with caution; he may have felt it politic under later emperors to exaggerate Caligula's antipathy towards him. Also, Seneca was skilled at adjusting his principles to suit the current ruler. In what may be his earliest surviving work, written under Caligula, the *Consolatio ad Marciam*, he abuses Sejanus. He may not in fact have suffered so badly under Caligula. It was only after Caligula's death that Seneca started to abuse him too.

4.66 Dio 59.19.7 But Lucius Annaeus Seneca, who in intellect surpassed all Romans of his time and many others, too, was almost destroyed, not for having done or appearing to have done any wrong but simply because he had spoken well in some case in the senate while Caligula was present. **8** Caligula ordered him executed but then released him, believing one of Seneca's mistresses that he had advanced consumption and would soon die.[84]

Further Reading

Humphrey, J. W. and P. M. Swan. 1983. "Cassius Dio on the Suffect Consuls of A.D. 39." *Phoenix* 37: 324–7.

Malloch, S. J. V. 2001a. "Gaius' Bridge at Baiae and Alexander-Imitatio." *CQ* 51: 206–17.

Simpson, C. J. 1980. "The 'Conspiracy' of A.D. 39." In *Studies in Latin Literature and Roman History*, edited by C. Deroux, 347–66. Brussels: Latomus.

Wardle, D. 1998. "Caligula and His Wives." *Latomus* 57: 109–26.

Woods, D. 2014. "Caligula Displays Caesonia (Suet. Calig. 25.3)." *RM* 157: 27–36.

---

[84] Seneca was banished by Claudius for an affair with Livilla, who was herself exiled, for a second time. Also, it was later claimed that he had an affair with Livilla's sister, Agrippina. Both might qualify as the mysterious unnamed female, but it is hard to explain why either name would have been concealed.

5

The Private Caligula

Appearance

As well as paying a powerful role in ancient Rome Caligula was also a human being, with all the foibles and idiosyncrasies of a human being, arguably with more than most. As well as being an interesting emperor he is also an interesting personality, one well worth studying. We might reasonably begin our consideration of Caligula the private individual with the very basic issue of his appearance. The ancient literary sources provide considerable detail on this topic, but much of their information is highly coloured, presumably reflecting a conviction that there was a strong link between appearance and character, and that a tyrant should look like a tyrant, or perhaps rather like an exaggerated version of a tyrant.

Seneca was a contemporary of the emperor and wrote for people who in many cases had seen him, and some, if fewer, of Pliny's readers also would have seen Caligula in person, so we can probably assume that there is at least an element of truth in their vivid descriptions. From them we might fairly safely conclude that Caligula was tall. The comment about him providing the shade in his tree house at Velletri (5.6) is clearly a joke, but it would be a joke without any point whatsoever if he was not a lanky individual. He seems to have had big feet and skinny legs, the last a family trait, since his father Germanicus also had skinny legs, although in his case they were seen positively (1.2). Also he was pale (not surprising in an insomniac, although this is taken by Seneca as a symptom of madness) and balding.

Caligula's coinage provides a useful test, since portraits on the coins issued by the official mint are generally realistic. Except perhaps in the provision of rich heads of hair the images of Caligula on the coins are individualized and distinct (Figure 13). They seem to suggest a large forehead (as noted by Suetonius), pointed nose and chin, and deep-set eyes, the last noted by Suetonius and given a more fiendish twist by Pliny and Seneca. But essentially the coins portray someone not particularly remarkable in appearance (unlike those, for instance, of the bloated Nero in his later years). Moreover, the pet names that the enthusiastic crowds heaped on him as he progressed from Misenum to Rome to accompany the lately deceased Tiberius (5.5) seem incompatible with someone whose appearance was as repellent as is suggested by the sources.

Caligula clearly had a propensity for exotic clothing, particularly for dressing up in the guise of deities (5.7). But we must be alert to the tendency of Suetonius to attribute a general pattern to what may have been specific and isolated events,

The Emperor Caligula in the Ancient Sources. Anthony A. Barrett and J. C. Yardley, Oxford University Press.
© Anthony A. Barrett and J. C. Yardley 2023. DOI: 10.1093/oso/9780198854562.003.0006

Figure 13 Brass sestertius. Yale University Art Gallery.

such as his wearing triumphal garb to honour Augustus on the dedication of his temple (3.46) or the breastplate of Alexander worn on the crossing of the bay of Naples (4.41).

5.1 Suet. *Cal.* **50.1** He was tall, very pale,[1] and had a large physique but neck and legs that were very thin;[2] his eyes and temples were sunken and his forehead broad and menacing; and his hair was sparse and missing on top, though he was otherwise hairy all over. So looking down on him from above when he passed or using the word "goat" for any reason was deemed a capital crime. Although his appearance was naturally hideous and repulsive he would deliberately make it more frightening by contorting it before a mirror into all manner of hideous and terrifying expressions.

5.2 Sen. *Const.* **2.18.1** Among the many vices to which the abusive man was prone, Gaius Caesar was also taken with an amazing fondness for pouncing on everyone for any strange physical peculiarity, despite being himself a most fertile source for ridicule. Such was the ugliness in the pallor of his face (which betrayed his insanity), so intense the grim look in those eyes lurking beneath a hag-like brow, such the hideousness in that head, bald but for a few scattered hairs! And add to that a bristle-besieged neck, the skinniness of his legs, and the hugeness of his feet.

5.3 Suet. *Cal.* **35.2** Whenever he came across good-looking men with hair he would have the backs of their heads shaved to spoil it.[3]

---

[1] Nymphidius, who as Praetorian prefect made an unsuccessful, and fatal, bid for power after Nero's death, in AD 68, claimed that he was Caligula's son, and it was thought that he might have inherited his father's lofty stature (Tac. *Ann.* 15.72.2).

[2] To the ancients, Caligula's disproportionate body would suggest a default of character. Nero and Domitian, both tyrannical emperors, had skinny legs too, combined with pot bellies (Suet. *Ner.* 52; Suet. *Dom.* 18.1).

[3] Further evidence of Caligula's sensitivity about his baldness. Seneca (*Ira* 2.33.3) identifies one such victim, the son of Pastor.

5.4 Plin. *NH* 11.144 The princeps Gaius' eyes were always in a fixed stare.

5.5 Suet. *Cal.* 13.1 Having thus acquired imperial power he fulfilled the prayers of the Roman people or, I might say, of the human race: he was the ruler most eagerly wanted by most provincials and soldiers since most had known him as a child, but also by all the urban plebs from their recollection of his father Germanicus and pity for a family almost entirely wiped out. Thus when he set off from Misenum escorting Tiberius' cortege in mourning dress and was proceeding between altars, sacrificial victims, and blazing torches, he was met by a dense, jubilant crowd of people that flocked to meet him, addressing him with names like (in addition to others of good omen) "star," "chick," "little fellow," and "my child."[4]

5.6 Plin. *NH* 12.10 Another example (sc. of a plane tree) is that of the emperor Gaius in the territory of Velletri[5] ... he dined on it ... personally forming part of the shade.

5.7 Suet. *Cal.* 52.1 In clothing, footwear, and the rest of his wardrobe he did not conform to either traditional or his citizens' norms or, indeed, even to male or ordinary human ones. He often made public appearances in embroidered jewelled cloaks or a long-sleeved tunic and wearing bracelets; occasionally he would be in silk and wearing a *cyclas*;[6] and sometimes he was in slippers or buskins,[7] or else in military boots[8] or women's low-heeled shoes. On many occasions he was actually sighted with a golden beard and holding either a thunderbolt, trident, or caduceus (the gods' emblems), and even dressed as Venus. Triumphal decorations he regularly wore even before a campaign, and sometimes even Alexander the Great's breastplate, which he had removed from his sarcophagus.[9]

Personality

Caligula clearly was possessed of a highly strung personality. The fainting fits that he suffered in childhood might suggest someone who had problems dealing with

---

[4] Tiberius headed a similar procession as he accompanied the body of Augustus from Nola to Rome (Dio 56.31.3). Tiberius had also previously accompanied the body of his brother Drusus to Rome in 9 BC (Dio 55.2.1).

[5] Pliny is here discussing plane trees. The ancient Volscian town of Velletri was located in the Alban Hills near Rome. Caligula presumably had a villa there; Seneca mentions that he retreated to a villa in the Alban Hills on the death of his sister Drusilla (4.30).

[6] The *cyclas* was an upper garment of light material, worn by women of rank.

[7] The *cothurnus* was a high boot worn originally by actors but adopted by kings in the Hellenistic period. It was a symbol of decadent luxury. The sole might be thicker than usual, to impart added height, hence its regular use in Greek tragedy.

[8] Precisely what form these might have taken is uncertain.

[9] Caligula is said to have worn Alexander's breastplate, as well as the triumphator's garb, in the procession over his bridge at Baiae (4.41). Claudius was granted permission to wear the garb of the triumphator when dedicating Pompey's theatre (Dio 60.6.9). It was clearly not a particularly unusual practice.

stress. The history of adult insomnia and sleep interrupted by nightmares rein-
forces that suspicion. His supposed self-diagnosis of mental weakness (5.8) might
well be a clue to a history of nervous breakdowns or anxiety attacks, although the
dangers of trying to psychoanalyse someone over a gap of two thousand years are
self-evident, and we cannot discount the possibility that the comment, as reported,
is a garbled version of what had been intended as a joke. The popular view, both
ancient and modern, of Caligula is of a quintessentially mad emperor. But the
ancient evidence, when examined closely, does not support that view. He was
clearly able to make rational decisions until the end, and the detailed portrait of
him that Philo provides, after meeting in person in the summer of AD 40 (5.40),
suggests someone who was certainly narcissistic, self-centred, arrogant, mischievous, cruel, callous, and self-obsessed, but not someone who was insane, or
anything approaching insane, in the clinical sense. Ancient authors often bandy
about expressions denoting mental incompetence to describe behaviour that may
be no more than eccentric, just as words like "mad" or "crazy" are used of
prominent leaders today. As an example, Tacitus asserts that Caligula was
"unsound of mind" (*turbidus animi*) in making changes in the command structure of the legion in Africa (7.4), but even if Tacitus is correct about Caligula's
motive (which is far from certain), that he made the change because he feared the
provincial governor, that motive is in fact a perfectly sane one, and the African
arrangements were left in place by subsequent emperors.

Perhaps the most striking aspect of Caligula's personality is that for all his
arrogance, if not megalomania, he does seem surprisingly insecure about his
status. He was sensitive about perceived disrespect when he was addressed, and
disliked being referred to by the affectionate military nickname of his childhood,
"Caligula," and even took offence at being called "Gaius," if the speaker was not
his social equal (5.11). Also, perhaps more surprisingly, he was extremely sensitive
about his age. He was already twenty-four when he became emperor, much
younger than his predecessors, Julius Caesar, Augustus, and Tiberius, when they
reached supreme power, but by ancient standards hardly a callow youth: Augustus
had already formed a triumvirate with Mark Antony and Lepidus at the age of
twenty, Alexander the Great became king of Macedon at that same age, twenty;
Nero was only sixteen when he succeeded Claudius in AD 54. So there was nothing
remarkable about Caligula's age. But he clearly was enraged whenever he thought
he was being treated like a child; it is perhaps understandable that he might have
resented Macro's efforts to make him behave properly (5.15, 21), but it is more
difficult to understand why he should be offended to be called a "Young Augustus"
(5.12), and why he should take umbrage at Domitius Afer's compliment about
having achieved so much when so young (4.45).

5.8 Suet. *Cal.* 50.2 His strength was good neither physically nor mentally.
After suffering epilepsy as a boy, although he could tolerate some physical
effort he was in his youth barely able to walk, stand, or pull himself together and

keep going.[10] He had even become aware of his mental weakness himself and quite often thought about retirement and clearing his brain. He is thought to have been drugged with a love potion by his wife Caesonia, but one that actually turned him crazy.[11] 3 He was especially prey to insomnia; for he could remain at rest no more than three hours a night, and even during those he would have no tranquil sleep but one fearful with bizarre apparitions, including, among others, thinking he saw the ghost of the sea conversing with him. So having enough of being awake and lying down most of the night, he was in the habit, whether reclining on his bed or wandering through his extensive colonnades, of repeatedly calling for daylight and waiting for it to arrive.

5.9 (see also 7.16) Tac. Ag. 13.2 It is beyond question that Gaius Caesar envisaged an invasion of Britain, but being temperamentally unstable he was quick to change his mind...

5.10 (see also 7.4) Tac. Hist. 4.48 Later, Gaius Caesar, who was unsound of mind and fearful of Marcus Silanus when he was governor of Africa, removed the legion from the proconsul...

5.11 (see also 2.5) Sen. Cons. 18.4 But it was this same Gaius who would take all comments as insults, those people unable to bear them being the most eager to inflict them. He was furious with Herennius Macer for having addressed him as Gaius,[12] and he did not allow a senior centurion go unpunished for calling him "Caligula." Since he was born in the camp and was the "baby" of the legion, that was what he was usually called, never being better known to the soldiers by any other name; but now that he wore big boots he judged the name "little boots" a demeaning insult.[13]

5.12 Dio 59.13.6 In addition, he was also very annoyed that when singing his praises they would call him "Young Augustus," for he did not think he was being congratulated for becoming emperor as a young man but rather that he was being criticized for holding such power at that age.

5.13 (see also 4.45) Dio 59.19.2 Then when, after erecting a statue of him, Domitius Afer set on it an inscription indicating that he was consul for the

---

[10] Caligula clearly suffered from childhood fits, and it may have been assumed that this was evidence of epilepsy. Such a diagnosis would have been reinforced by seeing parallels between Caligula and Julius Caesar, who apparently suffered from epilepsy (Suet. Jul. 45.1; Plut. Caes. 17.2); Britannicus, the son of Claudius, was believed to suffer from the same disorder (Suet. Ner. 33.3).

[11] Caesonia was supposedly blamed by some of the conspirators against Caligula for driving Caligula mad with a love potion (Jos. Ant. 19.193). The claim appears also in Juvenal (Sat. 6.614–17), and may have originated from a comment attributed to Caligula himself, who said that he wanted to torture Caesonia to find out why he was so passionate about her (Suet. Cal. 33).

[12] Herennius Macer is otherwise unknown.

[13] There seems to be a word play here. Seneca, if the text of the manuscript is correct, describes Caligula as cothurnatus, hence wearing the cothurnus, a large, often elegant, boot sported by men of high rank (see note on 5.7). It seems to be used here in contrast to the diminutive of caliga, the military boot or sandal, the source of Caligula's nickname.

second time at the age of twenty, 3 Gaius was annoyed, thinking that he was reproaching him for his youth and lawless conduct.

5.14 (see also 4.65) Suet. *Claud*. 9.1 When Lepidus' and Gaetulicus' conspiracy was finally exposed and Claudius was sent into Germany as one of the legates to congratulate the emperor, he came close to losing his life because Gaius was embittered and furious that it was his uncle in particular who had been sent to him[14] as though he were a boy in need of guidance, so much so that some have recorded that Claudius was even tossed into a river in the clothes in which he had arrived.[15]

5.15 Philo *Leg*. 53 (*Caligula commenting on Macro*) "Here comes the instructor of somebody who has no need to learn, the tutor of somebody who is no longer a child, the adviser of somebody smarter than himself, a man who believes that an emperor should obey his subjects..."[16]

Intellect

Caligula does not appear to have lacked intellectual ability, a trait he shared with other members of the Julio-Claudian family. His father Germanicus had something of a reputation as a literary scholar, and Caligula seems to have followed in his footsteps.[17] In AD 18, at the age of five, he is recorded as delivering a speech to the city of Assos (1.18), and in AD 29 he gave the funeral oration for Livia (2.4), when probably still sixteen. On Capri he came under the stewardship of Tiberius, who had a deep interest in learning and enjoyed the company of scholars. Josephus acknowledges Caligula's natural abilities and insists that he was inspired by Tiberius to accomplish great things in this sphere, seeking out the company of people who shared his interest in the higher things of the mind. The Byzantine encyclopaedia, the *Suda*, claims that he wrote a book on oratory.[18] Suetonius mentions his oratorical skill (5.18) and Tacitus alludes to his *vis dicendi* ("power of speaking") (5.19) and contrasts it with Nero's limited ability and reliance on

---

[14] Claudius led the delegation that was sent to congratulate Caligula on the suppression of the conspiracies in late AD 39 (see 4.57).

[15] This story, attributed to unnamed sources, must be treated with caution, and is nowhere else attested. If the supposed incident took place in Germany the river is probably the Rhine, the scene of Caligula's military activities. But Suetonius speaks of rhetorical competitions staged by Caligula in Lyon, involving much horseplay (5.20). The losers were apparently obliged to erase their entries with their tongues or be beaten and thrown into one of the two local rivers (Lyon lies at the juncture of the Rhône and the Saône). It is tempting to suspect that these two separate topics have somehow become confused.

[16] The comment is recorded within a wider discussion of Caligula's attitude towards Macro after his accession (Philo *Leg*. 41–56; similar thoughts recorded at Philo *Flacc*. 15). Macro had been Praetorian prefect for six years when Caligula succeeded, and had managed the succession flawlessly. He was no political amateur.

[17] See Chapter 1, n. 9.   [18] *Suda* 1.503 (Adler).

Seneca as his speech writer. The consul Domitius Afer supposedly made a show of being overawed by Caligula's oratorical skills (4.45), although surely with a huge helping of flattery on this occasion.

Caligula also demonstrated an interest in current literary questions. He condemned Seneca for his idle and decorative style. He exhibited little admiration for Homer, and threatened to remove the busts of Vergil and Livy from libraries (5.17).

5.16 Jos. *AJ* 19.208 Being besides an excellent speaker, perfectly fluent in Greek as well as in his native Latin...

5.17 Suet. *Cal.* 34.2 He even considered banning Homer's poems, asking why he should not be allowed to do so, just as Plato had been allowed to eject him from the state he was framing.[19] But he also came close to removing the works and busts of Vergil and Livy from all libraries, criticizing one as being a man of no talent and minimal learning, and the other as being long-winded and slipshod in his history.[20] In the case of jurists, too, he boasted (as if intending to do away with their entire profession) that he—damn it!—was going to see that they could give no judgement contrary to his.

5.18 Suet. *Cal.* 53.1 In the area of liberal arts he had little interest in literature but a lot in rhetoric, and in that he was as eloquent and fluent as one could wish, especially if he had to conclude a case against someone. When he was angry, words and ideas would keep coming to him, as would the manner of delivery and intonation, to the point that in his fervour he could not remain standing in one spot and would still be clearly heard by people standing at a distance. 2 At the point of summing up he would threaten to draw out "the sword of his late-night meditations," and he was so disdainful of a smooth, elegant style that he claimed that the then very popular Seneca was producing "mere trivialities" and was "sand without lime."[21] He also used to write responses to successful legal

---

[19] In the ideal state as envisaged by Plato there was no place for poets like Homer (*Rep.* 606e1–5). Emperors were often assigned eccentric views on literature. Hadrian was similarly said to have put down Homer, with equal conceit (*SHA Hadrian* 16.6, a source generally to be treated with considerable scepticism). In fact, Caligula seems to have been fond of quoting Homer (Suet. *Cal.* 22.1, 4). Close attention should therefore be paid to the phrase "he considered": in describing his outrageous behaviour the literary sources often have recourse to what Caligula supposedly *planned* to do rather than what he actually did.

[20] Such opinions were not unique to Caligula. Vergil was charged with plagiarism in his own day (Donat. *Vit. Verg.* 43–6); the historian Pompeius Trogus during Augustus' reign (Just. 38.3.11) described Livy as verbose, which Quintilian 10.1.32 seems to have considered a positive trait, *Livi lactea ubertas*. Likenesses of distinguished authors were displayed in medallions in public libraries, as, for instance, that of Germanicus in the Palatine library (Tac. *Ann.* 2.83.3).

[21] Suetonius does not identify "Seneca" here, and it is not impossible that the reference was to the elder Seneca. But Caligula is known to have had particular contempt for the younger Seneca.

The word that he uses for "trivialities" (*commissiones*) is something of a challenge. It comes from the context of theatre, and is strictly speaking the opening act in a performance (or possibly the performance itself). Caligula perhaps was suggesting that Seneca's writings were merely showy, light,

suits and work on prosecution or defence pleas of important men on trial in the senate; and it depended on how his writing turned out whether he would either sink or rescue anyone, the whole equestrian class being invited to listen to him—by order![22]

5.19 Tac. *Ann.* 13.3.6 Even Gaius Caesar's disturbed mind did not spoil the power of his speaking.[23]

5.20 Suet. *Cal.* 20.1 He also put on shows abroad: local games in Syracuse in Sicily, and a mélange of games at Lugdunum in Gaul; but there he also staged a contest in Greek and Latin rhetoric and in this, they say, losers had to give prizes to the winners and compose encomia on them. Those with the lowest approval ratings, however, were ordered to erase their compositions with a sponge or with their tongues, unless they preferred being beaten with sticks or to be ducked in the nearby river.[24]

Entertainments

When it came to private pursuits, Caligula' enthusiasms were essentially those of the masses and were focussed on the standard forms of entertainment (*spectacula*) available in the Rome of his time. They fell generally into three broad categories. There were the *ludi scaenici*, broadly, plays presented on the stage. On a more grandiose scale were the *ludi circenses*, events presented in the Circus, especially horse racing, along with other entertainments. Then there were gladiatorial contests, *munera gladiatoria*, which in Caligula's time were staged along with animal fights. In this context one of the most familiar fables from antiquity, the story of Androcles and the lion, is, in the first known version of the story, set in the arena while Caligula was presiding over the games (as recorded by the second-century AD writer Aulus Gellius).

---

entertainment lacking any real substance. Presumably the reference to sand without lime implies that his compositions were like shoddy buildings that would soon collapse. Caligula's stricture on Seneca might have seemed outrageous in his own day, but proved ahead of its time. A century and a half later such views had become almost mainstream, and Aulus Gellius (12.2.1) claimed that some thought Seneca the Younger had little value as a writer, that his style was commonplace, and the subject matter empty and affected.

[22] Caligula was presumably here writing responses as literary exercises, without legal authority, rather than overturning the verdicts of the courts.

[23] Tacitus is contrasting the oratorical skills of Nero with those of other emperors, including Caligula. The brief line contains two useful pieces of information, that Tacitus acknowledged Caligula's oratorical ability, and also that he expressed concerns about his mental stability (*mens turbata*).

[24] The games at Syracuse may possibly be dated to AD 38 when Caligula visited the city on the death of his sister Drusilla. Suetonius refers to *astici ludi* (strictly "city games") perhaps on the lines of the City Dionysia in Athens. The contest in Lugdunum presumably belongs to late 39, when he spent time there on his way to his northern campaign. The contest seems to have involved a good deal of tomfoolery (perhaps connected with the Saturnalia) represented here as serious penalties. The "nearby river" is probably the Rhône, but it could be the Saône.

The Stage

Caligula drew great pleasure from the company of actors. Tiberius had banished many of them from the city to safeguard public order, and on his accession Caligula moved quickly to have them recalled (5.21). He indulged them with financial gifts and even reputedly took some along on his expedition against Britain and Germany in AD 39. His very last public act before his death in 41 was to chat amiably with a company of visiting actors. Two stand out among his favourites. Apelles of Ascalon, the most celebrated performer of the time, was constantly in attendance (5.22, 7.30). And the famous pantomime Mnester was even said to have been Caligula's lover (Suet. *Cal.* 36.1 and 5.24).

Caligula was devoted to the theatre, and disapproved strongly of people arriving or leaving in mid-performance; if an audience member created the slightest noise while Mnester was on stage, according to Suetonius, Caligula would personally drag him out of his seat and whip him. He reputedly put off lawsuits and ended official periods of public mourning to allow attendance. He was not satisfied with being a spectator; Dio claims that he performed publicly in pantomimes and on the tragic stage. On Capri it is claimed that he would don a long robe and wig and perform dances and songs. Even after his accession he would join in the songs and the dances. These colourful stories of public displays are highly entertaining, but at variance with Suetonius' assertion that on the very day he died Caligula was making preparations for his very first venture on the public stage (5.25).

5.21 Philo *Leg.* 42 Now any time Macro noticed Caligula falling asleep at a dinner he would rouse him, both for the sake of respectability and also for his safety, since a man asleep is an easy target. Or if he observed him going crazy on seeing dancers (or sometimes even joining in the dance), or if he saw him responding to a mime of unbecoming scenes and dirty jokes, not with a gentle, dignified smile but with raucous, teenage laughter, or being thrilled with the harmony of harpists or choral singers, or sometimes even singing along with them, he would sit or recline beside him in order to nudge him and try to stop him.

5.22 Dio 59.5.2 For Tiberius it was a matter of ruling on his own and he used his underlings only for carrying out what he needed done; but Gaius was under the thumb of charioteers and gladiators, and in thrall to dancers and others with connections to the stage. In fact Apelles, the most noted tragedian of the time, he always had at his side even in public . . . 4 With the passage of time, however, he even went as far as entering and competing in many events; 5 for he drove chariots, fought as a gladiator, and did pantomime dancing and tragic acting. Such were his everyday practices, and on one occasion he urgently called the leaders of the senate at night for a supposedly critical meeting, and then danced for them.

5.23 Suet. Cal. 18.2 He was constantly putting on theatrical performances of various kinds and in different locations, sometimes even at night with the whole city lit up. He also tossed various gift tokens around and gave everyone baskets of food;[25] and during the feasting he once sent his own plate over to a Roman equestrian across from him who was eating with evident pleasure and gusto, while for the same reason he also sent a senator a document in which he was appointing him a supernumerary praetor.

5.24 Suet Cal. 55.1 To those for whom he felt particular affection his favour verged on madness. The mime actor Mnester he would kiss even during performances, and anyone making the slightest noise during Mnester's dancing he ordered dragged from his seat and then would beat him with his own hand.

5.25 Suet. Cal. 54.1 But he also applied himself with much enthusiasm to other very different kinds of arts. As a Thracian gladiator, a charioteer, or even as a singer or dancer he would fence with real fighting weapons[26] and drive a chariot in many custom-built locations; and so enthused was he with love of song and dance that not even at public performances could he keep from accompanying a tragic actor's delivery of his lines, and also quite openly mimicking a performer's gestures as though he were commending or correcting them. 2 And the day he died he had apparently declared a *pervigilium* for no other reason than to inaugurate his stage debut in an indulgent atmosphere.[27] In fact he would even sometimes dance at night; and he once called three former consuls to the palace at the second watch, seated them, and then, as they quaked on a bench with deadly fear, he suddenly leaped forward wearing a cloak and ankle-length tunic, danced to a song amid a deafening cacophony of flutes and heel-clappers, and left. And yet this man, so capable of learning everything else, could not swim.[28]

5.26 Dio 59.2.5 In fact, his expenditure on dancers (for he immediately had them recalled)[29] as well as on horses, gladiators, and other things of that sort knew no bounds...

5.27 Dio 59.7.5 So no one could have an excuse for not coming to the theatre (for he was terribly upset if any of them missed or left the performance halfway through), he adjourned all law cases and also suspended periods of mourning,

---

[25] *Missilia* were tokens that were distributed at random, to be redeemed for gifts of food or money, and reportedly also of animals or even farms (Suet. *Ner.* 11.2; Dio 66.25.5).

[26] Suet. *Cal.* 33.2 describes how Caligula fought a gladiator in a gladiatorial school using wooden swords for rehearsal, and when his opponent staged a fall Caligula stabbed him with a real dagger then ran a victory lap.

[27] A *pervigilium* was a performance put on at night.

[28] Gaius and Lucius Caesar, Augustus' grandchildren, were both taught to swim (Suet. *Aug.* 64.3), and Caligula's sister Agrippina reputedly was able to swim to shore when she fell from the ship she was travelling on (Tac. *Ann.* 14.5.3).

[29] Tiberius expelled actors from Rome because of their unruliness and sexual excesses (Dio 57.21.3).

as a result of which widowed women were permitted to marry before the proper time unless they were pregnant.[30]

The Arena

As a profession gladiators were much favoured by Caligula, and they supposedly joined the actors who accompanied him on his northern expedition in AD 39. He was particularly attached to the *parmularii*, who fought with small round shields, and, conversely, felt distaste for their rivals, the *murmillones*, equipped with large oblong versions. He is even supposed to have participated personally in their combats. Gladiatorial contests responded to a dark side of the human psyche, and Caligula's taste for this particular type of brutality seems to be more or less that of the typical Roman, and indeed he on one occasion reprimanded those spectators who enjoyed the gore.

5.28 Suet. *Cal.* 18.1 As for gladiatorial shows, some he staged in the amphitheatre of Taurus and some in the Saepta,[31] and in them he put on companies of the finest African and Campanian boxers from both regions. He did not always preside over the events himself but from time to time conferred that honour on magistrates or friends...[32]

5.29 Suet. *Cal.* 30.3 Some tunic-clad *retiarii*, five in number, had given up the fight when matched against the same number of *secutores*;[33] and when the order was given for them to be killed one took up his trident again and killed all the winners. This Caligula lamented in an edict as a horrific murder and also excoriated those who had had been able to watch it.

5.30 Gell. 5.14.5 At such an extraordinary occurrence, he says, the loudest of cries went up from the people, and Androcles was summoned by Gaius Caesar and asked why the fiercest lion had spared only him.

---

[30] Injunctions were placed on the speedy remarriage of a widow because of potential confusion over the paternity of subsequent children. During the republic a widow had to wait ten months to remarry. In the imperial period this was extended to one year.

[31] Statilius Taurus was an outstanding commander and supporter of Octavian. He celebrated a Triumph for military achievements in Africa and afterwards built the stone amphitheatre named after him, the first permanent structure for gladiatorial contests. It is generally thought to have been located in the southeast section of the Campus Martius, and was destroyed in the Neronian fire of AD 64.

The Saepta Julia, located in the Campus Martius, had been conceived as a great assembly hall for the casting of votes. It was begun by Julius Caesar and completed by Agrippa. It was in fact used for gladiatorial contests from a very early stage and in 7 BC funeral games were celebrated there in honour of Agrippa.

[32] The presidency of such events would have been considered a considerable honour. The president's role was more than simply honorific, since he could be called upon to decide life or death after a gladiatorial combat.

[33] *Retarii* ("netters") were armed with nets and tridents; their principal opponents were *secutores* ("pursuers"), armed with short swords and small shields.

The Racetrack

The private pursuit for which Caligula reportedly showed the greatest enthusiasm was horse racing. This was a passion shared by the majority of Romans. In this period stables of racing teams were distinguished by the colours worn by their drivers, and they could count on zealous, and thoroughly partisan, supporters. Blues and Greens came to be the predominant teams. Caligula's enthusiasm was apparently genuine. He even had his own track, the Gaianum, on his Vatican estate, and built a major public track, the Circus Vaticanus, which incorporated the famous obelisk that now stands in St Peter's Square. A frequent companion in Caligula's races was Aulus Vitellius, emperor himself, albeit briefly, in AD 69, who walked with a limp as the result of an accident suffered when driving with Caligula.

Caligula was a fanatical adherent of the Greens (5.33). He bestowed generous gifts on the teams and dined at their stables. He supposedly supplied his favourite horse, Incitatus, with a lavishly appointed stable, and soldiers (presumably Praetorian guards) would keep the surrounding area quiet before races. The claims that he went so far as to plan to make Incitatus consul (or a priest) no doubt originated from his own humorous quips (5.33, 34).

Romans generally would have been happy with an emperor who was devoted to the races, and when Suetonius mentions games in the circus where sand was coloured red and green and where men of the senatorial order drove chariots, he includes this among Caligula's meritorious activities. The number of races to be held each day during the games was raised from the standard ten (Dio 58.12.8) to a staggering forty (Dio 59.7.2–3). He organized circus games in honour of his mother Agrippina in 37 (3.26), in 38 he marked Tiberius' birthday with two days of horse races, and he celebrated the birthday of his sister Drusilla in similar fashion (4.29).

5.31 Suet. *Cal.* 18.3 He also put on many games in the circus that went from morning till evening, with intervals filled by panther-baiting or the Trojan game,[34] some of them especially grand, with the circus strewn with green and red pigment and the charioteers only men of senatorial rank.[35] He also gave games just on impulse after a few people asked for them from nearby verandas while he was surveying the circus preparations from the Gelotian house.[36]

---

[34] Caligula put on a performance of the Trojan game on the dedication of the Temple of Augustus (Dio 59.7.4) and in the funeral games of his sister Drusilla (4.27).

[35] The presence of men of the senatorial order may suggest some special event, when the traditional embargo on senatorial participation was relaxed. The green colouring reflects Caligula's adherence to the green faction. The addition of red is a little more puzzling, perhaps suggesting some sort of alliance between the two groups.

[36] The Gelotian house was located on the southwest edge of the Palatine, indicating that the circus in question was not Caligula's Vatican structure but the ancient Circus Maximus, located in the depression between the Palatine and Aventine hills.

5.32 Dio 59.28.6 And in addition to that he also made himself his own priest[37] and declared his horse his fellow priest; and a number of dainty and very costly birds would be sacrificed to him every day.

5.33 Suet. *Cal.* 55.2 To the Green racing faction he was so fanatically dedicated that he would regularly dine and spend the night in their stable, and in one of his drinking parties he gave a driver Eutychus 2 million sestertii among the takeaway presents.[38] **3** For his horse Incitatus he would on the day before the games have his soldiers enforce silence in the neighbourhood so he would not be disturbed, and in addition to a stable of marble, an ivory stall, purple coverings, and collars of precious stones he also gave him a house, slaves, and furniture so those invited in his name might be given a more elegant reception. It is also claimed that he intended making him a consul.

5.34 Dio 59.14.5 He then killed the best and most famous of them with poison. He would also do the very same thing with horses and chariot drivers of factions competing against his. **6** For he was an avid supporter of the team wearing the frog green, which from its colour was also called the "Leak Green," so that even now the place where he practised his charioteering is still called the Gaianum after him. **7** And one of the horses, which he named Incitatus, he used even to invite to dinner, throw golden barley corns before him, give him plenty of wine in golden cups, and swear oaths by his life and fortune; and he even promised to make him a consul. And that promise he would certainly have also fulfilled had he lived longer.

5.35 Suet. *Vit.* 17.2 For Vitellius was of enormous height, had a face usually flushed through excessive drinking, a fat belly, and one thigh quite disabled from being hit on one occasion by a four-horse chariot while attending on Gaius when he was driving.

Sex

While on Capri, portrayed in the later tradition as the centre of sexual indulgence and perversion during Tiberius' sojourn there, Caligula most likely lived a relatively sheltered life, with his first wife Junia for at least part of the time. At any rate Tiberius took strong measures in AD 32 against two individuals who claimed otherwise. When he became emperor Caligula reputedly devoted much of his energies to his vigorous and varied sex life, although we must be on our guard against the stereotype of the tyrant, who is traditionally a slave to lusty depravity.

---

[37] The manuscript is corrupt at this point.
[38] Caligula's adulation of Eutychus was legendary. Josephus records a story that after Caligula's assassination the perpetrator Cassius Chaerea facetiously anticipated that Eutychus would give the watchword in the absence of the princeps (Jos. *Ant.* 19.256–7).

5.36 Tac. *Ann.* 6.5 Next it was the turn of Cotta Messalinus, mover of all the most savage proposals and so an object of long-standing hatred.[39] As soon as an opportunity presented itself, he was accused of making numerous remarks about Gaius Caesar's "dubious manhood" and referring to a banquet he attended with the priests on Augusta's birthday as "a funeral dinner."[40]

5.37 Tac. *Ann.* 6.9.2 Next came a letter from Tiberius targeting the ex-praetor Sextus Vistilius, whom the emperor had transferred into his own cohort because he was a close friend of his brother Drusus.[41] What caused his displeasure with Vistilius was either that he had been the author of some writings impugning Gaius Caesar for his immorality or Tiberius' mistaken belief that he had done so.[42] Excluded from the emperor's circle over this, he tried the knife with his aging hand, but retied the veins; and after sending a letter begging for pardon and receiving a heartless reply, he opened them again.

5.38 Suet. *Cal.* 36.1 He had no respect for decency, either his own or anyone else's. He reportedly had sexual relations with Marcus Lepidus,[43] with the pantomimic actor Mnester,[44] and with a number of hostages,[45] engaging in reciprocal buggery with them. Valerius Catullus,[46] a young fellow from a consular family, openly declared that Caligula had been screwed by him and that his own strength had given out from his session with him. Apart from incest with his sisters and his notorious liaison with the whore Pyrallis,[47] there

---

[39] Cotta Messalinus was a powerful political figure and literary patron, a friend of the poet Ovid. He was consul in AD 20 and served as proconsul of Asia. He was a close ally of Tiberius. His comments at the very least suggest that unflattering reports were circulating about Caligula's sexual inclinations, but not too much should be read into that—the very privacy of life on Capri would have encouraged such speculation.

[40] Livia's birthday was January 30. She had died in AD 29, three years before the charge was made against Cotta. The precise point Cotta meant to convey is unclear but he may have suggested that the birthday celebration was the equivalent of the modest funeral banquet normally held nine days after a death. He seems to be alluding to the fact that Tiberius refused his mother special honours, including deification, after she died.

[41] Little is known about Vistilius apart from this entry. He had been a close colleague of Tiberius' brother Drusus, but does not seem to have advanced beyond the praetorship. He may have been the brother of Vistilia, the mother of Caesonia, Caligula's fourth wife. The severity of the punishment is unusual.

[42] The uncertainty expressed here is striking. At the very least it suggests that Tacitus had no *direct* acquaintance with the supposed texts.

[43] Marcus Lepidus was married to Caligula's sister Drusilla and was executed for his supposed involvement in a conspiracy (4.56, 59–61, 65). His inclusion among Caligula's lovers is not mentioned by any other source and makes its way into Suetonius probably on little more evidence than the close friendship of the two men.

[44] Mnester was much favoured by Caligula (5.24, 38). He later became the reputed lover of Claudius' wife Messalina, and was put to death after she fell.

[45] There are known to have been Parthian hostages in Rome during Caligula's reign, including Darius, who took part in the crossing of the bridge at Baiae (4.40).

[46] There is much speculation about the identity of Valerius Catullus, perhaps the son of the consul of AD 31. He has also been identified with the author of the mime Laureolus. Note that the behaviour of the first two is ascribed, as often, to rumour, but in the case of Catullus to a public admission/boast.

[47] On his sisters see 2.6–8. The identity of Pyrallis is unknown. Caligula has moved from homosexual partners, to incest, to Pyrallis as the final entry in the list. Her presence in this context is in fact strangely anticlimactic, and there may be something significant about her of which we are unaware.

was hardly any illustrious woman that he kept his hands off. **2** These women, who were usually women invited to dinner with their husbands, he would examine as they passed by his feet, doing it in a careful and leisurely manner, as merchants would, even lifting up any woman's face if she looked down from embarrassment; then, whenever he felt so inclined, he would leave the dining room, call for the one he most fancied, return a little later with the fresh marks of their sexual encounter and give it either praise or criticism, enumerating all the good and bad features of her body and the fucking.[48] To some he himself sent a divorce notice in the name of their absent husbands[49] and ordered it entered in the public records.[50]

Dark Wit

Caligula had a highly ironical view of the world, which was fed by his being thrust into a position of almost unlimited privilege, surrounded by people desperately anxious to please. As a consequence he developed a dark sense of humour, one that was invariably vindictive and sadistic, and in essence involved inflicting humiliation on captive audiences who had little choice but to accept it with as much good grace as possible.

Roman humour was very much an acquired taste. The following passages contain, or appear to contain, examples of Caligula's dark jokes, although in some cases their precise intent may be lost and grotesquely misrepresented by the source.

Suetonius sums up the nature of Caligulan wit nicely when describing the brutality of his language, and gives three examples of his humour, where he makes a "witty" comment about a grim situation.

5.39 Suet. *Cal.* 29.1 His horrific crimes he augmented with brutal language. There was nothing in his nature for which he had more praise and approval, he would say, than his, to use his own word, *adiatrepsia*, that is, his effrontery.[51] When his grandmother Antonia gave him advice, he, as if simply ignoring

---

[48] This seems to be a topos. Suetonius records (*Aug.* 69.1) that Antony claimed that he witnessed Augustus take the wife of an ex-consul away for sex during a dinner, and reported that when they returned the wife was similarly dishevelled. Suetonius seems often to draw general observations from specific instances, and this may have happened here. Caligula supposedly had an affair with Lollia Saturnina (perhaps his sister-in-law), the wife of Valerius Asiaticus, possibly one of the plotters in the final conspiracy (Sen. *Const.* 18.2), and at a banquet taunted Asiaticus about his wife's performance.

[49] The bill of divorce (*repudium*) had to be formally issued by the husband (or his father, the male head of his family, the paterfamilias) against the wife. There would have been no legal basis for Caligula to have done so. Again, this may have been a generalization based on a garbled account of a single incident.

[50] Biographical details of the lives of famous individuals were recorded in the Acta Diurna, the official gazetteer of public events. Suetonius noted that he found the birth of Caligula recorded there (1.4).

[51] The manuscripts here read *adiatrephia*. It is generally assumed that they are in error and that the original text read *adiatrepsia*. This word is not attested elsewhere (which would help to explain why the

her were insufficient, replied: "Remember, I have licence to do anything to anyone."[52] About to murder his brother and suspecting him of safeguarding himself with drugs from fear of poisoning, he said: "Hmm, an antidote against Caesar?"[53] After banishing his sisters, he made the threat that he had not only islands but swords too.[54]

It is perhaps hardly surprising that Caligula's cruel displays of humour have not always been recognized as humorous. A knowledge of the context is crucial. Take, for example, the story of his treatment of Lucius Vitellius, the commander who ably arranged the peace with Parthia at the beginning of the reign (7.1–3). This is often used to illustrate Caligula's madness, his belief that he could consort with the moon. But surely what is going on here is Caligula having fun at the expense of someone who, as Dio notes, was notorious for his flattery. Under the next emperor, Claudius, Vitellius would go so far as to carry the slipper of Claudius' wife Messalina on his person to demonstrate his loyalty. On this occasion Caligula entertained himself by putting Vitellius in an impossible situation—he would have to expose himself either as a toady or as mad. Vitellius' answer, however, was little short of brilliant, and goes a long way to explain why he was able to thrive under three different emperors.

5.40 Dio 59.27.6 And when Gaius once told him that he had sex with the moon and asked him if he could see the goddess with him, Vitellius looked in amazement, trembling a little, and with a half whisper, said, "Only you Gods, lord, are able to see each other." So after starting with this, Vitellius went on to surpass everyone else in flattery.

Inevitably Caligula's quips have been much distorted by posterity to show him in a bad light, often by being taken out of context and stripped of their humorous intent. Most of them were no doubt casual passing comments whose significance has been grotesquely exaggerated by the sources. What is arguably the best-known story associated with Caligula may have arisen from a cruel jest: it is almost

---

copyists got it wrong), but an unattested word is not necessarily a problem, since Suetonius does seem to suggest that the term is coined by Caligula. It is formed from the root *trep*, preceded by a negative particle *a*, so that it connotes the idea of "not turning," and since it is given a negative connotation here it would connote the idea of unbending or inflexible, perhaps in the sense of being pitiless or merciless. Presumably it all depended on context. Tac. *Ag.* 13.2 says that in fact Caligula was very prone to changing his mind rapidly (*velox ingenio mobili paenitentiae*).

[52] Ironically, Caligula's comment is an accurate summation of his constitutional position, since the senate, according to Suetonius, had granted him "supreme authority" (3.9, 11).

[53] Gemellus is of course Caligula's cousin and adopted son. The term "brother" is used presumably to emphasize the impiety of the act. Suetonius claims that Gemellus had been taking medicine to deal with a persistent cough (4.5).

[54] The reference is to the banishment of his sisters to Pontia after their involvement in the conspiracy of Lepidus. The simple message is that he can put to death as well as send into exile.

universally accepted at the popular level, and constantly restated, that Caligula appointed his horse to the consulship, a byword for the advancement of the totally incompetent, in circulation from at least the time of Gladstone, who compared an appointment of an official by his political rival Disraeli to Caligula's action. But the sources for the anecdote do not in fact say what is popularly attributed to them. Suetonius claims only that *it is reported* that Caligula *designated* (*destinasse*) his horse Incitatus for the consulship; Dio similarly says that he *promised* to do this. To confuse matters Dio adds in another context that he appointed Incitatus to a priesthood. It is hard not to conclude that this famous tale originated in a facetious comment about the stature of the candidates for the consulship, no more competent for the job, Caligula may well have suggested, than his horse.[55]

5.41 (see 5.33) Suet. *Cal.* 55.3 It is also reported that he planned to make it (sc. his racehorse) consul.

5.42 (see 5.34) Dio 59.14.7 He promised to appoint him (sc. his horse) consul. And he certainly would also have fulfilled that promise had he lived longer.

5.43 (see 5.32) Dio 59.28.6 [Caligula] declared his horse his fellow priest.

5.44 Suet. *Cal.* 29.2 From a retreat in Anticyra,[56] where he had gone for health reasons, a former praetor had often been asking for extensions to his leave,[57] and after ordering his execution Caligula added the comment that anyone who had received no benefit from hellebore after such a long time needed bloodletting.[58] Every tenth day he would confirm the list of those to be brought from prison for execution, and then say he was "clearing accounts."[59] After sentencing a number of Gauls and Greeks to death at the same time he declared triumphantly that he had "conquered Gallograecia."[60]

5.45 Suet. *Cal.* 27.1 Reviewing a line of men in custody, without examining anyone's criminal charges, he just stood in the middle of a colonnade and ordered them taken off "from baldhead to baldhead."

5.46 Dio 59.22.3 At one point when he saw a gathering of prisoners or the like he gave the famous command for them all to be killed "from bald-head to bald-

[55] It has been persuasively suggested that the joke derives from the names of Incitatus ("rapid") and one of the suffect consuls for 38, Asinius Celer ("swift ass").

[56] Anticyra was a port on the north shore of the Gulf of Corinth, In antiquity it was famed as a major source of the miracle drug hellebore, used to cure insanity, among other ailments.

[57] Senators were allowed to be absent from Italy for a maximum period of three years from the time of Julius Caesar (Suet. *Jul.* 42.1).

[58] Hellebore was apparently removed from the system by bleeding (Plin. *NH* 25.56).

[59] A ten-day delay was prescribed between the passing of a death sentence and execution (Tac. *Ann.* 3.51.2).

[60] Gallograecia refers to Galatia in Asia Minor, a Hellenized region settled by Gauls. The incident probably belongs to Caligula's sojourn in Gallia Narbonensis, with its mixed population of Greeks and Gauls, during his northern expedition. "Conquer" (*subigo*) might involve a wordplay, connoting either military or sexual conquest.

head." Playing dice at another time and realizing that he had no money, he asked for the census register of the Gauls and ordered the richest of them executed.

5.47 (see also 6.4) Suet. *Cal.* 37.1 In expenditure on extravagant living he surpassed every spendthrift's ingenuity ... repeating that a man had to be either thrifty or a Caesar.[61]

The Meeting between Caligula and Philo

Probably the most striking depiction of Caligula in jocular mood is Philo's account of the meeting between the emperor and the Jewish delegation from Alexandria in AD 40, headed by Philo himself (see Chapter 7), one of the most celebrated incidents of antiquity. Although Philo is usually much given to sententious ruminations on ethical and theological issues, his account of this meeting demonstrates that he possessed a superb narrative skill, much enlivened by possibly unintentional humorous detail. What makes the episode particularly fascinating is that it comes from the pen of a contemporary source. Not an unbiased one, of course—in Philo's eyes Caligula was the enemy of the Jews and of God—but unlike many of the anecdotes related by Dio and Suetonius long after the fact and often preserved in isolation, on this occasion the narrative of the events evolves in a sequence and provides context. It is noteworthy that despite Philo's undisguised distaste for the emperor, the Caligula he describes emerges from the episode surprisingly well. While he was clearly at his most mischievous, and Philo's comment that the whole affair was like something of a farce (5.48; 359) is surely not far off the mark, Caligula comes across as at worst an impish narcissist, a Wildean figure willing to go to any length just to deliver a funny line, far from the brutal and sadistic tyrant often depicted elsewhere. We also have intriguing minor details, the coterie of fawning courtiers applauding Caligula's every witticism, his nervous energy as he rushed from room to room to inspect the furnishings, and Philo's confirmation of Caligula as an enthusiast and spirited connoisseur of the arts, personally involving himself in the minutiae of how the pictures in the palace were to be arranged.

After the serious disturbances that broke out between Greeks and Jews in Alexandria under the governor Avilius Flaccus in AD 38 (7.23–4), Flaccus' replacement, Gaius Vitrasius Pollio, had determined that the conflict should be adjudicated by the emperor himself, and both sides were invited to dispatch a delegation to Rome. Philo led the Jewish group. We do not know when they

[61] "Caesar" was the cognomen of Gaius Julius Caesar and in the imperial age it became a title, with the force of "emperor" (as in the modern derivatives, Kaiser, Tsar). *Frugi* is an adjective, "frugal," but also a cognomen, the most familiar holder being Crassus Frugi, the father of Pompey, the arch-rival of Julius Caesar.

departed Alexandria; they sailed during the winter (*Leg.* 190) but whether that was the winter of AD 38 or of AD 39 is not made clear. At any rate the meeting did not take place until AD 40, after Caligula's return to Rome from his operations in Germany and the abortive campaign against Britain. Philo's delegation had in fact initially seen the emperor very briefly when he gave them a friendly greeting from his villa in the Vatican district on the west bank of the Tiber (Philo *Leg.* 181), just outside the city limits. But no business was conducted on that earlier occasion. In the following extended passage Philo describes their second meeting, held some time later in the emperor's residence in the exclusive Esquiline district. It was an ominous location, although neither side could have realized it, since it was here that Caligula would later receive his initial hasty burial after his assassination in AD 41 (8.12).

The meeting seems to have been inconclusive, but the chief concern of the Jewish members, over Caligula's decision to set up his own statue in the Temple in Jerusalem, proved in the end to be groundless. The sources claim that the scheme fell through because of the deliberate procrastination of Petronius, the governor of Syria, but it must be remembered that after Caligula's assassination it was in the interests of his loyal lieutenants to create the myth that they had been reluctant servants pretending to follow orders while in fact undercutting those orders. Caligula's threat to install the statue may have been nothing more than that, a threat designed to pressure the Jews into being more amenable to some sort of accommodation.

5.48 Philo *Leg.* 349 It is worth recording what we saw and heard when sent to attend the dispute over our status in the city. For as soon as we entered we could see from the look on his face and his reactions that it was not before a judge that we had appeared but a prosecutor more hostile than those who were our opponents. **350** For this is how a judge proceeds:[62] he sits down with his councillors, men chosen for their shrewdness since the matter under review is of vital importance, being one that has lain dormant for four hundred years and one being raised for the first time against the Alexandrian Jews;[63] the litigants stand with the people supporting their cause on one or other side of him, and he listens to the prosecution and defence in turn for as long as the water clock permits[64] and after this rises and discusses with his councillors a verdict that

---

[62] Philo here describes the procedure where the emperor's *consilium*, or body of advisors, would assist him in those cases that the emperor personally adjudicated. Philo is suggesting that Caligula ignored that sensible tradition, but of course his meeting with the embassy is not a formal judicial procedure.

[63] The figure of four hundred years is a rough approximation. Jews were supposedly involved in the foundation of Alexandria and their rights in the city were established either by Alexander the Great (Jos. *BJ* 2.487–8; *Ap.* 2.35) or by his successor in Egypt, Ptolemy I Soter (Jos. *Ant.* 12.8).

[64] Water clocks (*klepsydrae*) had been a standard feature of Athenian courts to allot time to individual speakers. They were introduced into Roman court procedures in the late republic.

they were openly to declare they thought fair. But no; the whole procedure was actually conducted by an unfeeling tyrant with an imperious frown.

351 For, apart from doing none of the things I have just mentioned, he summoned the procurators of the gardens of Maecenas and Lamia (they are close to each other and to the city, and he had been spending three or four days there), since that was where, in our presence, the drama directed against our whole people was to be staged, and he ordered them to leave all the residences there completely open—he wanted to inspect them carefully one by one.[65] **352** When brought before him we bowed low to the ground, and we paid honour to him with the greatest respect and deference[66] as soon as we set eyes on him, addressing him as "Imperator Augustus." So polite and so cordial was his response, however, that we lost all hope not only for our case but also for our lives: **353** "Are you the god-haters,"[67] he said, sneering and grimacing, "the ones who don't think I'm a god, a god that is recognized by now among all other peoples but not given that name by you?" He then stretched his hands to the sky and uttered an expression that it is not even proper to listen to, let alone reproduce the actual wording![68] **354** With what great joy were the opposing party's delegates immediately filled, believing as they did that their embassy had been crowned with success by Gaius' first utterance! They were gesticulating, dancing around, and calling him by all the gods' names.

355 Observing his delight over such salutations, suggestive of some suprahuman qualities, the abominable sycophant Isidorus[69] then said: "Even more, my lord, will you hate these people here, and those of their breed, when you know their animosity and ungodliness towards you. For when everyone else was offering thanksgiving sacrifices for your well-being, these alone could not

[65] The Horti Lamiani were possibly laid out by Lucius Aelius Lamia, consul in AD 3, and left by him to Tiberius, to become imperial property. They have supposedly been identified in recent excavations: https://www.romanoimpero.com/2018/02/horti-lamiani.html, accessed December 30, 2022. Adjoining them were the Horti Maecenatis, laid out on the Esquiline by Maecenas, transforming the area into a beautiful promenade, and possibly containing Maecenas' hot swimming pool, the first such amenity built in Rome. These became imperial property after the death of their founder, and Tiberius lived here on his return to the city in AD 2.

[66] *Proskynesis*, the act of prostration before a superior, is an ancient custom, performed before the kings of Assyria and in the later Persian court. Initially it seems to have conveyed little more than the respect shown to someone of high rank, but when adopted in Greece it became a form of worship. The most famous example of Caligula's reign is that of Lucius Vitellius, notorious for his obsequious flattery, who prostrated himself on encountering the emperor (5.38). Domitius Afer also supposedly threw himself to the ground when overwhelmed by Caligula's brilliance as a speaker (4.45). The distinction between treating someone as a god and giving them god-like respect is not a sharp one, but the Jews clearly felt obliged to walk that fine line.

[67] Caligula uses a pedantic term *theomiseis*, to convey the notion of "god-hater," possibly for humorous effect rather than to be particularly insulting.

[68] Caligula clearly uttered a form of the word "Jehovah," blasphemous only because of the context, since the name could be properly uttered in formal oaths and by priests in certain rituals.

[69] Isidorus was one of the two Greeks identified as members of the Alexandrian Greeks' embassy (Jos. *Ant.* 18.257 also names Apion). He was a notorious anti-Jewish agitator.

bring themselves to sacrifice. And in saying 'these' I am lumping the rest of the Jews in with them." **356** Together we all cried out: "Lord Gaius, we are falsely accused; we did indeed sacrifice, and we sacrificed hecatombs, too, not only pouring the blood on the altar and taking the flesh home for our dinner and festivities as people normally do, but also consigning the complete sacrificial victims to the holy fire, and doing that not once but three times already. The first time was when you succeeded to your realm, the second when you escaped from that serious illness that the entire inhabited world suffered together with you, and the third in hope of victory in Germany."[70]

357 "Yes," he said, that is true. "You did sacrifice, but to someone else, even if it was on my behalf. So what good is that? It wasn't to me that you sacrificed!" On hearing that after his earlier comment, a profound shudder immediately gripped us, which spread until it was clear to see. **358** And while he said this he was also pressing ahead with the residence inspections, noting the men's quarters and the women's, the features on the ground floor and those above—everything!—criticizing some as structurally faulty, while personally making plans for others and also ordering the more expensive. **359** Next, we were herded along, and we followed him up and down, scoffed at and cut up by our antagonists just as in stage comedies. In fact, the whole thing was a sort of comedy:[71] the judge had assumed the role of accuser and the accusers the role of bad judge, focused only on his personal hostility and not the real truth of the case. **360** When a judge charges a defendant, however, and the judge is such a powerful man, you have to hold your tongue. For by silence one possibly also has some means of defence, especially for those unable to respond to anything he was asking about and wanted, since our traditions and customs were holding back our tongues and shutting up and stitching up our mouths. **361** When he had made some arrangements for the buildings,

[70] The initial two sacrifices are easily dateable, the first to the beginning of Caligula's reign, March or at the latest April, of AD 37, the second to his recovery from his serious illness, in late October/early November of the same year. The third is more tricky. Those sacrifices were held in anticipation of victory in Germany. The projected northern expedition was supposedly common knowledge at the time of the bridge of Baiae (4.40) which is supposed to have occurred in mid-39 (that date is far from certain). The campaign might just have taken place in late 39 (see Chapter 7) but more likely belongs to early 40; in fact the ancient accounts of the northern expedition are so utterly chaotic that it is virtually impossible to work out the sequence of events. At most we might say that the third set of sacrifices might have been conducted in late summer/autumn AD 39, by early AD 40 at the very latest.
[71] Philo here used the word *mimeia*, to be differentiated from the modern concept of "mime," in which meaning is conveyed by gesture without words. The ancient form originated in Greece as a dramatic sketch portraying events from daily life. The Roman mime evolved into indecent and riotous farce. The actors were both men and women, performing barefoot without masks, playing stock characters like the deluded husband or the errant wife and her lover. By Caligula's day mimes were immensely popular and remained so until the end of the empire.

however, he asked a very weighty and serious question: " Why don't you eat pig's flesh?"[72]

The question met with such great bursts of laughter from our adversaries (some of whom were genuinely pleased, but others, being merely practised flatterers, wishing to make what he said appear smart and chic) that one of the servants behind him was angry at this perceived irreverence towards an emperor in whose case even a half-hearted smile was unsafe for those not in his inner circle. 362 When we replied, "There are different customs for different people, and some things are forbidden to us as others are forbidden to our opponents" and someone then retorted, "Just as many people don't touch lamb, which is a common food," he laughed, saying, "Yes, that's because it's not tasty." 363 Facing nonsense and abuse like this we were at a loss. Then, mockingly, he finally said, "We want to be told what rights of citizenship you enjoy."[73] 364 After we started speaking and explaining, and he had got a taste of our plea and realized it was not a paltry one,[74] he even cut off our preliminary arguments before we could get to the stronger ones, and he ran at full speed to the large house and, walking around it, ordered its windows to be restored all round with diaphanous stones (which do not block the light but do keep out the wind and the intensity of the sun). 365 He then went ahead in no hurry, and in a more relaxed manner he asked, "What is it you are saying?" but after we began what was to come next he started running again into another room and gave orders for its original paintings to be set up there.

366 So, with our case torn up and suspended, and all but shredded and shattered, we abandoned it; and in despair and exhaustion we anticipated nothing other than a death sentence, and we no longer had our spirits within us—these, in our anguish, had abandoned us, leaving us to beg the real god to hold back the anger of the one falsely bearing that title. 367 And God, taking pity on us, turned the man's heart to compassion; he, now put in a gentler mood, said this: "They seem to me unfortunate rather than bad men, and just stupid in not believing that I have been made a god," and with that he took his leave, telling us to go as well.

---

[72] The mirthful response of the hangers-on to Caligula's question about the Jewish dietary prohibition of pork, and Philo's concession that for some the laughter was genuine, suggests strongly that the phrase conceals a clever witticism, recognized, but not explained, by Philo, and a complete mystery now, mainly because we do not know what immediately preceded it.

[73] Despite his external frivolity Caligula seems to have grasped the crucial issue that lay at the heart of the problems in Alexandria, the tricky question of the status of the Jewish residents and the degree to which they could be considered citizens (Chapter 7).

[74] For all Philo's description of the proceedings as farcical, these brief comments suggest that in fact the issues were discussed seriously. There clearly was no resolution, but, that said, it is far from given that the problems were in fact resolvable.

Further Reading

Flory, M. B. 1986. "Caligula's *Inverecundia*: A Note on Dio Cassius 59.12.1." *Hermes* 114: 365–71.

Goodyear, F. R. D. 1984. "Tiberius and Gaius: Their Influence and Views on Literature." *ANRW* 2.32.1: 603–10.

Newbold, R. F. 1975. "The Spectacles as an Issue between Gaius and the Senate." *PACA* 13: 30–5.

Woods, D. 2008. "Concealing Caligula's Epilepsy." In *Studies in Latin Literature and Roman History*, edited by C. Deroux, 306–12. Brussels: Latomus.

Woods, D. 2014. "Caligula, Incitatus, and the Consulship." *CQ* 65: 772–7.

6

The Public Caligula

When we look at the celebrities of the past, and of the present too, it is often hard to separate their private from their public lives. Making that distinction in Caligula's case can be a major challenge, because the sources often depict his activities as emperor as the wild follies of a madman, rather than what we expect of an executive official in the conduct of his duties. Thus much of the material included in this chapter might well have been assigned to the previous one. The basic criterion for deciding where to place it is the degree to which the incidents seem to have an impact on the Roman populace generally, rather than merely on Caligula and his immediate entourage. The distinction is not a sharp one.

Cruelty

Within some two years of coming to power Caligula seems to have begun to suspect that there was well-established opposition to his rule, and within four years of his accession it became clear that his suspicions were not just paranoia. It might be argued that reasonable people had reasonable grounds for opposing this particular emperor. Perhaps so, but equally it would not have been unreasonable for him to take measures for his own self-preservation, and inevitably some of those measures would be brutal. But as the sources present the events Caligula went beyond the heartless treatment of his potentially dangerous opponents to a different plane of ruthlessness, of quite arbitrary cruelty indulged in for its own sake, resulting sometimes in acts of pure sadism, without political motivation, often in petty attempts to belittle and humiliate. How much faith we can place in the anecdotes that have been passed down is difficult to assess: much of his reported behaviour belongs to the category of the familiar excesses of the stereotypical tyrant.

6.1 Suet. *Cal.* **26.2** He was no more courteous or gentle with the senate: some members that had held the highest positions he allowed to run toga-clad beside his carriage for some miles and when he dined to stand in linen tunics, sometimes at the back of his couch and sometimes at his feet;[1] others, after

---

[1] Suetonius' words should be noted carefully. Caligula is not portrayed as inflicting these humiliations on the senators; rather he is castigated for allowing them to humiliate themselves. The implication is that we have here the obsequious activities of toadies, with members of the Rome elite

he had secretly executed them, he would continue to summon as if they were still alive, lying some days later that they had died from suicide. 3 When from forgetfulness the consuls omitted to declare his birthday he annulled their office, and for a three-day period the republic was without its most important officials.[2] He had his own quaestor, who had been charged with conspiracy, flogged, removing his clothing and setting it under the soldiers' feet for them to have a firmer footing for beating him.[3]

4 He dealt with the other classes with similar high-handedness and violence. When disturbed by noise from people taking up the free seats in the Circus Maximus in the middle of the night, he chased them all away with cudgels;[4] in that melee more than twenty equites and as many married ladies were crushed to death and countless others, too. Sowing seeds of discord between plebeians and equites at theatre performances, he would give out *decimae* in advance so that equestrians' seats could be taken by any commoner.[5] 5 At a gladiatorial show he would sometimes have the awnings drawn back in blazing sunlight and forbid anyone to leave;[6] and replacing the normal fine display he would put on decrepit animals and age-weary gladiators, and rather than stage amateur

---

playing the role of slaves at his table. The unlikely and otherwise unattested story of the senators in their togas running along with his chariot may be a distorted generalization of a specific incident. When Caligula visited the Rhine armies in 39/40, the new commander, Galba, a stern disciplinarian, distinguished himself by running for 20 miles behind Caligula's chariot, the activity being portrayed by Suetonius in a very positive light (7.17). A route march of 20 miles was standard training in the late empire (Veg. 3.4) and a similar regimen could well have been in force in the early empire too.

[2] Caligula's claim here is unconvincing. The likelihood of the consuls forgetting his birth date seems very remote. Dio provides more details (4.46), that they failed to celebrate the birthday adequately, and to make matters worse they had celebrated the victories of Augustus over Antony.

[3] Seneca identifies the quaestor as Betilienus Bassus (8.3).

[4] The Circus Maximus ran along the southwest edge of the Palatine. Caligula had a residence on the Gelotiana region of the hill, overlooking the circus, and could watch events from his balcony (5.31). Clearly the location had its disadvantages also, but the precise background to the rowdy situation described here is unclear. Dio reports two occasions when tickets were free. He says that Caligula provided free games to mark the birthday of Drusilla (4.28), and that Hadrian provided free games on his own birthday (69.8.2). Suetonius here seems to suggest an occasion when only a portion of the tickets were free. It is not clear if his reference is to the games celebrated in honour of Drusilla.

There is some evidence of pre-dawn queuing for the theatre in the notoriously unreliable *Historia Augusta*, which claims that the emperor Heliogabalus would release snakes among the crowds lining up there (*SHA Hel.* 23.2). Caligula would himself sometimes arrive before dawn (Dio 59.13.5).

[5] Caligula's actions are far from clear here. He seems to have pre-distributed some sort of ticket (the Latin text reads *decimas*). The first fourteen rows of the theatre were reserved for the knights, and occasionally there were not sufficient seats for everyone (Sen. *Ben.* 7.12.3–6). It seems that if the equestrian seats were not all occupied by a certain hour, they were made generally available, which Caligula may have subverted by allowing non-equestrians early admission. Admittedly, not the most vicious behaviour.

[6] Dio 59.7.8 records that at least in his first year Caligula allowed senators to wear sun hats at performances (as well as providing cushions for them to sit upon), and, when it became excessively hot, performances were moved to the Diribitorium (voting hall) on the Campus Martius, which was covered. Even in the summer of AD 39, when the political climate had darkened, he put awnings over the forum because of the severe heat.

fighters he instead used reputable heads of families who were, however, known to have some physical handicap.[7]

6.2 Suet. *Cal.* **27.1** The viciousness of his character can especially be seen in the following examples. When the price of cattle for feeding wild animals at a gladiatorial event was becoming rather high, he earmarked convicts to be torn to pieces.[8] **2** He demanded fulfilment of a vow from a man who had promised to fight as a gladiator in return for Caligula's return to health, and he watched him fight with the sword and would not let him off unless he won, and then only after he made many appeals to him. Another man, who had vowed his own death for the same thing, he passed on to his slaves when he balked at it, ordering them to chase him through the streets still wearing ceremonial branches and woollen headband, and to insist that he fulfil his vow—until he was finally thrown off a rampart.[9] **3** Many men of high status he condemned to mining and road-building after first disfiguring them with branding irons, or he had them thrown to wild animals, or shut them up in a cage on all fours like animals, or cut them to pieces with a saw; and it was not always for serious offences, but for having a poor opinion of his shows[10] or because they had never taken an oath by his *genius*.[11] **4** He would make parents attend sons' executions;[12] and when one pleaded poor health he sent him a litter, while another he invited to dinner straight from witnessing the execution, and with fulsome affability tried rousing him to laughter and gaiety. He ordered the supervisor of his games and hunting to be beaten in his sight, in chains, for three days in a row, and he did not put him to death until he was nauseated by the smell of his rotting brain. A playwright of Atellan farces he burned alive in the middle of the arena of the amphitheatre over a humorously ambiguous line.[13] When

---

[7] There is a manuscript problem here. *Paegniarii* were clowns who performed mock fights with dummy weapons during the midday intermission. They seem to have been an established institution; the outrage lay in his obliging/allowing Romans of good standing to perform.

[8] Dio 59.22.3 places this event in Lyon, thus during Caligula's absence from Rome in 39/40. Note that prisoners would regularly be fed to animals during the performances as part of the show. The disgrace here was that they were simply used for routine feeding.

[9] The reference here is to whoever had vowed to fight as a gladiator if the emperor's life was spared (3.54). Dio 59.8.3 identifies the would-be gladiator as a knight, Atanius Secundus, and the other individual who vowed his life as Afranius Potitus, a plebeian. It may be that the punishments were ritual, not real, meant to humiliate individuals who had been guilty of gross flattery.

[10] Dio 59.13.5–6 claims that Caligula was upset with people for not showing enough enthusiasm for the shows or for applauding the wrong performers.

[11] See 6.25.   [12] See 8.4.

[13] Atellan farces may well owe their name to the town of Atella in Campania. They were broad comedies, performed by masked actors playing stock characters, highly popular in Rome. Many of the lines were ambiguous, and it is not clear here if Caligula took exception to the sexual innuendos, displaying the kind of prudery that led to the banning the *spintriae* (3.49), or if the offending lines were political in nature—they could of course be both, as in the allusion to an old goat in a farce of the time of Tiberius (Suet. *Tib.* 45). If Suetonius' claim is true the punishment would be excessive. An Atellan performer who referred allusively to the murders of Claudius and Agrippina suffered only exile from Nero (Suet. *Ner.* 39.3).

a Roman knight was thrown to wild animals and proclaimed his innocence, he pulled him out, cut out his tongue, and put him back.[14]

28.1 When he asked someone who had been recalled from long exile what he used to do there, the man, to flatter him, replied, "I always begged the gods for what has come to pass, that Tiberius would die and you would become emperor." Thinking then that people he had exiled were also praying for *his* death, he sent men around the islands to slaughter everyone.[15] When eager to have a particular senator torn to pieces, he induced some men to attack him suddenly when he entered the curia, call him a public enemy, stab him with their styluses, and hand him over to the others to be mangled; and he was not satisfied until he saw the man's limbs, body parts, and guts dragged through the streets and dumped in front of him.[16]

6.3 Suet. *Cal.* 30.1 He did not punish anyone negligently, doing so only with many slight wounds, his regular and soon well-known order being: "Strike so he can feel he is dying."[17] When someone other than the earmarked person was killed through a mistake in names, he said that man, too, had deserved the same fate.[18] He often uttered the tragic poet's familiar line of: "Let them hate, provided they fear."[19]

Extravagance

The emperor Tiberius was notoriously parsimonious, and his reign so austere that whoever succeeded him was almost bound to seem a wildly extravagant spendthrift by contrast. We can assume a genuine change in spending patterns when Caligula came to power, but the picture of irresponsible waste that the sources portray, with the accumulated surplus of Tiberius soon squandered and the state close to bankruptcy, should be viewed with considerable caution. There were certain expenditures that would reasonably have had to be met, such as the cost of raising two new legions

---

[14] Dio 59.10.3 offers another version, and both stories may go back to one apocryphal tale, that he cut out the tongues of bystanders and fed them to the beasts when there was a dearth of criminals available for this form of execution.

[15] Flaccus, the former prefect of Egypt, was a notable example. He was exiled first to the island of Andros, then was executed (Philo *Flacc.* 185–9), and Josephus records the similar fate of Anteius (Jos. *Ant.* 19.125–6). Caligula's brother Nero had previously been banished to an island, then forced to commit suicide (2.12).

[16] Dio identifies the victim as Scribonius Largus, in late 40 (Dio 59.26.2), the death incited by Caligula's freedman Protogenes, and adds the detail that he was torn to death.

[17] The tables were reputedly turned on him at the time of his assassination. Josephus claims that Caligula was killed by a series of deliberately restrained blows so that he would die more slowly (Jos. *Ant.* 19.106).

[18] Dio 59.22.4 tells the story of Julius Sacerdos, a Gaul of moderate means, put to death by Caligula for his money in mistake for another man with a similar name.

[19] The line (*oderint dum metuant*) supposedly came from the *Thyestes* of the playwright Accius, and is quoted by a number of individuals, including, in a slightly different form, Tiberius (Suet. *Tib.* 59.2).

for the planned campaign against Britain and Germany, or the restoration of kingdoms to their former rulers and the consequent loss of revenue for Rome. Moreover it seems that Claudius, on his accession, found the treasury in a healthy enough condition to be able to abolish Caligula's new taxes and also to finance his own campaigns, initially in Germany and subsequently in Britain.

6.4 (see also 5.47) Suet. *Cal.* 37.1 In expenditure on extravagant living he surpassed every spendthrift's ingenuity, devising a new kind of baths and the most bizarre sorts of food and dinners; he would bathe in hot and cold unguents,[20] drink the most precious pearls dissolved in vinegar,[21] and serve his fellow diners breads and other snacks set in gold, repeating that a man had to be either thrifty or a Caesar.[22] In fact, he even threw coins of no small denomination to the crowd from the roof of the Basilica Julia over a number of days.[23] 2 He also built ten-banked Liburnian galleys that had gem-studded sterns, multicoloured sails, capacious warm baths, porticoes, and dining rooms, as well as a large assortment of vines and fruit trees, so that when reclining on board he could sail along the Campanian coast enjoying singing and dancing.[24] In constructing his mansions and country houses expense was no concern, and there was nothing he ever wanted to do more than bringing off what was said to

---

[20] The use of hot and cold water in bathing was standard in the Roman world. The addition of perfumes was the quintessence of decadence. The dining room of Nero's Golden House reputedly had a rotating device that sprinkled perfume on the guests (Suet. *Ner.* 31.2). In his compendium of Roman history, the fourth-century historian Eutropius (*Brev.* 7.14) claims that Nero's custom of washing in perfumes was in imitation of Caligula. Pliny *NH* 13.22 provides the detail that Caligula sprinkled the sides of his bath tubs with perfumes.

[21] Dissolving pearls in vinegar was a byword for extravagance. There was a famous story of how Cleopatra bet Antony that she could spend 10 million sestertii on a meal, and proved her point by dissolving her pearl earring in vinegar (Pliny *NH* 9.119–21; Macrob. *Sat.* 3.17.16–18). Interestingly, Seneca (*Cons. Helv.* 10.5) says that Caligula spent the same sum, 10 million sestertii, the equal of the tribute of three provinces, on a single day of eating. The Cleopatra anecdote seems to have been reassigned to Caligula, with different elements of it surviving in Pliny and Seneca. Josephus *Ant.* 18.289–91 claims that Herod Agrippa put on a banquet that exceeded even Caligula's in its extravagance and was admired for this by the emperor.

[22] On the joke, see 5.45.

[23] Dio dates the donative securely to Caligula's return to the city after his northern campaign, identifying it as an attempt to win popular support in his quarrel with the senate (7.20). Josephus (*Ant.* 19.71) claims unconvincingly that the coins were gold and silver, echoed in Dio, who adds, equally unconvincingly, the story that people were killed because the loot included pieces of iron—in fact the fatalities were probably caused by the greedy scramble, a phenomenon observed by Seneca (*Ep.* 74.8).

In the republican period, Tuditanus, wearing a cloak and buskins, was in the habit of throwing coins to the crowds from the rostra in the forum, and was considered mad (Cic. *Phil.* 3 (VI) 16; Val. Max. 7.8.1).

[24] A Liburnian galley was strictly speaking a fast warship, and there seems to be a humorous application of the word here. The extravagance of these boats is confirmed by the survival of what are presumably two similar vessels recovered from Lake Nemi in the Alban Hills. The ships were sunk in the lake and there were efforts to raise them as early as the fifteenth century. This was finally achieved through a project beginning in the late 1920s, when the lake was drained. The recovered vessels were destroyed, along with their museum, when the Germans evacuated the area in 1944. They were identified as Caligulan on the basis of inscribed water pipes, but were probably still in commission under Nero. They had mosaic floors and running water, and matching columns of marble and fine bronze ornamentation.

be impossible. **3** So moles were built in dangerously deep waters, rocks of the hardest flint cut out, plains raised with infill to the height of mountains, and mountain ridges levelled to ditches, everything done with amazing speed, since delay was paid for with execution. And to sum it all up he spent immense fortunes, including two thousand, seven hundred million sestertii of Tiberius Caesar's, when not even a year had gone by.[25]

6.5 Suet. *Cal.* 39.1 Also, when he was in Gaul he sold off the jewellery, house furnishings, slaves, and even the freedmen of his sisters, whom he had condemned to death, at enormous prices; and enticed by the money he made he demanded to have all the property in the old palace moved from the city, with hired vehicles and baker's mules commandeered for its transportation, so that there were frequent shortages of bread in Rome and many people with lawsuits saw their cases fail through being absent and unable to appear to meet their bail.[26] **2** In selling off these goods there were no lengths of cheating and pandering he would not employ, now berating various people for avarice and not being ashamed to be richer than he was, and then feigning regret over giving ordinary people the opportunity to acquire the property of emperors. He had discovered that a wealthy provincial had paid his major-domo two hundred thousand sestertii to be slipped into one of his banquets, and he had not been upset that the honour of dining with him was so highly prized; and when this man was sitting at his auction the following day he sent someone to him to hand him a piece of trash for two hundred thousand sestertii and tell him he was to dine with Caesar by personal invitation.[27]

Alongside Caligula's purely personal expenditures there were various building and engineering projects that would have drawn heavily on the treasury. One of his undertakings illustrates nicely how useful it is to have more than one source available for a given topic, and how the information the literary sources provide can be enlivened by an inscription. Dio informs us that Caligula flooded the Saepta Julia, the great enclosure on the Campus Martius begun by Julius Caesar and completed by Agrippa for naval shows, but that he found the site unsatisfactory and demolished the building to construct new stands (6.6). Suetonius also alludes to this new building project, but he in addition provides its general

---

[25] Nero supposedly admired Caligula for spending all the money frugally saved by Tiberius (Suet. *Ner.* 30.1). Dio records two variant amounts for the funds left in the treasury by Tiberius, either 2,300,000,000 or 3,300,000,000 sestertii, but says that in any case Caligula had spent it all before the end of his second year.

[26] We do not know how far north Agrippina and Livilla had accompanied Caligula when he went to Gaul on his way to his northern campaign. It seems unlikely that they could have taken with them much in the way of movable furniture.

[27] Invitations were conveyed to banquets by individuals known as *vocatores*, the term that Suetonius uses here. They had considerable control over who was invited, and Martial makes fun of a friend who failed to invite him to his dinners, and blames it on his *vocator* (Mart. *Ep.* 7.86).

Invitations to Caligula's dinners were highly prized. Suetonius (*Vesp.* 2.3) claims that Vespasian, during his praetorship, thanked him in the senate for a dinner invitation.

location, reporting that the new structure was still located in the neighbourhood of the Saepta (6.7). But to cap all this we have a building inscription from the area, in which Claudius parades his repair to the Aqua Virgo aqueduct, which ran west of the Saepta, and, luckily for the historical record, brings the episode to life, since Claudius used the occasion to berate Caligula for the damage that his construction projects had caused to Rome's water supply (6.8).

> **6.6 Dio 59.10.5** He put on these games in the Saepta at first, digging up the entire area and filling it with water to bring in just one ship, but then he actually moved them to another spot where he demolished large numbers of huge buildings and set up benches; for he felt only contempt for the amphitheatre of Taurus.[28]

> **6.7 Suet.** *Cal.* **21** He also started work on an aqueduct in the Tibur region[29] and an amphitheatre next to the Saepta, the one later completed by his successor Claudius and the other abandoned. At Syracuse he had walls restored that had collapsed from age, as well its temples of the gods.[30] He had also intended to rebuild the palace of Polycrates on Samos,[31] to complete the Didymaeon in Miletus,[32] and to found a city on the upper slopes of the Alps,[33] but his highest priority had been to dig a passage through the Isthmus in Achaea, and he had already sent a senior centurion to survey the work.[34]

> **6.8 Building inscription on Aqua Virgo, Rome AD 46 (Smallwood 308b)**
> Tiberius Claudius Caesar Augustus, son of Drusus, pontifex maximus, in his fifth tribunician year, acclaimed Imperator eleven times, Father of the Country, consul designate for a fourth term, constructed and thoroughly restored from the foundations the arches of the Aqua Virgo severely damaged by Gaius Caesar.

Taxes

Adding to the financial difficulties, the abolition of the sales tax, whether at 0.5 per cent or 1 per cent (4.22, 23), meant that Caligula was obliged to raise revenue from a variety of other indirect taxes.

---

[28] On the amphitheatre of Taurus see 5.26.

[29] Suetonius refers to this aqueduct again in *Claud.* 20.1. Pliny and Frontinus record two aqueducts begun by Caligula and completed by Claudius, the Aqua Claudia and the Anio Novus (Front. *Aq.* 1.13; Pliny *NH* 36.122). They pass relatively close to Tibur.

[30] Perhaps connected with the visit to Syracuse that he undertook after the death of Drusilla (4.26). Augustus had repaired some of the walls, damaged during the recent civil war (Strabo 6.2.4).

[31] Polycrates was the famous sixth-century BC tyrant of Samos. No trace of the supposed restored palace has been discovered on the island.

[32] The temple at Didyma in Miletus (6.12–14).

[33] This seems implausible; Suetonius may have been referring to road-building activities.

[34] The dream of constructing a canal across the Isthmus of Corinth began in at least the sixth century BC with the local tyrant Periander, but it was Nero who initiated actual construction (Paus. 2.1.5). It was not until 1893 that it was completed.

6.9 Suet. *Cal.* 40 He levied fresh, unprecedented taxes,[35] first through his *publicani*[36] but later, as the money kept pouring in, through his centurions and praetorian tribunes, and he passed over no kind of commodities or people on which he could impose some kind of tax. On foodstuffs sold throughout the city a fixed, standard charge was levied; for lawsuits and judicial proceedings in any location[37] it was one fortieth of the amount involved in the litigation, not without a fine imposed on anyone found to have reached a settlement or abandoned the proceedings; for porters it was one eighth of their daily wages;[38] for prostitutes' takings it was what she earned for one session of sex;[39] and a codicil was added to that particular section of the law that people earlier in the business of prostitution or brothel-keeping were also subject to the tax, and that even being married offered no exemption.[40]

41 When taxes of that sort had been imposed but not actually put in writing[41] (since many of the offences were committed through ignorance of the promulgated laws), he eventually at the people's insistence[42] posted up the law, but in miniscule letters and also in a very cramped space so no one could write it down. And to leave no sort of profiteering untried he opened up a brothel on the Palatine, and setting apart numerous rooms (and furnishing them

[35] Dio 59.28.8–11 and Jos. *Ant.* 19.24–7 place the new taxes in the final period of the reign. Dio 60.4.1 claims that they were revoked by Claudius.

[36] Although in some provinces direct taxes in the form of tribute might be raised by the communities themselves, elsewhere the collection of revenues was assigned to private contractors, who would perform the function for a profit, the *publicani* (collectors of "public" revenues), attested from the third century BC on. Some of them operated independently but others would be organized in companies (*societates*), who carried out other tasks too, such as the management of public property or public works, like the maintenance of roads or temples. In the early principate they lost the collection of taxes in the provinces. But *publicani* continued to be widely employed in Italy. They were much criticized for their avarice, familiar to us from the New Testament (e.g. Mark 2:16), and under Nero there was public concern over their widespread abuses (Tac. *Ann.* 15.30). Soldiers had been used in the provinces to collect the taxes before Caligula—under Tiberius the Frisians rebelled because of the exactions of a centurion assigned to the task (Tac. *Ann.* 4.72.1); but Caligula may have been innovative in using the Praetorians to collect these funds, which had the advantage that the taxes in their entirety would be paid into the treasury without a cut going to the *publicani*.

[37] The phrase "in any location" suggests that these taxes were imposed throughout the empire. Their purpose may have been to discourage frivolous suits.

[38] Dio 59.28.8 refers to taxes on wage-earning slaves, presumably with reference to the same tax. Porters (*geruli*) are commonly attested in funerary inscriptions, which means that they could afford proper burials, and they might be of a somewhat higher status than men engaged for such tasks as unloading material or carrying litters; perhaps they were employed to carry letters or documents. One eighth is a relatively high imposition.

[39] Caligula's tax on prostitution seems to be an innovation in Rome, although there were precedents in the Greek world. It is not clear to what period of earning this tax relates; suggestions range from the earnings of one day to those of one month. If we can use the steep rate assigned to porters as a guide, one day might be more attractive here.

[40] One could not evade the tax by claiming to have given up prostitution, even by ending it through marriage.

[41] The suggestion is that Caligula avoided publication in the hope that people would transgress out of ignorance, and Dio 59.28.11 says that he was thus able to raise new revenues from the penalties that they would incur.

[42] Jos. *Ant.* 19.26 claims that some people were killed, adding to the disgust felt by the assassin Cassius Chaerea for the regime.

appropriately for the area's class) in which ladies and freeborn youngsters could stand on show,[43] he then sent pimps around forums and basilicas to invite young and old to come for their pleasure; money on interest was offered to them on their arrival, and people were stationed to take a clear note of the names contributing to Caesar's revenues.

6.10 Suet. *Cal.* 38.2 The wills of primipili who from the start of Tiberius' reign had not named him or Caligula as an heir he revoked as being a sign of ingratitude;[44] and he also rendered null and void those of any others that stated they had Caesar designated as their beneficiary on their deaths. In this way he aroused fear, and when he was named as heir by strangers among close friends and by parents among their children, he would say they were mocking him because they kept on living after making such a commitment, and to many he sent poisoned delicacies.[45]

3 He would try cases of this kind after first reckoning up the amount he thought he needed to acquire, and only after acquiring it would he finally leave.[46] And unable to stand a moment's delay he once, and with a single sentence, found more than forty people guilty that were on trial for various offences, and waking Caesonia from her sleep he bragged about how much business he had completed while she was taking her siesta.[47]

6.11 Dio 59.15.1 And as for ways of raising money, a vote was earlier taken that any people still alive who had said they wanted to leave something to Tiberius should now leave it to Gaius when they died;[48] to make it seem that he had the right to inherit and accept such gifts even in spite of the laws (since he then had neither a wife nor children), he proposed an ordinance to that effect. In this present instance, however, eschewing any decree, he simply took for himself all the property of any who had served as centurions and who, after his father's Triumph, had left it to someone other than the emperor.

---

[43] Claudius' wife, the notorious Messalina, was previously said to have turned the palace into a brothel (Dio 60.18.1–2, 31.1; Pliny *NH* 10.172), but that was meant in an essentially figurative sense.

[44] Primipili were senior centurions. An important Roman legal principle was the notion of obligation to members of one's family. Caligula seems to have viewed the emperor as someone presiding as father over the state as whole and as such entitled to consideration on the basis of *pietas*.

[45] The suggestion seems to be that by continuing to live after they had made the bequest they were mocking the emperor and thus were guilty of *maiestas*. It seems very likely that a misrepresented joke is at the basis of this claim.

[46] Presumably Suetonius is suggesting that Caligula presided over the *maiestas* trials of the individuals mentioned in the previous section and that when he had raised a certain amount of money he would end the operation for that day.

[47] The suggestion may be that he ignored the statutory delay of ten days after sentencing (see 8.5) before carrying out the execution. The role given to his fourth wife, Caesonia, places the incident no earlier than AD 39.

[48] His requirement that he should inherit the estates that had been bequeathed to Tiberius was a significant legal development. It meant that that there was an understanding that bequests made to the princeps were made not to him personally but to the individual who happened to occupy the position of princeps; this would become a formal rule (*constitutio*) in the late second century, under Antoninus Pius (Gaius *Dig.* 21.56).

Divinity

Of all the stories of bizarre behaviour that circulated about Caligula it is probably his reputed insistence that he be recognized as a god that has sealed the popular perception that he was crazy. The evidence for this topic is particularly murky and confused, to be treated with great caution.

Romans, in common with many other ancient peoples, did not observe the sharp distinction between the human and the divine generally maintained in most parts of the modern world. Hence the notion of emperor worship did not seem as outlandish then as it generally does now. The roots of the phenomenon can be traced back to the republican period, with local worship of Roman officials in the provinces, particularly the eastern provinces.[49] It was inevitable that with the evolution of the imperial system the emperor would become the focus of such attention. At the official level the policy under Augustus and Tiberius was to allow official provincial worship of the emperor only in association with Rome or the Roman senate. At the more local level any such restrictions appear to have been widely neglected. Even in Italy emperors from the outset were worshipped daring their lifetimes at the local municipal level, while in Rome itself there was a casual tendency to equate the emperor with the gods. But in the city of Rome there was a strong aversion to the idea of the *formal* worship of a living man as a god. It could happen after death, of course, and the official apotheosis of Julius Caesar after his death created a precedent for the posthumous treatment of later deserving emperors and members of their family.

Following his accession Caligula was recognized as divine from the outset in provinces in the east. In the congratulatory despatch sent to him by the League of Greek states (1.18) he is explicitly described as a god (*theos*), while a decree of Cyzicus in Asia Minor calls him "the new sun" (*ho Helios neos*, Smallwood 401.3). But the most complete evidence for his worship in the east comes from the city of Miletus, on the west coast of Asia Minor, at the mouth of the River Meander. Miletus had long held ambitions to be a major player in the imperial cult, losing out in AD 26 to the city of Smyrna as a cult centre for a temple to Tiberius, Livia, and the senate. The precedent had been established earlier by Pergamum, which had been granted a temple to Augustus and Rome during the emperor's reign. But the worship of Caligula at Miletus broke with tradition. He did not have to share the billing with others—the temple there was to the emperor standing alone in his own right.

Miletus was famous in antiquity for its great Temple of Apollo, built within its territory at Didyma, something actually used against Miletus' bid to secure the Temple of Tiberius in AD 36. The Didyma temple was destroyed by the Persians

---

[49] An example is the temple decreed for Cicero in his province of Asia, which he refused (Cic. *Q.Fr.* 1.1.26).

(variously reported, either by Darius or by Xerxes), and Alexander the Great began its replacement, a task still not completed in the second century AD when Pausanias described the area (Paus. 7.5.4). The relationship between Caligula's temple and that of Apollo is unclear. Suetonius lists the emperor's intention to complete the Temple of Apollo at Didyma among his praiseworthy actions. But Dio attributes to him a much less worthy scheme, of taking over Apollo's uncompleted temple for his own use. This is not impossible, given what we are told of Caligula's plans for the Temple in Jerusalem, but it seems unlikely that the literary sources would have passed up the opportunity to castigate him if he had entertained similar plans for Miletus.

An inscription discovered close to the southwest corner of the Temple of Apollo is particularly valuable for the rich evidence it provides for local organization of the imperial cult, and also for confirming that this cult was based not within the city of Miletus itself but rather in Didyma, which falls within Milesian territory. The inscription records the dedication of a cult statue of Caligula, probably in the precinct mentioned by Dio. It demonstrates that in the provinces the imperial cult was as much a matter of regional pride as of religion, and the local worthies mentioned clearly felt that they enhanced their own status by undertaking the responsibilities, and the expenses, of holding up to three offices within the local organization, each meticulously noted and preserved in perpetuity.

Apart from the office holders, thirteen *neopoioi* ("temple officials") are mentioned. These individuals came from various cities of the province of Asia, and it is possible that they formally represented those cities: Julia,[50] Miletus, Pergamum, Antiocheia on Maeander, Cyzicus, Apamea, Laodicea, Caesareia (Tralles?), Adramyttium, Philomelium, Halicarnassus, Smyrna, and Sardis. The officals are further described as *philosebastoi* ("devotees of the Augustus"), which may indicate some sort of formal office but might also simply be an honorific title. Since they are from thirteen separate cities it may be that the temple was financed by the province as a whole, like that to Augustus at Pergamum or to Tiberius, Livia, and the senate at Smyrna, but this is not proved.

6.12 Inscription (to accompany statue). Didyma at Miletus: AE 1912.134 (Smallwood 127)

[Gaius] Caesar Germanicus, [Imperator], divine Augustus, son of Germanicus. His senior temple officials during the time when Gnaeus Vergilius Capito[51] was high priest of the Temple of Gaius Caesar at Miletus[52] for the first time and of Asia for the third, and when Tiberius Julius Demetrius, the son of Menogenes

---

[50] Presumably of Julia Gordos in Lydia.
[51] Vergilius Capito was a prominent individual who later, under Claudius, became prefect of Egypt.
[52] Presumably Miletus is used here not to distinguish the city from Didyma, but to signify the whole region of Miletus, including Didyma, as opposed to the province of Asia.

was legislator, high priest for the second time and temple warden[53] of the temple at Miletus, and when Protomachus, son of Glyco, of the city of Julia, was *archineopoios*[54] and *sebastoneos* and *sebastologos*. At their own expense the following made the dedication: Protomachos, son of Glyco, of Julia; Neon, son of Artemon of Miletus, Friend of Gaius;[55] Theopompos Asklepiogenes, son of Theopompos, of Pergamum; Sochares, son of Sochares, of Antiocheia; Peithias, son of Pytheos, of Cyzicus; Diocles, son of Moutas, of Apamea; Glycon, son of Euarchos, of Laodicea; Hierokles, son of Artemidoros, of Caesareia; Daimenes, son of Antigonos, of Adramyttium; Pylades, son of Pantaleon, of Philomelium; Aspasios, son of Aristokles, of Halicarnassus; Olympianos Hieronymos, son of Poplios, of Smyrna; Hermippos, son of Hermippos, of Sardis, Friends of Augustus, their names appended in the order determined by lot.

6.13 Suet. *Cal.* 21 He had also planned on...completing the Didymaeon in Miletus...

6.14 Dio 59.28.1 Gaius ordered that in the province of Asia a sacred precinct in Miletus must be set off for his worship. His choice of this city he explained by saying that Diana had taken Ephesus before him,[56] Augustus had taken Pergamum, and Tiberius had taken Smyrna; but the fact was that he wished to take over the great and very beautiful temple that the Milesians were building for Apollo.

The Beginnings of the Reign

According to Dio, Caligula at the outset of his reign behaved with restraint and even with decorum in matters relating to his worship, which accords with his general conduct in this early phase. He prohibited images of himself and sacrifices to his *genius* (on which, see below). It is likely that Dio had in mind restrictions applied only in Italy, but we have a vivid illustration of his general initial restraint in an inscription dated precisely to August 19 (AD 37), hence only a few months into his accession. This takes the form of a letter from Caligula to the officials of the city of Acraephia in Boeotia (6.16). In the letter it is clear that what appears to be a newly formed *koinon* ("league") of Greek states had sent a delegation to Rome

---

[53] Demetrius was *neokoros*, charged with the task of keeping the temple clean.

[54] The *archineopoios* had the responsibility for supervising the people who tended to the upkeep and expenses of the temple.

[55] Only Neon is singled out for this distinction, which refers specifically to Caligula and not to the emperor in the abstract, perhaps because Neon represented Miletus, where the dedication took place.

[56] The Temple of Diana at Ephesus was one of the traditional ancient Wonders of the World. Constructed in the sixth century BC on the site of earlier predecessors, it was destroyed by a mad arsonist, Herostratus, in 356 BC, rebuilt, and finally razed by the Goths in AD 262. Little of the temple remains *in situ*.

to congratulate the emperor on his accession, and had offered a number of honours, including statues.[57] Caligula courteously agreed to the formation of the *koinon* and accepted some of the honours, but diplomatically suggested that they not go to the expense of extra statues beyond those to be set up at the sites of the great games.

6.15 Dio 59.4.4 Moreover, after first forbidding anyone to set up likenesses of him he even went on to make statues himself, and after once resolving that a decree for sacrifices to his *genius* be annulled, and then even going so far as to have an inscription made of it, he nevertheless ordered temples to be built and sacrifices offered for him as a god.

6.16 *ILS* 8792 (Smallwood 361). Acraephia, Boeotia, August 19, AD 37
Imperator Augustus Caesar, descendant of the god Augustus, grandson of Tiberius Caesar, Pontifex Maximus with Tribunician Authority, greetings to the *koinon* of Achaeans and Boeotians and Locrians and Phocians and Euboeans. On reading the resolution submitted to me by your delegates and on recognizing that you omitted no lavishness in the zeal and piety you exhibited towards me, each one of you sacrificing individually for my welfare,[58] and communally celebrating a festival, and voting for the greatest honours possible—for all of these I praise you, and acknowledging the distinction of each of the Greek peoples from early times I grant permission for you to assemble together. With reference to the statues that you voted me, give up the large part, if it is acceptable, and limit yourself to those to be set up at Olympia and Nemea and Delphi and the Isthmus, in order that...and you burden yourselves less with expenses.

The delegates whose names are added [*presented*] the decree to me. [*My Greetings!*]. The senior delegate... [*fragmentary names follow*]
Issued on August 19, Rome.

On occasion he showed himself to be a stickler for traditional religious rules. Hence, when in January 39 a traditional oath was being administered in the senate, he prevented the Flamen Dialis (priest of Jupiter) from taking part, on the grounds that the swearing of an oath was one of the activities forbidden to that specific priest.

---

[57] The *koinon*, initially a federal association of independent Greek states, formed primarily as a military alliance, is a well-known feature of Greek history, most notably the Aetolian and Achaean leagues, which became powerful from the third century BC and played key roles during Rome's expansion through Greece. When Lucius Mummius defeated the Achaean League in 146 and ruthlessly destroyed Corinth, such leagues were abolished, but Rome later relented and allowed them to continue in modified form (Paus. 7.16.9–10). They lost their political independence, but small *koina* were allowed, mainly for cult purposes, as illustrated by this inscription.
[58] Clearly each individual state carried out sacrifices, but collaborated in presenting a festival.

6.17 Dio 59.13.1 On later becoming consul again, Gaius forbade the priest of Jupiter to take the oath in the senate (for even then they were taking the oath as in Tiberius' time), but he personally took it from the rostra, which had been enlarged, both when he entered and left office, like everybody else.

The Temple of Diana on the Alban Mount

An ancient Temple of Diana stood on the Alban mount overlooking Lake Nemi, southeast of Rome, the site of Caligula's celebrated luxury boats (see Chapter 5). The priest of Diana, the "king at Nemi," was, according to a very old tradition, a runaway slave who stayed in office until another slave came along and challenged him by plucking a twig from the sacred grove (the subject of Fraser's celebrated *The Golden Bough*). The challenger would take over as king if he killed the incumbent. Unsurprisingly the strict observance of the ritual had fallen into neglect by Caligula's day and the current office holder was very elderly. Suetonius suggests that Caligula found someone to come forward as challenger. There is no mention however of anyone suffering harm, and the procedure may have been formal and ritualistic, rather than bloody (and perhaps had always been so).

6.18 Suet. *Cal.* **35.3** As the "King of Nemi" had by now held his priesthood for many years, Caligula procured a challenger who was stronger.

Claim of Divine Recognition

One of the problems we face in trying to assess Caligula's insistence on being recognized as a god in Rome is that the great body of the evidence provided by Dio is included under the year 40. Dio also appears to suggest that the actual cult of the emperor belongs to the spring of that year, since on his return from his military expedition Caligula was annoyed with the senate for failing to vote him divine honours.

6.19 Dio 59.25.5 On entering the city, however, Gaius almost did away with the entire senate for not having voted him honours beyond the human ...

This does not necessarily mean that all the events assigned by Dio specifically to AD 40 occurred in that year. It is very possible that he found some of them in undated contexts and that he lumped them together conveniently in one place, a commonly observed practice of his. Moreover we must be very cautious in assessing what both he and Suetonius have to say on this issue. First of all, it is at variance with the material evidence. There is no surviving inscription from

Rome, Italy, or any western province that contains even the slightest hint that Caligula aspired to divine honours. In the Arval record we interestingly find that Caligula's successor, Claudius, is referred to as *divinus* when emperor and still alive (Smallwood 14.8, 24), while nowhere in that record is there any indication of Caligula claiming this status. Of course inscriptions recording divine attributes of Caligula would have been leading candidates for destruction after his death, but it is still striking that not a single one has been found in the west.

The same negative evidence is provided by the official coinage of Caligula. Coins would be an excellent tool for Caligula to demonstrate to the world how he saw himself and how he wanted to be seen. Although his official coins are highly innovative in the range of images that appear on them, they are traditional and modest in the depiction of the emperor and in the legends that describe his status, with not a single claim to worship. In particular it is noteworthy that no official Roman coin bears the image of Caligula wearing the "radiate crown." This symbol of a crown with the rays of the sun suggests divine qualities without necessarily identifying the wearer with the gods. By contrast, the emperor Nero is depicted with such a crown on his official coinage, even though he is on record as specifically refusing divine honours in Rome (Tac. *Ann.* 15.74.3).

Moreover, we are fortunate in that Philo, who headed the Jewish delegation to Caligula, and was very hostile towards him, was present in Rome in AD 40 and met the emperor there (5.48). Philo was highly sensitive about religious issues, particularly those connected with the imperial cult, and Caligula's demand that he be worshipped as Zeus in the Temple at Jerusalem horrified him. Yet he never asserts that Caligula claimed formal divine honours specifically from his fellow Romans. The same was true of Seneca, also a contemporary of Caligula in Rome and who similarly makes no explicit reference to a claim of divine honours. The elder Pliny, another contemporary of Caligula, who is scornful of him and is not reluctant to recount his outrageous behaviour, also says nothing in the *Naturalis Historia* about any such demand for divine status.

Philo takes it as a sign of madness that Caligula was in the habit of impersonating various gods, running the whole gamut from Dionysus to Apollo (Philo *Leg.* 78–113). This penchant is reflected in the passages of Suetonius and Dio below (6.20, 21). But when it came to impersonations of the divine, both Dio and Suetonius agree that he would dress as the female deities too, and Suetonius describes Caligula's impersonation of the gods in the context not of a claim for immortality but rather of a simple love of dressing up, whether as a god or as a real human like Alexander the Great. Caligula was not alone in attracting censure on this issue. Even Augustus had caused a scandal when he presided over a banquet with himself and his guests dressed in the guise of various deities—the indignation stemming not from the potential disrespect for the divine but because such frivolous activities occurred during a time of great hardship in Rome (Suet. *Aug.* 70). The story recounted by Dio of the Gallic cobbler moved to laughter at the sight of Caligula in the garb of Jupiter delivering oracles, and

Caligula's cheerful reaction, suggests that he did not take the impersonations too seriously (6.23).

6.20 (see also 5.7) Suet. *Cal.* 52.1 On many occasions he was actually sighted with a golden beard and holding either a thunderbolt, trident, or caduceus (the gods' emblems), and even dressed as Venus.

6.21 Dio 59.26.6 Then again, since he had bridged so much of the sea, he would pose as Neptune, and also as Hercules, Bacchus, Apollo, and the rest of them, and not just males but often the females as well: Juno, Diana, and Venus. In line with the name changes he would adopt all the appropriate characteristics so as to appear just like them. 7 At one time he would be looking effeminate, holding a mixing bowl and thyrsus, and at another very manly and have a club and lion's skin or helmet and shield. He could be smooth-skinned and then bearded; sometimes he carried a trident, and then he was wielding a thunderbolt. He would be dressed to look like a girl out hunting or at war, and a little later was just like a woman. 8 So by regularly changing his appearance and using make-up and wigs he could convincingly vary his parts, and he wanted to appear to be anything other than a man and an emperor.

6.22 Dio 59.26.10 This was the figure he would present whenever he made himself out to be a god, and the appropriate supplications, prayers, and sacrifices would be offered for him; and on other occasions he would appear in public in silk and in triumphal dress.

6.23 Dio 59.26.8 On one occasion a Gaul laughed when he saw him delivering oracles from a high platform dressed as Jupiter; Gaius summoned him and asked, "What do you think I am?' And he replied (I shall quote his actual words) "a complete idiot." And yet he came to no harm, for he was just a shoemaker. I suppose people of that sort can tolerate the bluntness of everyday folk more easily than what comes from people of high status.

Numen and *Genius*

Another potential area of confusion is that Romans had a way of what amounted to worshipping an emperor during his lifetime, but of doing so indirectly. This they achieved by means of two related notions. All Romans were endowed with a *genius*. This is not be confused with its modern English derivative. The Roman *genius* was an essential spirit that could be passed on from generation to generation and comprised all the qualities that our ancestors had endowed it with. To worship a human was to step beyond the borders of propriety. To worship the *genius* of a human was within the range of acceptability. The second concept is that of the *numen*, from the Latin for "nod," which signifies the power that resides in someone, especially the power associated with the gods. Hence to worship the *numen* of the emperor was to worship the divine power that resides within him. One might argue that the distinction is a very abstract one but Romans seemed happy to give lip service to it. In this context it is interesting to note that when Suetonius speaks of Caligula having a temple dedicated to himself in Rome he does not say that it was dedicated actually to *him*, but rather to his *numen*. If Suetonius is speaking precisely here, possibly deriving his information from the imperial archives, this could reflect a situation where Caligula did not step beyond the traditional boundaries, but instituted only the worship of his *numen* (or perhaps *genius*, the two tending to be used interchangeably in such contexts). This may in fact be borne out by Persius, a satirical poet a generation later than Caligula, who says that among the celebrations planned for the return of Caligula from his splendid campaigns in Germany the speaker will put on a show with a hundred pairs of gladiators in honour of the gods and of the *genius* of the commander, to mark his splendid achievements (6.24). And certainly, Caligula is said to have punished upper-class Romans for refusing to take an oath by his *genius* (6.25). This more modest cult may well have become misrepresented in the literary tradition.

Deserved or not, Caligula's reputation for demanding divine worship persisted. Aurelius Victor, writing in the fourth century, comments that Caligula and Domitian distinguished themselves as being the only emperors before Diocletian (succeeded AD 284) to insist on being addressed as a god.

6.24 Pers. *Sat.* 6.48 Accordingly, for the gods and our commander's *genius*, I am staging a hundred pairs of gladiators to honour his magnificent achievements.

6.25 (see also 6.2) Suet. *Cal.* 27.3 Many high-ranking men he condemned... because they had never taken an oath by his *genius*.

6.26 Aur. Vict. *Caes.* 39.4 For after Caligula and Domitian, Diocletian was the very first to allow himself openly to be called "master" and be worshipped and addressed as a god.

6.27 Suet. *Cal.* 22.2 However, advised that he had risen above the level of both princes and kings, he then started laying claim to divine status for himself. He gave orders for statues of gods that were known for their sanctity and outstanding artistry, that of Olympian Jupiter included, to be brought from Greece so he could take off their heads and set his own in their place;[59] and he extended a

---

[59] Pheidias' statue of Zeus at Olympia was widely admired in antiquity. Memmius, the former husband of Caligula's third wife, Lollia Paulina, and legate of Macedonia and Achaea from AD 35, was ordered in 40 to arrange its transportation to Rome, and reputedly procrastinated over the instruction (6.29; Jos. *AJ* 19.8–10). This apparent disobedience might have been expected to lead to his death but he, like many others who had flourished under Caligula, supposedly won a reprieve with the timely

section of the palace all the way to the forum.[60] He transformed the Temple of Castor and Pollux into its vestibule,[61] and to those who came there he would often present himself between the two divine brothers to be worshipped;[62] and there were some who addressed him as "Jupiter Latiaris."[63] **3** He even established a personal temple dedicated to his own divine status, with priests and the most exotic sacrificial victims. In the temple stood a lifelike golden statue of him, and every day it would be dressed in such clothing as he himself wore. All the wealthiest people would try to achieve a senior priesthood, competing for them with the highest bids.[64] The sacrificial victims to him were flamingos, peacocks, grouse, Numidian and Abyssinian guinea fowl, and pheasants, which were variously offered up by species on a daily basis.[65] **4** At night, too, he would invite the moon when it was full and shining to his embraces and his bed, but in

death of the emperor. It must be remembered, however, that after Caligula's assassination it was in the interests of his loyal lieutenants to create the myth that they had been reluctant servants pretending to follow orders while in fact undercutting those orders (see also Petronius, at 7.31).

[60] The comment about the extension of the palace is a puzzling one. Attention tends to focus on the 15,000-m² platform of the monumental structure located on the western side of the Palatine, the Domus Tiberiana. Despite its name it is highly unlikely that this was built by Tiberius. Nero is a far better candidate. At the time of Caligula it does not seem that there was a unitary structure there. Josephus comments, describing events after Caligula's assassination, that the imperial palace consisted of a conglomeration of buildings erected by the previous emperors (Jos. *AJ* 19.117). At the northern edge of the Palatine the Domus Tiberiana overlies republican houses, which appear to have been refurbished after the Tiberian period. These restored houses might represent the expansion mentioned by Suetonius. Caligula's properties would now be overlooking the forum.

[61] Suetonius, supported by Dio, seems to suggest that the palace of Caligula extended beyond the top of the Palatine and down the slope as far as the Temple of Castor and Pollux. This stood in the southeast corner of the forum; the reconstructed version, completed by Augustus in AD 6, with its high podium, is still partially standing today. Suetonius speaks of Caligula using the temple as a sort of vestibule, which could be little more than a reference to its location close to the palace. Dio goes further, suggesting a structural alteration that would have made the temple more formally part of the palace. Suetonius may have meant that Caligula inserted a passage in the rear of the building, to allow access to his residence. Some structural alteration is implied by Dio's claim that Claudius afterwards restored their Temple of Castor and Pollux (Dio 60.6.8).

[62] It is not clear what Suetonius meant by this. It might be no more than a distortion of some account of Caligula engaging in tomfoolery. But it is also possible that he placed a statue of himself in the temple's inner chamber, the *cella*. This was commonly done in ancient Rome, not with the intention that a statue would be a cult object, but simply as an offering to the temple. Tiberius, for instance, who made a point of displaying restraint, insisted that if statues of himself were deposited in a temple it should be made clear that they were to be among the accoutrements of the temple and not among the gods (Suet. *Tib.* 26.1). But that distinction was clearly not generally observed. In 54, for instance, in response to successes against Parthia, the senate voted a statue of Nero for the Temple of Mars Ultor. It was to be the same size as Mars' statue, which implies that they would stand side by side (Tac. *Ann.* 13.8.1).

[63] The cult of Jupiter Latiaris, the god of the Latin League, was an ancient one, first established on the Alban Mount. Since Suetonius goes out of his way to observe that "some people" venerated Caligula, the worship seems not to have been formal or official.

[64] Caligula saw the cult as an opportunity to raise revenues. Dio comments that it bankrupted Claudius, although he gives the entry figure as 8 million, rather than 10.

[65] It is to be noted that these birds were regularly found on the menu of exotic Roman banquets. The emperor Vitellius' speciality was a dish called the "shield of Minerva" which contained, among other dainties, the brains of pheasants and peacocks, and the tongues of flamingos (Suet. *Vit.* 13.2). Dio seems to imply that the six exotic birds were sacrificed in a six-day cycle (5.30).

daytime would hold a private conversation with Capitoline Jupiter, at one moment whispering and lending him his ear and at the next more audibly and not without belligerence. For his voice was heard uttering the threat "Lift me up, or I'll lift you!" until (so he would claim) he was won over, and then, invited to share the god's lodgings, he brought the Palatine and Capitoline together with a bridge that went over the Temple of the Deified Augustus.[66] Then, to be even closer, he not much later laid down foundations for a new house in the precinct of the Capitoline.

6.28 Suet. *Claud.* **9.2** Eventually obliged to pay eight million sestertii for entry into a new priesthood, Claudius so diminished his family resources that he could not cover what he owed the treasury, and to meet the shortfall his property was put up for sale by order of the prefects[67] under the law relating to confiscations.

6.29 Dio 59.28.2 After that he went even further and built two temples to himself right in the city of Rome, one voted to him by the senate and the other on the Palatine, built from his own resources. For he had built some sort of quarters on the Capitoline hill so he could, as he put it, live there in company with Jupiter;[68] **3** but thinking it beneath him to take second place in the cohabitation, and remonstrating with the god for taking the Capitol before him, he hurriedly erected another temple on the Palatine and wanted Olympian Zeus' statue transferred there with its appearance changed to his own. **4** But unable to manage that—for the ship built for transporting it was struck by lightning and guffaws of laughter were heard whenever people approached to touch the pedestal—he uttered threats against it and set up another one himself.

---

[66] It is to be noted that Suetonius here does not exhibit his common practice of presenting the emperor's intentions, essentially speculating on what was going on in his mind, but asserts as a fact that the Temple of Augustus lay in the low ground between the Palatine and the Capitoline. It is conceivable that Caligula constructed a causeway of some sort, resting on the roof of the Temple of Augustus. If this is so, the structure might to some degree be reflected in the Elder Pliny's strange and exaggerated statement that Rome had seen itself encircled by imperial dwellings, Nero's (the Golden House) and Caligula's (Pliny *NH* 36.111).

[67] The state treasury was located in the Temple of Saturn in the forum. In 28 BC Augustus placed it under the control of two prefects, chosen from men of praetorian rank (Suet. *Aug.* 36). Claudius later reverted to the republican system, whereby the treasury was administered by the quaestors (Suet. *Claud.* 24.2).

[68] The accounts of Caligula's temple in Rome seem very confused. Dio here suggests that there were two temples, but he is the only source to do so. Dio does provide details, asserting that one, on the Capitoline, was paid for by the senate, and the other was provided at Caligula's own expense. This is confused by his report that Caligula erected some sort of lodge on the Capitoline (is this the same as the putative temple?). Suetonius also speaks of the new accommodation on the Capitoline, suggesting that it had not progressed beyond the foundation stage. But Suetonius refers to one temple only. And if such a temple did exist it is probably best located on the Palatine, which appears in both sources and which already had a shrine to Augustus, dedicated by Livia after his death (Pliny *NH* 12.94; Suet. *Aug.* 5.1; Dio 56.46.3, this last without mention of the Palatine).

5 He split the Temple of the Dioscuri in the Roman Forum in two and between the statues made an approach to the Palatium so that he should, as he would say, have the Dioscuri as gate keepers. Calling himself "Jupiter Latiaris," he conscripted his wife Caesonia, Claudius, and the wealthiest citizens as his priests, taking 10 million sestertii from each of them for it. 6 And in addition he also made himself his own priest and declared his horse his fellow priest, and a number of dainty and very costly birds were sacrificed to him every day.

A Supposed Challenge to Jupiter

Seneca relates a challenge that Caligula made to Jupiter, inspired by the one made by Ajax to Odysseus in Homer's *Iliad* (*Il.* 23.724), when they were deadlocked in a wrestling match and Ajax called out "Lift me, or I'll lift you!" (reflecting, incidentally, Caligula's familiarity with Homer, see 5.17). This story gained much currency. There is an echo of it in the above passage of Suetonius (6.27.4). Dio relates it also, in his account of Caligula's thunder machine, a device that somehow could reciprocate when there was real thunder and lightning, adding the detail that he would hurl a spear at a rock when he made the challenge. Suetonius and Dio suggest a claim of communication with the gods. Seneca, writing an almost contemporary account, offers a more mundane narrative. When Caligula planned some open-air theatrical show in which he intended to make a personal appearance, a thunderstorm ruined the whole event, and he yelled out the familiar challenge, which turns out to be little more than a blasphemous outburst uttered in anger (or mock anger), a common enough human response to sudden bad weather ruining a special treat.

6.30 Sen. *Ira* 1.20.8 ... Gaius Caesar was angry at the sky for thundering over some pantomime performances that he was mimicking more carefully than he was watching, and also because his partying was being upset by lightning flashes (certainly far from accurate), and so he challenged Jupiter to fight, even to the end shouting out that verse of Homer: "Lift me up, or I'll lift you!" 9 What craziness that was! He must have thought either that he could not be harmed even by Jupiter or that he could actually harm Jupiter.

6.31 Dio 59.28.6 When there were thunder claps he would return them from some device that he had and to lightning flashes he would send back lightning; and whenever a thunderbolt fell he would hurl a spear at a rock, adding with each throw Homer's words "Lift me up or I'll lift you."

Further Reading

Barrett, A. A. 1998. "Caligula's Quadrans Issue." *Latomus* 57: 846–52.

Carlson, D. N. 2002. "Caligula's Floating Palaces." *Archaeology* 55: 26–31.

McGinn, T. A. J. 1998. "Caligula's Brothel on the Palatine." *EMC* 17: 95–107.

Simpson, C. 1981. "The Cult of the Emperor Gaius." *Latomus* 40: 489–511.

Simpson, C. 1996. "Caligula's Cult: Immolation, Immortality, Intent." In *Subject and Rule*, edited by A. Small, 63–71. Ann Arbor: Journal of Roman Archaeology Supplement 17.

7

Outside Rome

Although it would be misleading to talk about a Roman emperor's "foreign policy" in the modern sense of the phrase, it is reasonable to speak of each emperor putting his own distinctive stamp on the approach that Rome adopted in dealing with the issues that arose on the frontiers of its territories. Tiberius' approach had been one of restraint, reluctant as he was to extend Rome's *imperium* beyond where it had stood on his accession. Caligula was far less predictable, far more expansionist, seemingly far more reckless, and in several areas on the fringe of the Roman world we witness quite dramatic events. Unsurprisingly, at times it is difficult to understand what he was trying to achieve. As a general principle, activities in the frontier areas tended in all periods to be much misunderstood by the literary sources, who had their focus very much on goings on in Rome and Italy. When the centre of gravity moved temporarily into the hinterland they more often than not found themselves in very alien territory and their narratives can become particularly confused and unreliable.

Parthia

In the east serious problems arose at the very outset of the reign, during Caligula's stable "honeymoon" period, and there we can observe a careful and thoughtful response to the unfolding challenges. The arrangements skilfully put together by Caligula's father Germanicus nearly twenty years previously, which saw the agreement of Parthia to the installation of a pro-Roman king, Zeno, in Armenia, were seriously unravelling. By AD 37 it was fully anticipated that Artabanus, king of Parthia, would launch an invasion of Syria. Happily, that province was governed by a decisive and competent legate, Lucius Vitellius, who quickly moved his troops up to the Euphrates. His enterprising action applied enough pressure to give Artabanus second thoughts, and peace talks were arranged in neutral territory, in a pavilion in the centre of the river. The details of the agreement that they reached are now lost, but Artabanus seems to have yielded, even surrendering his son Darius as hostage (Darius was present when Caligula later rode over his bridge on the bay of Naples, probably in AD 39 [4.40]). Caligula cannot in any meaningful way take full or even major credit for this diplomatic coup, since Tiberius was still alive during the initial stages of the crisis. But it was said that while Artabanus despised Tiberius he (like almost everyone else, it sometimes seems) felt

The Emperor Caligula in the Ancient Sources. Anthony A. Barrett and J. C. Yardley, Oxford University Press.
© Anthony A. Barrett and J. C. Yardley 2023. DOI: 10.1093/oso/9780198854562.003.0008

considerable affection for Caligula's father Germanicus. This may well have at least encouraged him to place his faith in an arrangement with his son, the new emperor. At the very least Caligula showed himself willing to heed Vitellius, the commander on the spot, and to confirm his settlements. In the event the agreement proved to be short-lived, but even at the very best of times stability was rarely a feature of Rome's eastern frontier.

7.1 Jos. *AJ* 18.101 On hearing this Tiberius felt he should have a treaty with Artabanus. When Artabanus gladly accepted the invitation to discuss the matter, he and Vitellius proceeded to the Euphrates. **102** The river was bridged, and they each came to the meeting at the middle of the bridge with their guards around them. Since their discussions were tending towards agreement, the tetrarch put on a feast for them, erecting a very costly pavilion at midpoint.[1] **103** Artabanus sent his son to Tiberius as a hostage, together with many gifts, including a 7-cubit Jewish man called Eleazorus.[2] Because of his size he was known as "The Giant."

7.2 Suet. *Cal.* 14.3 In addition to his own people's deep love for Caligula there was also remarkable affection shown by foreigners.[3] For the Parthian king Artabanus, who always made clear his hatred and contempt for Tiberius,[4] actually sought Caligula's friendship and came to a meeting with his consular legate,[5] after which he crossed the Euphrates and paid homage to the Roman eagles and standards, and to the death masks of the Caesars.[6]

7.3 Dio 59.27.2 Now Lucius Vitellius was neither low-born nor unintelligent but a man who actually had a good reputation from his administration of Syria.

---

[1] The tetrarch mentioned here is one of Herod the Great's sons, Herod Antipas, reputedly called a "fox" by Christ (Luke 13:32). He had been bequeathed the tetrarchy (the term used for the divisions of Herod's kingdom) of Galilee and Peraea by his father, which was confirmed by Augustus. He was brought up in Rome, and was a good friend of Tiberius. When Antipas fell in love with Herodias, sister of Herod Agrippa, he divorced his wife, who fled to her father, King Aretas of Nabataea, this leading to clashes between Antipas and Aretas. Tiberius instructed Vitellius to go to the assistance of his old friend Antipas, but on Tiberius' death Vitellius broke off his preparations (3.21). Antipas seems to have tried to score a diplomatic coup by acting as mediator between Vitellius and the Parthian king Artabanus, and he stole some of Vitellius' thunder by being the first to report the news of the settlement to Caligula. Ultimately Antipas came to an unhappy end. He was banished and his kingdom awarded to Herod Agrippa.

[2] Lazarus. Seven cubits would be about 10 ft 6 in. (3.2 m).

[3] The reference to Caligula's popularity may seem surprising: Suetonius had just described the great outpouring of emotion when he fell ill early in his reign (3.53–5).

[4] Tiberius had in fact supported the cause of Tiridates III, who succeeded in briefly replacing Artabanus as king of Parthia (AD 35–6).

[5] The expression can be confusing. Vitellius had consular rank since he held the office of consul in AD 34 (he would go on to hold the office twice again, under Claudius), but in Syria he would have served at the lower rank of praetor (as propraetor, rather than proconsul), as did other provincial legates, so as not to rival the consular authority of his commander, the emperor.

[6] Josephus has the two meet in the centre of the river, Suetonius makes Artabanus' submission more total by having him cross into Roman territory and do homage to the Roman standards, echoed in Dio's account.

Apart from his other brilliant achievements 3 he also stole a march on Artabanus when he planned an assault on the province after receiving no retribution for his actions in Armenia.[7] Vitellius caught him off-guard when he encountered him close to the Euphrates and then drew him into negotiations and made him offer sacrifice to the statues of Augustus and Gaius, while also granting him a peace on terms favourable to the Romans and taking his sons as hostages.

Africa and Mauretania

In Africa too we find what seems a commendable approach to the problems that Rome faced. The core of the Roman province of Africa lay in what is today Tunisia. The original province (Africa Vetus, "Old Africa"), conquered in the second century BC, was joined by Augustus to Africa Nova ("New Africa"), essentially the old kingdom of Numidia, to form Africa Consularis, one of the most prosperous regions of the empire. This new province was anomalous from the start, since it was governed by a proconsul selected by the senate (considered a highly desirable appointment) but because of the constant military threat from the south, stemming to a large degree from the displacement of settlers by newly arrived immigrants, Africa housed a legion (Legio III), which fell under the command of the senatorial proconsul rather than of the usual imperially appointed legate. This was not a unique arrangement under Augustus, but only in Africa did it continue after his death.

The anomaly was removed by Caligula, and seemingly for good reasons. Senatorial control of both a legion and a rich province represented a potential threat to imperial authority, and there was also a need for proper coordination of the military campaign to be conducted to the west, in Mauretania (see later in this section). The change that Caligula instituted, placing the army under an imperial legate, was a rational one, although it did not solve the problem entirely. The absence of a clear dividing line between the responsibilities of the senatorial proconsul and those of the imperial legate was bound to lead to confusion. Eventually, at the end of the second century AD, the emperor Septimius Severus detached the sensitive military zone from the province of Africa and created a distinct imperial province of Numidia.

The two surviving accounts of Caligula's reorganization illustrate very well the challenges presented by the source material for the period (see Chapter 1, section "The Problem"). Tacitus makes the plausible case that Caligula had been afraid of

---

[7] Something of an exaggeration. Artabanus attempted in AD 35 to impose his son on Armenia and, faced with both Roman and internal opposition, was forced to flee Parthia for a time, eventually regaining control.

Marcus Junius Silanus, the proconsul of Africa, and had therefore removed the command of the legion from him. Silanus was a member of a powerful aristocratic family and had married Aemilia Lepida, granddaughter of Augustus. Dio on the other hand suggests that, from similar fears, Caligula removed Lucius Piso, the son of Calpurnius Piso, the former governor of Syria and arch-nemesis of Caligula's father Germanicus. A good case can be made for either candidate and it is virtually impossible to resolve the issue.

7.4 (see also 5.10) Tac. *Hist.* 4.48 The legion in Africa and the auxiliary forces stationed there for the defence of borders of the empire were commanded by a proconsul when the emperors were Augustus and Tiberius. Later Gaius Caesar, who was unsound of mind and fearful of Marcus Silanus when he was governor of Africa, removed the legion from the proconsul and transferred it to a legate sent out specifically for that post. The number of appointments was then divided between the two, and through some confusion over their responsibilities, quarrelling broke out and was increased through perverse rivalry. The legates' power grew because of the length of their term, or perhaps because the lesser the rank the greater the competition; all the most illustrious proconsuls were more concerned about their safety than their power.

7.5 Dio 59.20.7 When Lucius Piso, son of Plancina and Gnaeus Piso, was allotted the governorship of Africa,[8] Caligula feared that Lucius might through his arrogance be led to revolt, especially since he was to have a powerful force of both citizens and allies; and, splitting the region in two, he gave someone else command of the military and the neighbouring nomadic tribes; and since then this arrangement has lasted until today.

During the Caligulan period the main focus of Roman attention in this part of the world lay to the west of the province of Africa, the huge region of Mauretania, comprising very roughly modern Morocco and western Algeria. From 25 BC it had been ruled under Augustus and Tiberius by Juba II, who had been king of Numidia until its annexation by Rome under Augustus, after which Juba was recognized as king of Mauretania. He had been heavily dependent on Roman assistance in suppressing rebellious elements among his own people. His son, Ptolemy, born to Juba and Cleopatra Selene, daughter of Mark Antony, was thus related to Caligula, grandson of another of Antony's daughters, Antonia. Ptolemy succeeded his father in Mauretania in AD 23, and seems also to have met with little success in dealing with the unrest. Tacitus says that he "ruled with a young man's negligence," but all the same, in AD 24, in a show of solidarity, he was honoured by

---

[8] Governors of public (senatorial) provinces were chosen by lot, but the process was less arbitrary than might seem to be the case, since only the suitable candidates were included in the selection process.

a senatorial delegation from Rome, which awarded him a triumphal toga and ivory sceptre.[9] Ptolemy at that point drops out of the record for a while, and his re-entry during the reign of Caligula is extraordinary. What went on between him and the emperor is clothed in obscurity and presented by the sources in terms very hostile to the emperor.

Under AD 40 we have a fragmentary statement in Dio's account that Ptolemy was put to death by Caligula, and at that point Dio's manuscript frustratingly breaks off. Other sources provide further cryptic details. Suetonius says that Caligula executed Ptolemy because he was offended when Ptolemy wore a splendid cloak to enter a gladiatorial show. Seneca claims to have seen him in prison before execution. This all seems to suggest that Ptolemy was summoned to Rome in early 40, met Caligula on the latter's return from his northern campaign, then was imprisoned and executed. It is almost impossible to disentangle the truth from the fragments of evidence. The fine cloak might suggest that after Caligula had decided to incorporate Ptolemy's kingdom he had lured him to Rome under false pretences, perhaps the promise of new honours. But even if Ptolemy was to lose his kingdom it is surprising that he was put to death and not allowed the usual fate of former client kings on dismissal, a comfortable exile. We cannot rule out the possibility that he had somehow been drawn into the political intrigue associated with Caligula's northern campaign (see Chapter 4) and had to pay the price.

The incorporation of Mauretania into the empire, perhaps inevitable given Ptolemy's lax rule and the constant threat to the stability of the province of Africa, proved to be a long and bloody business. There is archaeological evidence for destruction in towns like Volubilis, Lixus, and Tamuda. Ultimately the old kingdom became two separate provinces, Mauretania Tingitana and Mauretania Caesariensis, with the River Malua separating them. There is much uncertainty about when it was actually incorporated into the empire. The initial policy was clearly Caligula's, but the final implementation of that policy may have awaited his successor Claudius' reign. The first recorded governor of Mauretania, Marcus Fadius Celer Flavianus, did not take office until AD 44 (Smallwood 407a), three years after Caligula's death.

7.6 Dio 59.25.1 While they were doing this, Gaius meanwhile (sc. early AD 40) sent for Juba's son Ptolemy, and learning that he was rich he executed him, and... (manuscript breaks off)

7.7 Suet. *Cal.* 35.1 He had Ptolemy, whom I mentioned earlier, come from his kingdom, and after welcoming him with honour he suddenly executed him for no other reason than that when Caligula was putting on a show Ptolemy had attracted people's attention by coming into the performance in a splendid purple cloak.

[9] Tac. *Ann.* 4.23.1, 26.3.

7.8 Sen. *Tranq.* **11.12** King Ptolemy of Africa and the Armenian king Mithridates we saw in Gaius' hands...

7.9 Pliny *NH* **5..11** Roman weapons were first employed in Mauretania during Claudius' principate, when the freedman Aedemon was out to avenge King Ptolemy's death at the hands of Gaius Caesar.[10]

Aedemon's Rebellion

An inscription from Volubilis (near modern Meknes) confirms Pliny's assertion that the resistance to Rome was led by Aedemon (these are the only surviving references to him) and reveals that Aedemon did not enjoy the undivided loyalty of the populace in his struggle against his Roman enemy. The inscription takes the form of a dedication made to Marcus Valerius Severus, the son of Bostar (that name is Latinized, representing Punic Bodastart or Bod'star) by his wife Fabia Bira, daughter of Izelta. Marcus was a *sufes* (a Punic term for an official) and *duovir*, perhaps similar to a *sufes*, and became first priest in the imperial cult, presumably of Claudius. He commanded the auxiliary forces in the war against Aedemon. Volubilis benefited from his service, since the inscription goes on to say that Marcus was part of a delegation sent to the deified Claudius ("deified" some time after this event, of course) and obtained Roman citizenship and other rights for the city.

7.10 Inscription, Volublilis, after AD 54 (Smallwood 407b)

To Marcus Valerius Severus, son of Bostar, of the tribe Galeria, aedile, suffete, duumvir, senior flamen in his town, prefect of auxiliaries against Aedemon,[11] who was defeated in war...

Client Kings

Ptolemy's treatment cannot be taken to reflect Caligula's general policy towards client kings, as we can see from the brief references to other rulers. Caligula was clearly determined to put Roman interests first, and those kings who had not served Rome well, or whose continued rule did not suit Rome's larger strategy, were removed. But they were not normally put to death. Mithridates, of the kingdom of Iberia (in modern Georgia), had been installed as king of Armenia under Tiberius. He was removed from his kingdom by Caligula, possibly as a consequence of the negotiations between Vitellius and Artabanus. He was then

---

[10]   Ptolemy clearly commanded considerable loyalty, as the action of Aedemon reveals.
[11]   Marcus commanded a unit of auxiliaries, non-citizen troops normally of either five hundred or a thousand men, probably recruited locally.

imprisoned in Rome, but his treatment was quite different from Ptolemy's, and he was in fact restored to his kingdom after Caligula's death.

Also, on the death of Antiochus III of Commagene in AD 17, Antiochus' kingdom had been incorporated into the Roman empire,[12] the process overseen by Germanicus. Suetonius and Dio tell us that Caligula restored the kingdom to his son, Antiochus IV, with an enlargement of territory to include the coastal zone of Cilicia, along with a repayment of the revenues that had accrued (7.12, 13). Caligula and Antiochus were on very close terms, and the latter was identified, along with Herod Agrippa, as one of the emperor's "tyrant-teachers" (7.11). Dio is the only source to give Claudius the credit for restoring Antiochus' kingdom, explaining that Caligula had in fact taken the kingdom back, without explaining why (7.15). Dio might have got things confused. Antiochus may have been technically dismissed in AD 41 with the cancellation of Caligula's acts after his death, and he would need to be formally restored by Claudius. A nice illustration of the constant difficulty of understanding the events of Caligula's reign.

7.11 Dio 59.24.1 And they were especially worried because they learned that both kings were with him—Agrippa as well as Antiochus—like some trainers of tyrants.

7.12 Dio 59.8.2 For to Antiochus son of Antiochus he gave Commagene, which his father had ruled, together with the coastal area of Cilicia . . .

7.13 Suet. *Cal.* 16.3 To any kings to whom he restored kingdoms he also granted any tax income and revenue accruing in the intervening period (like the hundred million sestertii in the treasury for Antiochus of Commagene).

7.14 Tac. *Ann.* 11.8.1 I noted above how Mithridates became king of Armenia and was later imprisoned on the orders of Gaius Caesar. Now at about this time, on Claudius' advice and relying on the support of Pharasmanes, the king returned to his kingdom.[13]

7.15 Dio 60.8.1 After that Claudius restored Commagene to Antiochus (for although Gaius had himself given it to him, he had then taken it back), and Mithridates—the Iberian that Gaius had sent for and then imprisoned—he sent home to take up his throne again.

Britain and Germany

To the Romans, Germany was a wild and untamed place. Britain was even more remote, a distant and almost mythical island located in the Oceanus that

---

[12] Tac. *Ann.* 2.42.

[13] Phrarasmenes was king of Iberia, brother of Mithridates. There was a later falling out between the brothers, and Pharasmenes supported the claim of Rhadamistus to Armenia.

surrounded the settled world. It was seen as the last inhabited outpost of the west and its conquest, hesitantly attempted by Julius Caesar and routinely anticipated under Augustus, was symbolically interpreted as the extension of Rome's *imperium* to the utter western limits. The military exploits initiated by Caligula in late 39 illustrate perfectly the dark confusion that tends to prevail in the sources when we move away from events in Rome and Italy. Those sources clearly had no understanding of his intentions, and his campaigns are presented both as a frivolous last-minute enterprise decided on the spur of the moment and yet at the same time as a major undertaking with serious and sustained recruitment of troops to raise the new legions that would be required. This last thesis is probably the most persuasive and indeed it has long been argued from epigraphic evidence that two new legions, XV Primigenia and XXII Primigenia, were raised and stationed in Germany to replace those used intended for the planned invasion of Britain, a project eventually brought to fruition by Claudius in AD 43.

Moreover, there were sound strategic reasons for undertaking an expedition against Britain at this time. Its southern coast was in the process of falling to tribes that were hostile to Rome. Certainly by the time of the Claudian invasion of 43 much of the territory south of the Thames had been occupied by two rulers, the brothers Togodumnus and Caratacus, fiercely nationalistic and fiercely hostile to the Romans. Ancestral links between the various tribes of Gaul and Britain were very strong, and there was a clear risk of trouble being fermented in Gaul if enemies of Rome took power on the other side of the Channel.

In the literary sources Caligula's enterprise appears to be directed against both Britain and Germany. But it is highly unlikely that there could have been a serious intent at this time to launch a major invasion of Germany with the aim of permanently extending Roman power far beyond the Rhine—the disaster of Quinctilius Varus in the Teutoberg Forest in AD 9, and the near disasters experienced during Germanicus' campaigns, would have discouraged any such venture against the fearful Germanic tribes. Tacitus certainly implies that Caligula's main thrust was the conquest of Britain (7.16). But, as Tacitus further suggests, any planned invasion of Britain would have to be preceded by a strengthening of the insecure Rhine frontier. This would be crucial, in order to prevent the legions transported to the island being cut off from their supply lines. Caligula's most prudent policy on the Rhine would have been to make an aggressive show of strength along the river, without committing himself to a major operation. The political aspects of the situation in the German military zones are discussed elsewhere (see Chapter 4) but it can be noted that the lax commander, Gaetulicus, was replaced by the energetic and capable Servius Sulpicius Galba, who was able eventually to restore discipline. His initial priority would presumably have been to put an end to the frequent incursions over the frontier into Gaul.

Both Suetonius and Dio are highly critical of Caligula's northern campaign, but a problem far more serious than mere bias is that they clearly had no proper understanding of what occurred, and their accounts are confused, even incoherent. In the case of Dio the problem is aggravated by the loss of a considerable portion of his text right in the middle of his narrative of the campaign, and this loss has to be made good by recourse to the Byzantine epitomes (see Introduction, section "Literary Sources: Cassius Dio"). According to Dio, Caligula left Italy in AD 39; he went first to a suburb then set out with a motley gang of attendants, and "on arrival" progressed a short distance beyond the Rhine, then went to the coast, with a pretence of invading Britain, then somehow we are in Gaul, where Caligula engages in inflicting various torments on the citizens. Frustratingly, it is at this point, at the end of 39, that the manuscript breaks off, obliging us to turn to the epitomes. We are now back at the Channel, where bizarre things occur and we next find Caligula in Rome (we have, of course, only summaries of the text). This account, with Caligula on the Channel in both AD 39 and 40, is chaotic at best. Suetonius is barely more helpful. He never mentions Gaul, which looms large in Dio's account, and he *appears* to place the surrender of the British prince Adminius before the activities on the Channel, although strictly speaking while he mentions this surrender first as the only achievement of the whole campaign, he does not actually specify that it *happened* first.

A rational sequence of events might be that Caligula left Italy in late 39 and proceeded to Gaul, where he spent the winter, while Galba beefed up discipline in the Rhine legions. Caligula could then have proceeded to the Rhine early in AD 40, and taken part in minor actions intended to convince the Germans of a strong Roman presence on the Rhine. He could then have gone on to the Channel to receive the submission of Adminius. The insecure state of the Rhine defences probably precluded any real military undertaking against Britain—in fact actions by Galba aimed at subduing the Germans continued for two years after Caligula's death in AD 41 down to Claudius' successful invasion of Britain in AD 43, and Tacitus suggests that the lack of progress on the German frontier was a key element in Caligula's decision not to proceed with the British invasion. Adminius' surrender could have provided a nice diplomatic cover for abandoning the full-scale invasion, and that surrender could be presented as a major victory over the Britons. When it came to his victory celebrations, however, the emphasis seems to be on Caligula's victories in Germany rather than Britain. It may be that Caligula set out with the intention of invading Britain, and when that ambition was decisively thwarted he boosted his achievements in Germany as a kind of diplomatic compensation. That of course is speculative, but most of what we can say about the northern campaign is essentially speculative. Caligula's contemporaries seem to have had huge difficulty grasping exactly what his strategies were—it is hardly surprising, then, that we are so much in the dark about them today.

7.16 (see also 5.9) Tac. Ag. 13.2 It is beyond question that Gaius Caesar envisaged an invasion of Britain, but being temperamentally unstable he was quick to change his mind, and his massive incursions into Germany had not worked out as planned.

7.17 Suet. *Galb.* 6.2 Galba was appointed legate of Upper Germany by Gaius Caesar in place of Gaetulicus, and the day after he reached the legions he suppressed their applause at a traditional festival that happened to be taking place, circulating an order for them to "keep hands under cloaks"; and this was immediately bandied about the camp: "Learn to be a soldier, soldiers; this is Galba, not Gaetulicus."

3 With similar stringency he refused leave applications. The veteran and the fresh recruit he toughened up with constant work; he soon checked the barbarians who had already even forced their way into Gaul, and when Gaius was also there he earned such approval both for himself and the army that of the countless troops brought together from all the provinces none earned greater commendation or more prizes; and he personally won great distinction because while supervising military exercises carrying his shield he even ran alongside the emperor's chariot for 20 miles.

7.18 Suet. *Cal.* 43 Of war and military matters he had only one taste, and that not intentional; after setting off for Mevania to visit its grove and the River Clitumnus and being reminded about augmenting the number of the Batavian troops that he used to keep around him,[14] he had a sudden impulse to launch an attack on Germany.[15] He did not delay either, but marshalling legions and auxiliary forces from all around, with troop levies held everywhere in the strictest manner, and amassing all kinds of supplies as never before, he set out on the march in such a prompt and speedy manner that the praetorian cohorts were, contrary to custom, forced to put the standards on pack animals and keep up with him like that;[16] but sometimes he did it in such a lethargic and dainty fashion that he would be carried on an eight-man litter and demand that the roads be swept for him by people from neighbouring towns and sprinkled because of the dust.

44.1 After he reached the camp,[17] to show himself a keen and exacting leader,[18] he dismissed in disgrace any legates who had been somewhat late in bringing

---

[14] Augustus was the first to recruit German bodyguards, specifically from Batavia (located in the Rhine and Meuse deltas, now part of the Netherlands). They constituted a unit quite separate from the Praetorian guard.

[15] The notion of invading Germany on a "sudden impulse" is inherently absurd, and totally contradicted by the massive preparations described in the next sentence. Suetonius here mentions only Germany, and ignores Britain, possibly because of the preceding reference to the Batavians.

[16] Although an elite element of Rome military forces, the Praetorians were reportedly somewhat enervated by their service in Rome. When Otho decided to use the Praetorians in his bid to become emperor in early 69 they found it hard to march long distances over mountains and grumbled about the discipline and the meagre supplies (Tac. *Hist.* 1.23.2).

[17] Confusingly Suetonius provides no information on where this camp may be located. The legionary base at Mainz, the military headquarters of Upper Germany, is a good candidate.

[18] In fact the strict discipline was imposed by Galba, Gaetulicus' replacement, who did his work effectively, and the soldiers themselves noted the difference between his professionalism and that of his predecessor, a change which Suetonius in a different context admires (7.17).

auxiliaries from various locations; and on reviewing the army he cashiered several senior centurions who were already well on in years, some of them even only very few days before their time was up, and contrary to normal practice making age and frailty the excuse in each case; and then, berating the others for their greed, he cut back emoluments for completed service to 6,000 sestertii.

2 But he achieved no more than receiving the surrender of Adminius, son of Cunobelinus, king of the Britons, who, after being driven out by his father had fled with a tiny force and submitted to him. Caligula, however, as if the entire island had surrendered,[19] sent a pompous letter to Rome, ordering couriers to head straight for the forum and the curia and deliver it only to the consuls in the Temple of Mars, and before a plenary senate.[20]

45.1 Shortly afterwards,[21] having inadequate forces for a war,[22] he ordered a few Germans from his bodyguard[23] to be ferried over the river and hidden there and a report to be brought to him in confusion after lunch that the enemy was at hand. When that was done, he charged out to a nearby wood with his entourage and a number of praetorian cavalry, cut down some trees, decorated them like trophies, and then returned by torchlight—and those who had not gone with him he rebuked for their fear and cowardice, while bestowing on his companions who participated in the "victory" crowns of an extraordinary kind, termed "exploratory crowns," decorated with representations of the sun, moon and stars.[24] **2** On another occasion a number of hostages were removed from an

---

[19] Cunobelinus (barely recognizable as Shakespeare's Cymbeline) is the most famous of the British kings of the Roman period, although not, as Suetonius seems to suggest, king of *all* the Britons. Initially anti-Roman he may later have sought some sort of rapprochement with Augustus, to judge from the large quantities of Roman goods imported into his kingdom. Under Tiberius, Cunobelinus seems to have become aggressive again, and to have encroached on the pro-Roman tribes south of the Thames.

Adminius has been identified with a ruler minting coins in Kent with the coin legends A, AM, or AMMINUS. Pro-Roman, he may have been restored to his kingdom later by Claudius. Suetonius does not specifically associate Adminius with Caligula's activities at the Channel, but Orosius (*Pag.* 7.5.5), writing almost two centuries later, says that Caligula went to the Channel after Gaul and Germany and received the surrender of the son of Cunebolinus, returning then to Rome because military deficiencies made an invasion unfeasible.

[20] Suetonius makes a distinction here between the forum and the senate house. The latter was located in the old Forum Romanum, while the Temple of Mars Ultor ("the avenger") was built by Augustus in 2 BC as the showpiece of the quite separate great forum he constructed and which carried his name, the Forum Augustum. Augustus decreed that the senate should convene there to consider the claims made by victorious generals for Triumphs (Suet. *Aug.* 29.2).

[21] The transition that Suetonius makes here (Latin *mox*) is confusing. The two incidents can hardly have happened in sequence.

[22] Suetonius' text is ambiguous. He may be saying that Caligula was denied the opportunity for a proper war.

[23] Suetonius describes the Germans as *ex custodia*, either from his bodyguard or from the prisoners being held under guard. The latter seems unlikely, given that Suetonius suggests that no campaign had taken place, but his account is admittedly very confused here.

[24] The description of the crowns as "exploratory" is baffling, but Suetonius does emphasize that they were novel. The Latin word *exploratoriae* is otherwise used only once before, by the military writer Vegetius, where he applies it (4.37) to spy ships, painted the colour of the sea; a similar notion suits activity by Caligula intended mainly to control and pacify a frontier rather than to engage in full-fledged conquest.

elementary school and furtively sent ahead of him, at which he suddenly quit a banquet, chased them with his cavalry as if they were prisoners on the run, and on catching them brought them back in irons, a charade again revealing behaviour beyond the pale. When on his return to the meal some men declared that the troops were assembled he told them to take their seats just as they were, in their cuirasses; and with Vergil's famous line he also told them to "hold out and save themselves for better days."[25]

46.1 Eventually, as if intending to end war, he deployed a battle line on the sea shore with ballistas and other artillery laid out, and when no one had any idea what he was going to do he suddenly gave the order for them to pick up shells and fill their helmets and the folds of their tunics—"spoils of the Ocean," he called them, "owed to the Capitol and the Palatine"[26]—and to commemorate his victory he constructed a high tower from which fires would flash forth to guide ships on their course at night like the Pharos;[27] and announcing a donative of 100 denarii for each of the men, he said—as if he had surpassed every instance of generosity—"Leave happy, leave rich."[28]

47.1 After that,[29] he turned to arranging his Triumph; and in addition to barbarian captives and deserters he also chose all the tallest Gauls and (as he put it himself) those "triumph-worthy," along with a number of their chieftains, and set them aside for his procession. He forced them not only to dye their hair red and grow it long but also to learn the German language and take barbarian names. Furthermore, he ordered the triremes with which he had embarked on the Ocean to be transported to Rome, mostly overland;[30] and he also sent his procurators written instructions to organize his Triumph at the lowest possible

[25] From Verg. *Aen.* 1.207, Aeneas attempting to rouse the spirits of his men after they had been battered in a storm conjured up by Juno. Elsewhere (5.17) Suetonius claims that Caligula wanted to ban Vergil from the libraries.

[26] The incident of the shells is one of the most celebrated events of Caligula's reign and has inspired a wide range of explanations, that Caligula intended to humiliate the soldiers, that the shells were to be used as missiles, that the "shells" were in reality tents or boats. In fact they should not occasion surprise. It was the custom for generals to display spoils from defeated lands in the grand display of the Triumph, to be dedicated as an offering on the Capitoline. The shells could be seen as plunder from Oceanus, hence highly appropriate tribute, since the conquest of Britain was commonly depicted as the conquest of Oceanus.

[27] The Pharos was the famous lighthouse of Alexandria, one of the traditional wonders of the ancient world. The lighthouse built by Caligula at Boulogne, to assist with the invasion of Britain, was still standing in the sixteenth century, known as the Old Man (a corruption of the Celtic Alt Maen ["high stone"]), a polygonal pyramid over 35 metres high (the original Caligulan structure had no doubt been enhanced by Claudius and others).

[28] 100 denarii (400 sestertii) is a low figure when compared to the large donatives made to the praetorians on Caligula's accession (3.17). Germanicus gave regular legionaries 600 denarii each for not mutinying (Tac. *Ann.* 1.36.3; Dio 57.5.3). But of course the soldiers at the Channel had not in reality engaged in military combat.

[29] "After that" is vague. Suetonius seems to suggest that the Triumph was to be connected with the activities at the Channel.

[30] These have not been mentioned by Suetonius, although a brief sortie on board a ship is mentioned later (7.20).

cost but on a hitherto unprecedented scale, since they had jurisdiction over everybody's property!

7.19 Dio 59.21.1 By now Caligula had already spent virtually all the money there was in Rome and the rest of Italy, wherever it came from and whatever he had to do to get it. Then, when there was now no substantial amount to be found there or any practical way of gathering it, and his expenses were becoming oppressive, **2** he set off for Gaul with a pretext of taking some action against the hostile Celts that were on the warpath (though really it was to squeeze money out them—abounding in wealth as they were—and also out of the Spaniards).[31] He gave no immediate forewarning of his campaign, however, but instead went off to some suburb[32] and suddenly set off from there, bringing along with him numerous dancers and numerous gladiators, horses, women, and all sorts of other luxurious appurtenances.

3 On arriving[33] he inflicted damage on none of the enemy; for after advancing a little beyond the Rhine he immediately turned back, then proceeded as if to launch a campaign against Britain, but withdrew right at the sea's edge and was very angry with his legates, who had achieved hardly any success at all—but it was on his subjects, his allies, and his citizens that he inflicted the most and the heaviest punishments. **4** For on the one hand he would fleece those who had anything, using any pretext to do so; and on the other there would be private citizens and cities bringing him huge gifts—"willingly," of course. Some he put to death claiming that they were rebelling against him, others that they were plotting against him. In fact the charge against everyone was the same, namely, being rich. **5** By personally hawking off their possessions he even raised far more cash from this process—for everybody was forced to buy them no matter what, and at a far higher price than they were worth, as I have explained. He therefore sent for and auctioned off the monarchy's finest and most treasured heirlooms, selling the reputation of those who had once used them along with the articles themselves. **6** So on each item he would add a comment like "this was my father's," "this was my mother's," "this was my grandfather's," "this was my great-grandfather's," and "Antony owned this Egyptian item—it was Augustus' victory prize!" While doing this he would also point out (so no one else could keep pleading poverty) why he had to sell them, and along with each article he sold them its reputation.

[31] The reference to the Spaniards here is totally bewildering and symptomatic of the chaotic nature of Dio's account of the campaign.

[32] Dio's suggestion that Caligula went to a "suburb" is perhaps a misunderstanding of his source; Suetonius' precise and detailed allusion to Mevania is far more convincing.

[33] A good example of how confused Dio's narrative is. He does not say where Caligula arrived but seems to place the German campaign immediately after the arrival, then his account seems to morph somehow into Caligula's presence in Gaul.

22.1 He failed to build a surplus, however, but still maintained his usual sort of expenditures—putting on some games at Lugdunum, for example—but especially on the legions; **2** for he mustered 200,000 soldiers or, as some have it, 250,000.[34] And he was acclaimed emperor by them on seven occasions, or so he thought, despite having never won a battle or killed an enemy.

7.20 Dio 59.25.1 (in the epitome of Xiphilinus, following a gap in the text) When he reached the ocean it looked as if he was about to embark on a campaign in Britain, and he had his soldiers all prepared in battle order on the shore, **2** whereupon he stepped aboard a trireme and after setting out only a short distance from shore sailed back again.[35]

After that he ensconced himself on an elevated dais, and giving the soldiers the signal for battle and urging them on with his trumpeters he then suddenly ordered them to gather sea shells! **3** On taking this "plunder" (for clearly he needed these spoils of war for his triumphal procession) he was very pleased with himself, as if he had mastered the entire ocean, and he lavished donatives on the soldiers. He took the shells back to Rome with him to show the plunder to people there as well.

4 The senate had no idea either how to handle this, having come to realize how conceited he was, or how to offer him praise; for if one heaps great praise on a "courageous feat" that is of little or no account he is suspected of ridiculing or deriding it. **5** In any case, on entering the city he was on the verge of wiping out the entire senate for not having voted him honours beyond the human. Assembling the people, however, from a point high above he threw large amounts of silver and gold down on them, and many died trying to grab it; he is said by some to have mixed bits of iron in with it.

5a Because of his adulterous behaviour, after "subduing" all Germany and Britain, he was frequently hailed as Imperator, and also as Germanicus and Britannicus.[36]

7.21 Pers. *Sat.* 6.43-7 A laurel sprig has been sent from Caesar for his defeat of Germany's young men, and the cold ashes are being shaken off the altars; and now Caesonia is putting out contracts for arms to be set over the gates, for royal cloaks, for yellow woollen cloaks for the captives, and for chariots and huge effigies of the Rhine.

---

[34] The huge numbers given here, even allowing for exaggeration, are in stark contrast to the claims that the northern campaign was a frivolous venture, undertaken on the spur of the moment.

[35] If Caligula was engaged at this point in receiving the submission of Adminius, he may have staged a submission at sea. Had Adminius landed first in Gaul before meeting the emperor, it would perhaps have suggested that he arrived as a defeated fugitive.

[36] Caligula inherited the cognomen Germanicus from his father. There is no evidence that he claimed the cognomen of Britannicus. The assertion may have arisen from a witticism centring on the ambiguity of the word "subdue" in both the military and sexual sense.

The Jewish World

One broad sphere outside of Italy where an unambiguous deterioration is evident during Caligula's reign is in Rome's relations with the Jews. The issues were complex, involving two different Jewish communities, those who lived in the original area of Jewish settlement, broadly Judaea, and the Jews of the diaspora, especially the Jews residing in the Egyptian city of Alexandria, where they lived in awkward proximity to the dominant Greek population. It would probably be unfair to brand Caligula as overtly antisemitic. He had excellent relations with individual Jewish leaders, most notably Herod Agrippa, and his behaviour towards the Jews was probably no more cavalier than towards other groups. But the particular nationalistic and religious sentiments of the Jews required a deft diplomatic touch, and this he was sorely lacking.

Herod Agrippa

The account of the treatment of Herod Agrippa after Caligula's succession illustrates well the extent to which we are at the mercy of whatever sources are available. Caligula's major expedition to the north, and his extensive operations in Africa cannot be properly understood because of the fragmentary and often contradictory information available to us. But because of Josephus' interest in the career of Agrippa we are told with considerable precision how Agrippa was appointed king of much of the realm of his grandfather Herod the Great, and are even informed of the individual districts which he came to rule.

> 7.22 Jos. *Ant.* 18.237 Not many days later, however,[37] Caligula invited Herod Agrippa to his house, had his hair trimmed, changed his clothes, and then set a diadem on his head and ensconced him as king of the territory of the tetrarchy of Philip,[38] giving him also the tetrarchy of Lysanias; and in addition he replaced his iron chain with a gold one of equal weight.[39]

---

[37] Herod Agrippa had been held as prisoner in Rome on the orders of Tiberius. When Macro travelled to Rome on Tiberius' death he supposedly carried a letter to the prefect of the city with orders to move Agrippa from the prison into house arrest (3.2). When Caligula later arrived personally in Rome with the body of Tiberius, his grandmother Antonia advised him that as a show of respect to his predecessor he should allow an appropriate interval between the funeral and Agrippa's complete release.

[38] Philip was the son of Herod the Great, and after Herod's death had ruled part of the old kingdom as the tetrarch of Batanea, with Trachonitis and Auranitis, until he died in AD 33/4, when Tiberius assigned responsibility for his tetrarchy to the governor of Syria. Caligula now bestowed the region on Agrippa with the title of king.

[39] It seems that Caligula added to Agrippa's kingdom the district of Abilene, previously ruled by Lysanias (Luke 3:1). Presumably Lysanias had died by 37.

Alexandria

It was in Alexandria where the problems first arose, ironically, since down to the time of Caligula Alexandrian Jews had looked upon the Romans as the defenders of their political and religious rights. The prefect of Egypt, Aulus Avilius Flaccus, appointed by Tiberius in AD 32, had governed with energy and ability at the beginning of his term but if we are to believe Philo he seems to have started to lose his grip by the time of Caligula's accession, reputedly omitting, for instance, to forward to Rome a resolution from Alexandrian Jews honouring the new emperor. Philo claimed that Flaccus was under the influence of extreme Greek nationalists, but we must bear in mind that Philo, as a prominent figure in the Jewish community, was hardly an impartial observer. The growing tensions exploded in 38 on the arrival in Alexandria of Herod Agrippa, who paraded through the city in a showy display of his imperial favour, boasting of the benefits he could bring to local Jews. This provoked serious disorder, during which synagogues were burned and demolished. Agrippa himself managed to escape only by slipping quietly out of the city. Flaccus responded by imposing strict controls on the Jews, moving them into two specific quarters of the city. If anything, he seems to have aggravated the problem. Tensions increased, leading to considerable violence, even murder. Flaccus then tried to control the chaos by arresting prominent Jewish leaders. By October 38, he had been replaced as prefect by the more diplomatic Gaius Vitrasius Pollio, who was able to impose a level of calm. Delegates were sent to Rome to present their cases from both the Greek and the Jewish communities, the latter led by Philo, and they did so at a meeting with the emperor in AD 40, after he had returned from his northern expedition. Philo has left us a vivid account of this meeting (5.48), conducted in a mood of near desperation on the Jewish side, since while in Rome they received news that the Temple at Jerusalem was to be converted into a centre of the imperial cult (7.30). In the event, the discussions had no practical impact, since Caligula was assassinated before reaching a decision.

7.23 Philo *Flacc.* 8 For when Flaccus took on the prefecture for what was supposed to be a six-year term,[40] for the first five, while Tiberius was still alive, he preserved the peace and also governed so vigorously and studiously that he outdid all his predecessors. **9** In his final year, however, after Tiberius died and Gaius had succeeded as emperor, he started to sit back and let things slip.

---

[40] There was no fixed term for the prefects of Egypt, who served at the pleasure of the emperor. Flaccus' predecessor Galerius held office for fifteen years. Since Flaccus himself had been kept in office for five years under Tiberius it can probably be assumed that he was a competent administrator.

7.24 Philo *Flacc.* 103 For when the king Agrippa came home and we explained the scheme concocted against us by Flaccus,[41] he corrected the matter, and after promising to send the decree did send it, so we gather, explaining the time factor, that it was not just recently that we learned to revere the house of our benefactors, since we had been zealously respecting them from the start, but through the governor's terrible conduct had been deprived of any opportunity to show it.[42]

7.25 Philo *Flacc.* 55 So what do they do on receiving the permission? There are five sections in the city, all named after the first five letters of the written alphabet; two are called the Jewish districts from the fact that there are mostly Jews living in them;[43] but there are also some, though not many, in the other areas. So what did they do? From four named with the letters they ejected the Jews and then forced them together into the cramped space of only one. **56** These, because of their large numbers, spread out over the beaches,[44] dunghills, and tombs, robbed of everything that belonged to them. And those people, overrunning their empty houses, turned to pillaging and split up their plunder like spoils of war, with no one to stop them; and breaking open the Jews' workshops, which were closed through grieving for Drusilla, they carted off whatever they found—and there was a great deal of it—and took it through the middle of the agora, treating other people's property as though it were their own.[45]

7.26 Philo *Flacc.* 65 For as soon as they were seized by the people who had set the unruly mob on them they were treacherously murdered, and dragged along and trampled underfoot through the entire city; they were completely annihilated, with not the slightest piece of them left for any communal burial; **66** many thousand others they also overwhelmed, resorting to all manner of vicious behaviour, and maddened with cruelty to the point of becoming like wild animals—for wherever they came upon or caught sight of Jews they would

[41] Agrippa came to Alexandria in August 38. The tone of this passage suggests that Philo met him in person, which is entirely plausible (Philo's brother had loaned Agrippa money: Jos. *Ant.* 18.159).

[42] No explanation is given for how the Jews could have known that Flaccus had failed to pass on their oath of loyalty to Caligula.

[43] Alexandria had been divided into districts from the earliest Ptolemaic times and named, as Philo explains, after the first five letters of the Greek alphabet, alpha to epsilon (note that Greek letters also served as numerals, hence districts 1–5). As Philo indicates, Jews historically did not strictly live in a ghetto in the sense of being required to reside there (Jos. *Ant.* 14.117–18, citing Strabo, gives the wrong impression that they were so required); up to now at least they resided by choice mainly in two districts, the chief one being district Delta (Four) (Jos. *BJ* 2.495), and were scattered also throughout the remainder of the city. In the disturbances of AD 38 Philo describes the creation of what comes close to a ghetto proper, presumably the Delta district.

[44] District Delta was in the northeast of Alexandria and bordered the sea.

[45] There seems to be a chronological problem here. Drusilla died on June 10, AD 38 (4.25), but Herod Agrippa did not travel to Alexandria from Rome before the end of July of that same year (he had waited for the Etesian winds, in mid-July: Phil. *Flacc.* 26) and the riots are described as taking place at the time of Caligula's birthday on August 31 (Phil. *Flacc.* 83).

either stone them to death or cut them down with sticks, but not immediately aiming blows on their vital areas so that they should not escape the agonies they deserved by dying too quickly.[46] **67** Emboldened by impunity and licence for their offences and having no patience with their blunted weapons, some even took up the arms that were the most effective of all, fire and iron, and killed many with swords and destroyed no small number with fire; **68** and the most merciless of all of them sometimes burned whole families in the middle of the city, men with their wives, and young children with their parents, not sparing old age or youth or the innocent tender years of babies. And whenever they ran short of pieces of wood they gathered dry sticks together and murdered them with smoke rather than flames, devising a more pitiful and lingering death for these unfortunates, whose corpses lay around half-burned and in no order, a grievous, agonizing sight.

Stability in Alexandria

The final chapter of these events belongs to the reign of Claudius. After his succession Claudius imposed firm control over events in Alexandria and a fascinating papyrus has survived in the form of a letter to the city. In it Claudius appears judicious and even-handed, calling on both parties to show forbearance but threatening harsh measures should they fail to do so. It also happens that Josephus has preserved the same decree, and his version is in some respects quite different from the surviving papyrus, suggesting that Josephus was very cavalier with his sources, and might even have reconstructed the decree from memory. In particular, Josephus has Claudius blaming the problems on Caligula's madness, which seems a total invention. This demonstrates how cautious we need to be when Josephus raises the topic of Caligula's madness in other contexts.

7.27. Letter to Alexandria. November 10, AD 41 (Smallwood 370.81–9)

Accordingly yet again I (sc. the emperor Claudius) bear witness that Alexandrians behave gently and generously towards the Jews, who have been residents of the same city for a long period, and that they not disrespect the traditions followed by them in worshipping their god; rather that they permit the Jews to observe the customs prevailing during the principate of the deified Augustus and which I myself confirmed after giving a proper hearing to both parties.

---

[46] The vagueness of the numbers is not untypical of ancient reports of disasters, which are often rhetorical rather than statistical. The "thousands" is particularly suspect.

7.28 Jos. *Ant.* 19.284 (Claudius determined) that the Alexandrians had become stirred up against the Jews among them in the days of Gaius Caesar because with his terrible madness and deranged mind he had humiliated them for refusing to transgress Jewish religion and to worship him as a god; **285** "My wish," he said, "is that none of the rights of the Jewish people should fall by the wayside through Gaius' insanity and that their former rights should be safeguarded while they abide by their own customs, and I direct both parties to take the greatest care to ensure that there be no disturbances after this ordinance of mine is posted."

Judaea

The precise sequence of events in Judaea proper during Caligula's reign is almost impossible to reconstruct, but there can be no doubt that they took a serious turn for the worse. Tacitus, drawing a contrast between the state of Judaea under Tiberius and what happened under his successor, makes the famous comment that under Tiberius all was peaceful.[47] This was no doubt a considerable exaggeration, but such problems as existed in the Tiberian period were mainly of a local character, and settled after the suspension of Pontius Pilate, prefect of Judaea, by Vitellius, the legate of Syria (to which office the prefects of Judaea were subordinate). On his accession, Caligula sent out a new prefect to Judaea, the little-known Marullus. The appointment was largely irrelevant, since events took such a serious turn that they required the direct intervention of the new legate of Syria, Publius Petronius. Trouble first broke out in the coastal town of Jamnia (modern Yavne), probably in the winter of 39, when a group of Jews tore down an altar to the imperial cult. An enraged Caligula responded by decreeing that the Temple of Jerusalem would be converted into an imperial shrine, to house a huge statue of himself in the guise of Jupiter.

Repercussions were inevitable. Riots broke out in Syria, leading to attacks on Jews and the burning of the synagogue. Petronius used his diplomatic skills as best he could but he was met by the adamant refusal of the Jewish leaders to accept what they saw as the desecration of the Temple. Demonstrations throughout Judaea, and a deliberate decision to neglect the harvest, convinced Petronius that a disaster was in the offing. He shrewdly intimated to the sculptors in Sidon, who were working on the massive statue there, that they should proceed slowly, and alerted Caligula to how serious the security situation had become. The emperor reputedly refused to believe Petronius and suspected that he had been bribed, but was supposedly dissuaded from going ahead with his plans for the

---

[47] Tac. *Hist.* 5.9.4.

Temple by his good friend Herod Agrippa, who had been so dismayed by the scheme that he had fallen seriously ill.[48] The moral dimensions of this episode cannot accommodate the idea that Caligula might have listened to reason and moderated his policy; hence we are told that he changed his mind once again, but this time died before the revived plans could be put into effect.

How far Caligula can be held personally responsible for the serious disintegration of good relations is difficult to determine, so confused are our sources of information. Jewish writers like Josephus and Philo were persuaded that he hated the Jews and was planning a massive war against them. This is not convincing. Romans found it difficult to distinguish between religious and political fervour. Acts such as the destruction of the altar at Jamnia would have been seen as a challenge to imperial authority, and the provocations by the more extreme zealous Jewish factions certainly aggravated the situation. After Caligula's death Jews in Alexandria tried to even scores, and drawing on previously stored caches of weapons they went on a rampage against the Greeks. This was but one of a long series of bitter clashes following Caligula's death, leading eventually to the final confrontation and the devastating sack of Jerusalem fewer than thirty years later.[49]

7.29 Tac. *Hist.* 5.9.2 Under Tiberius there was peace. Then, when they were ordered by Gaius Caesar to place his statue in their Temple they preferred to take up arms, an uprising that was ended by Caesar's death.

7.30 Philo *Leg.* 201 Hearing from visitors how enthusiastic Gaius was about his own deification and how antagonistic he was towards the whole Jewish race, and so thinking also that a suitable opportunity for an attack had come their way, these people erected a shoddy altar from the most low-grade materials, using clay bricks, just to engineer a plot against their compatriots;[50] for they were sure that these would not tolerate any transgression of their customs (which, in fact, turned out to be the case). **202** For on seeing it and finding it intolerable that the sanctity of their holy land was being defiled, they got together and destroyed it;[51] and they immediately came to Capito, who was the architect of the whole drama. He then, thinking he now had the stroke of luck that he had long been looking for, wrote to Gaius, boosting the affair to the skies. **203** And after reading it Gaius then ordered a gilded colossal statue, something more expensive and magnificent than the brick altar set up as an insult in Jamnia, to be erected in the Temple in the capital[52] and employed as advisors the best and wisest men—Helicon, that noble slave, idle gossip, and

[48] Phil. *Leg.* 188–336; Jos. *Ant.* 18.261–309, *BJ* 2.184–203.   [49] Jos. *Ant.* 19.278–92.
[50] The altar seems to have been built in the winter of AD 39–40. It may be associated with Caligula's expedition to the north, either to help him secure success or to celebrate his victories there.
[51] Philo ventures no criticism of the Jewish conduct, even though it was the kind of behaviour that was threatened with draconian reprisal in Claudius' letter to the Alexandrians (7.27).
[52] Jerusalem.

pettifogger, and a tragedian Apelles, who they say in his early years hawked his good looks around, and when past that took to the stage.[53]

7.31 Philo *Leg.* 245 To good men God seems to supply good ideas by which in benefiting others they will also benefit themselves, something that also happened to Petronius.[54] So what were his ideas? **246** Not to hound the workers, but rather just persuade them to bring the statue to completion while trying as much as possible not to fall short of the most famous exemplars, but taking plenty of time...

Further Reading

Bilde, P. 1978. "The Roman Emperor Gaius (Caligula)'s Attempt to Erect His Statue in the Temple of Jerusalem." *STh* 32: 67–93.

Fishwick, D., and B. D. Shaw. 1976. "Ptolemy of Mauretania and the Conspiracy of Gaetulicus." *Historia* 25: 491–4.

Gruen, E. S. 2002. *Diaspora: Jews amidst Greeks and Romans*. Cambridge, MA: Harvard University Press.

Malloch, S. J. V. 2001. "Gaius on the Channel Coast." *CQ* 51: 551–6.

Wardle, D. 2006. "The Bald and the Beautiful: Imperial Hair-Envy and the End of Ptolemy of Mauretania." *Arctos* 40: 175–88.

Woods, D. 2000. "Caligula's Seashells." *G&R* 47: 80–7.

---

[53] The freedman Helicon was the most significant of a group of Alexandrian Greeks in Caligula's service, noted for his stinging witticisms and constant companionship of the emperor. He was eventually executed by Claudius, for reasons unknown. Apelles was a particular favourite of Caligula (5.22). Given the timing of the Jamnia incident we would perhaps have to assume that the information was conveyed to Caligula in Gaul and that the two were present with him there. Philo may of course simply be speculating here.

[54] Petronius had apparently been impressed by demonstrations at Ptolemais and had appreciated that the installation of Caligula's statue in the Temple would provoke bitter resistance (Jos. *Ant.* 18.269–72; Jos. *BJ* 2.192–201). That said, the report of Petronius' tactics might also suggest an attempt by a favoured commander to create the later image that he procrastinated in carrying out the emperor's orders (see also Memmius at 6.27).

8

Assassination

Fear of assassination is a mindset that we associate generally with autocratic rulers, and Roman emperors, including Caligula, were no exception. A fear of assassination might be one of the reasons why, when he returned from his northern campaign at the end of May in AD 40, Caligula chose to wait just outside Rome's city limits, and in fact delayed his entry into the city proper for three months, until August 31, his birthday, to celebrate the Ovation that the senate had voted him. It was not an irrational fear, as later events would prove.

On his was back to Rome Caligula was met by a senatorial delegation. The sequence of events is a little confused but it seems that the senate had sent two previous missions, one in late AD 39 to offer him an Ovation for his suppression of the conspiracy, which offended him because it was not grand enough and because of the participation of Claudius (4.57, 5.14), and a shadowy grander one some time later, reporting the award of unspecified honours (59.23.6), which he apparently met kindly. That happy mood passed, and he made clear to the third, final, delegation that he was returning to the city in a truculent mood.[1]

8.1 Suet. *Cal.* 49.1 So when he was met en route by the distinguished order's envoys who were begging him to make haste, he shouted at the top of his voice: "I'll come, I'll come, and this will come with me"—and he repeatedly beat the sword hilt at his side. He also announced that he was coming back, but only for those who wanted him, the equestrian class and the people—for he would be neither a fellow citizen nor princeps for the senate ever again.[2] 2 He also forbade any of the senators to meet him.[3] Then renouncing, or deferring, his Triumph, he entered the city on his birthday with an Ovation; and within four months he was dead,[4] having dared to commit monstrous crimes and while still planning even greater ones (for he had intended to move to Antium, and then to

---

[1] We should not rule out entirely the possibility that the supposed second and third delegations, although reputedly having different outcomes, are in fact a doublet of one single event.

[2] Caligula remained popular with the masses right to the end. His relations with the equestrians were more complex, and there are many stories of the humiliation and punishment he inflicted on members of the order.

[3] In the senate Caligula sat on high platform and had an armed guard (Dio 59.26.3); that said, his successor Claudius similarly made use of a guard when in the senate house (Suet. *Claud.* 12.1).

[4] He in fact died within five months, as Suetonius knew.

The Emperor Caligula in the Ancient Sources. Anthony A. Barrett and J. C. Yardley, Oxford University Press.
© Anthony A. Barrett and J. C. Yardley 2023. DOI: 10.1093/oso/9780198854562.003.0009

Alexandria,[5] after first murdering the leading members of both orders). **3** So none should doubt this, two notebooks were discovered among his personal effects, each with a different title, one called "The Sword" and the other "The "Dagger";[6] and both contained names and notes on people marked out for the death penalty. Also found was a huge box filled with different sorts of poisons, and when these were later thrown into the sea by Claudius it is said that the sea was poisoned, not without killing fish, which the tide threw up dead on adjacent shores.

There are indications that after the completion of his northern campaign Caligula took action against some of the leading senatorial families.

8.2 Suet. *Cal.* 35.1 He took their old family insignia from all citizens of the highest nobility,[7] from Torquatus his torque,[8] from Cincinnatus his lock of hair,[9] and from Gnaeus Pompeius the cognomen "Great" that came from his ancient ancestry.[10]

---

[5]   The supposed charge of planning to move the capital to Alexandria was a familiar one. It was made also against Julius Caesar (Suet. *Jul.* 79.3) and Nero (Dio 63.27.2). Caligula did in fact intend a visit to Alexandria (Philo *Leg.* 172, 250–1; Jos. *Ant.* 19.81). Antium was his birthplace, and he spent time there not long before his death (Plin. *NH* 32.4).

[6]   Presumably the dagger represented those who would be dealt with summarily if apprehended in a plot of some nature. He dedicated three daggers (swords, according to Suetonius) in the Temple of Mars on the exposure of the conspiracies of AD 39 (4.56, 59).

[7]   Suetonius groups the fates of these members of famous families with that of Ptolemy (7.6–9) but the connection is tenuous. Romans with distinguished lineages were humiliated and deprived of those elements of their names that recorded their illustrious ancestors, especially ancestors who had won fame in battle, while Ptolemy was actually put to death. The putative link is perhaps merely the danger posed by celebrity status.

[8]   Decimus Junius Silanius Torquatus was the son of Marcus Silanus and Aemilia Lepida, daughter of Julia the Younger, herself the daughter of Augustus' daughter Julia (the Elder). His cognomen "Torquatus" was derived from the achievement of an ancestor who in 361 BC killed a Gaul in single combat and removed the metal collar, the torque, from his neck. Decimus is recorded in an inscription as a member of the Salii priesthood in AD 40 (*ILS* 9339), still then called Torquatus (the name is fragmentary), and the humiliation reported here must be later than the inscription. Suetonius' statement is cryptic but Caligula may have suspected Decimus of dynastic designs. The family seems to have been very proud of its history (Tac. *Ann.* 15.52.1).

[9]   Cincinnatus was a descendant of Lucius Quinctius Cincinnatus, a much revered figure, who as dictator had been called from his farm to save Rome from an internal uprising in the fifth century BC and had famously retired afterwards. The cognomen seems to have been dropped after the fourth century. The descendants of the famous dictator were long undistinguished, although the Quinctii did see a revival of their fortunes under Augustus, with consulships in 9 BC and AD 2, and they may have resumed the famous cognomen in that period. On the other hand Cincinnatus means "curly-haired" and it is possible that the punishment echoes some lost witticism (the theme of Caligula's baldness is a persistent one), and that the inclusion of Lucius Quinctius (otherwise unknown) with the other two scions of distinguished families is unmerited.

[10]   Gnaeus Pompeius Magnus was the son of Marcus Crassus Frugi (possibly himself the butt of one of Caligula's jokes [see 5.47, 6.4]) and of Scribonia, descendant of Pompey the Great (to be distinguished from Augustus' wife Scribonia). Gnaeus drew his title "Magnus," which had lapsed after the death of Pompey the Great's sons, from his mother's side, thus deliberately, and somewhat injudiciously, recalling her great-grandfather. Along with Decimus Torquatus, Gnaeus was a member of the Salii in AD 40, and clearly in high favour then. According to Dio, who also mentions the deprivation of the cognomen, Caligula supposedly pondered killing him, then decided he was too contemptible to be

But Caligula did not stop at demotion and humiliation. In the months leading up to his death we have reports of a series of brutal executions. Some of these appear in Seneca, and since many of Seneca's readers would have been alive in Rome when the dramatic events supposedly occurred, it seems unlikely that the executions could have been concocted out of very thin air, although the details may well be coloured to highlight Caligula's brutality. But Seneca's account of Caligula's motives, that he carried out the executions purely for sadistic pleasure, should be treated with extreme caution. In fact it may well be that Caligula had concrete evidence of plots being hatched against him. If so, of course, their ultimate success demonstrates that the intelligence he was receiving came short of complete or perfect.

The first case involves a Sextus Papinius. Nothing certain is known about this individual beyond what Seneca and Dio tell us here. Dio reports that Papinius and his father, whom he identifies as Anicius Cerialis, were tortured. Dio notes that the accused were suspected conspirators—they were not simply victims of arbitrary cruelty, which Seneca implies. Dio also adds the detail that Papinius betrayed not only Anicius but also others, who were executed, while Papinius himself presumably survived. But we know that this information cannot be correct. Anicius Cerialis in fact survived Caligula to be executed much later, in AD 66, under Nero. To confuse an already confused situation, Tacitus mentions that Anicius' death at that later date elicited little sympathy because *he, Anicius*, had previously betrayed a conspiracy under Caligula (Tac. *Ann.* 16.17.1, 8), arguably what we might expect of an individual who had earlier displayed cringing flattery by proposing that a temple be erected to the deified Nero after exposure of a conspiracy (Tac. *Ann.* 15.74.3). It is very possible, then, that under Caligula Anicius betrayed a number of Romans, including Papinius, and that Dio got things mixed up, adding the dramatic but spurious touch that Anicius and Papinius were father and son. Betili(e)nus Bassus seems to have died at the same time, and he may well have been one of Anicius' victims. Clearly Dio did not use Seneca as his exclusive source here, if he consulted him at all. Confusingly, in Seneca's account Betili(e)nus Bassus is Papinius' *father*, while Dio gilds the lily by giving him the role of the *son* of yet another character, Capito. An ancient historiographical can of worms, to say the least.

8.3 Sen. *Ira* 3.18.3 Recently Gaius Caesar in a single day flogged and tortured Sextus Papinius, whose father had been a consul, Betilienus Bassus, his own quaestor, and the son of his procurator, as well as other men, both senators and Roman *equites*, not to interrogate them but simply out of malice.[11] 4 Then, so

taken seriously (Dio 59.5.9). He recovered the title under Claudius and was important enough to marry Antonia, Claudius' daughter, and to be permitted to stand for office before the official age. He was put to death probably in early 47 (Sen. *Apoc.* 11; Suet. *Claud.* 27.2; Dio 60.5.7–9).

[11] Suetonius, presumably referring to this Betilienus, describes the scourging as particularly brutal (6.1).

impatient was he with his pleasure being delayed, an enormous pleasure for which his cruel nature required immediate fulfilment, that he decapitated a number of them by lamplight as he sauntered with some ladies and senators in the terrace of his mother's gardens.[12]

8.4 Dio 59.25.5b (*in epitome*) Living like this, he was sure to face plots. He found out about the coup, and arresting Anicius Cerealis and his son Sextus Papinius he tortured them; and when Anicius divulged nothing, he persuaded Papinius with a promise of his life and immunity to denounce a number of others, whether truthfully or falsely, and then immediately had Anicius and the others killed before his eyes. 6 After ordering Betilinus Bassus' throat cut, he even forced his father Capito to attend the actual execution, though Capito was guiltless and had not been arraigned. When he asked permission to close his eyes Caligula also ordered him executed. 7 Facing such danger, Capito pretended he had been one of the conspirators, promised to identify all the others, and then named Gaius' companions and those associated with his wanton violence and brutality. He would in fact have destroyed large numbers of them had he not lost his credibility by also accusing the prefects as well as Callistus[13] and Caesonia. He thus met his end, but this actually precipitated Gaius' own downfall.

Another victim named by Seneca is Julius Canus, a philosopher, whose school is not specified here but who can be securely identified, from his comments, as a Stoic.[14] Founded in the third century BC, in Athens, Stoicism advocated a rational life, one lived according to nature, and saw virtue as the true good and the only source of genuine happiness. It made an impact on the educated Roman upper classes, and by the latter part of Nero's reign Stoics frequently appear among the more prominent opponents of the emperor. In practice they seem to have been broadly willing to reach some accommodation with a temporal ruler; the unhappiness of Stoics under Caligula and Nero may not have been so much with the principate *per se* as with the arbitrary abuse of power by individual emperors. Canus is the first adherent of the creed recorded as a victim of imperial hostility. It should be noted, however, that while Seneca attributes Canus' downfall to Caligula acting alone, the senate might have played a role in the affair. The period that elapsed between his conviction and execution, ten days, was precisely that prescribed as the required interval after trials in the senate,[15] and it is therefore possible that Canus was actually convicted by the senate and that his conviction followed a proper legal process.

---

[12] Caligula's mother Agrippina had owned an estate in the Vatican area, which he would have inherited.
[13] The powerful freedman Callistus may in fact have been involved in the final conspiracy against Caligula, on which see below (8.8, 10).
[14] He is identified as a Stoic in a fragment of Plutarch (*Frag.* 211).
[15] Tac. *Ann.* 3.51.3 (there is a problem in the manuscript); Dio 57.10.4.

8.5 Sen. *Tranq.* 14.4 Julius Canus was a truly great man, admiration for whom is not limited by his being born in our day. When he was in dispute with Gaius and that Phalaris[16] said to him as he was leaving, "In case you are deluding yourself with foolish hope, I have ordered you executed," he replied, "I thank you noble lord" . . .

6 Can you believe he spent the ten days right up to his execution without a care? It beggars belief what that man said, what he did, how calm he was. **7** He used to play board games. A centurion who was hauling off a crowd of condemned prisoners, ordered him to be brought out, too. When summoned he counted the pieces and said to his companion, "See that after my death you don't lie that you won." Then nodding to the centurion he said, "You will be the witness that I am one ahead." Do you think Canus was playing a game on that board? He was joking. His friends were sad at the prospect of losing such a man. **8** "Why so sad?" he asked. "You want to know if souls are immortal; I'll know soon." And he did not stop seeking the truth right to the end and using his own death for the enquiry. **9** He had his own philosophy teacher with him, and as they approached the hillock on which daily sacrifice took place to our god Caesar[17] he asked, "What are you thinking about now, Canus? What's in your mind?" "I have decided," replied Canus, "to observe whether, at that fleeting moment, the soul will be aware that it is leaving the body." And he promised that, whatever he found, he would go around his friends and report on just what souls really are.

Portents

Conspiracies are best planned in secret, and their details are best kept hidden. It is hardly surprising, then, that the events of a conspiracy will be misunderstood by later generations. An added complication is that the ancients took it as given that such major events took place to some extent through the agency of the divine, and that the divine, very accommodatingly, would often arrange portents of great

---

[16] Seneca sees a parallel between Caligula and Phalaris, the notoriously cruel sixth-century BC tyrant of Agrigentum, in Sicily. He reputedly roasted his enemies alive in a bronze bull, and would eventually suffer the same fate himself. Although somewhat rehabilitated later, he is here still the epitome of the brutal tyrant, which should put us on our guard, since Seneca's depiction of Caligula's conduct generally adheres to the stereotype of the ruthless tyrant.

[17] A much-discussed passage, which might be taken to suggest that Seneca was aware of a cult of Caligula in Rome. But we should be cautious. We cannot even be sure which Caesar is intended here; it could be the deified Julius Caesar, or Augustus, rather than Caligula. Also, the reference to a *tumulus* (basically a hillock, but used frequently in the sense of a funeral mound) rather than a temple or shrine is unusual. It might be an allusion to the dome-shaped Mausoleum of Augustus (which would place Canus on the Campus Martius). Or it might be a dark allusion to the Tarpeian rock on the Capitoline, from which condemned criminals were traditionally thrown: in that case the reference could indeed be to Caligula but made ironically, in that those sacrificed are the victims of the megalomaniac tyrant who behaves as if he was a god. Certainly the sequence of the narrative suggests that when Canus saw the tumulus it brought the realization that he was to die imminently. In any case it is hard to believe that Seneca could have meant the expression "our god" (*deo nostro*) seriously.

events. As a bonus, events could be resurrected and understood retrospectively in the light of later developments to have in fact been unmistakable (although, admittedly, previously mistaken) signs of what was to come.

8.6 Suet. *Cal*. 57.1 The forthcoming assassination was preceded by numerous prodigies. At Olympia the statue of Jupiter, which he had wanted dismantled and moved to Rome, suddenly let out such a loud guffaw that its scaffolding fell apart and the workmen ran off;[18] and a man named Cassius immediately arrived there claiming that he had been instructed in a dream to sacrifice a bull to Jupiter.[19] 2 The Capitol at Capua was struck by lightning on the Ides of March,[20] as also was the chamber of the Palatine major-domo in Rome.[21] Nor was there any shortage of people conjecturing from the one omen that its master faced danger from his guardians,[22] and from the other that there would be a murder just as memorable as one committed in the past on the same day. When Gaius consulted him about his horoscope the soothsayer Sulla also maintained that his murder was coming soon. 3 There was also further warning from the Fortunes at Antium to "beware of Cassius";[23] and because of that he had given an order for the execution of Cassius Longinus, then proconsul of Asia, not remembering that Chaerea's name was Cassius.[24] The day

[18] Caligula had reputedly intended that the statue be brought to Rome and its head replaced by his own. Memmius had been charged with its transportation but had delayed the commission (Jos. *Ant.* 19.9); the reference to scaffolding here suggests that plans for moving the statue were still in place, although we cannot be sure how long before the assassination the supposed omen occurred.

[19] The thinking here is presumably that Caligula had made the god his own victim but that he would instead be sacrificed as a victim to the god. The Cassius in question is otherwise unknown, beyond his having the same nomen as Cassius Chaerea, Caligula's eventual assassin.

[20] A curious portent. A lightning strike might well portend a death, as it supposedly did for Augustus (Suet. *Aug.* 97.2: a lightning flash melted the letter C in his name Caesar, showing that he would live fewer than a hundred days) and for Claudius (Suet. *Claud.* 46: his father's tomb was struck by lightning). The precise day of Caligula's assassination is disputed but it must have been in late January. Hence the damage at Capua had to have happened the best part of a year earlier, on the anniversary of Caesar's assassination. Although Shakespeare famously has Spurinna warn Caesar to "beware the Ides of March," Suetonius reports that the warning was that danger could befall him at any time *up to* the Ides of March, a far less precise prediction (Suet. *Jul.* 81.2).

The connection between Caesar's death and Caligula's death is forced, to say the least, as Suetonius seems to realize when he goes on to say that in Caligula's case the omen suggested a significant death, just as the death on the Ides of March was significant.

[21] The versatility of ancient omens is illustrated here. When Augustus' home on the Palatine was similarly hit by lightning he took it as a positive sign that Apollo had revealed that his temple should be built on the spot (Suet. *Aug.* 29.3).

[22] The analogy seems to be that Cassius Chaerea was the steward of Caligula's person, and would cause his destruction—of course the steward on the Palatine was a totally innocent bystander.

[23] There was a celebrated Temple of Fortune in Antium, where she was worshipped in double form and where oracles were dispensed. Antium was Caligula's birthplace, and a favoured retreat; it was appropriate that the two Fortunes should look out for him.

[24] Gaius Cassius Longinus was the brother of Lucius Cassius Longinus, Drusilla's first husband. Suffect consul in 30, he had gone on to be governor of Asia. He may well have been a more dangerous figure than Suetonius suggests here. Although apparently favoured by Claudius, and appointed governor of the important province of Syria, he was suspected by Nero of stirring up dissatisfaction, as a descendant of Gaius Cassius, the assassin of Caesar, whose bust he kept in his home with the inscription "the leader of the cause." As a consequence, he was exiled by Nero to Sardinia (Tac. *Ann.* 16.7, 9.1; Dio 59.29.3; Suet.

before his death he had a dream that he was standing in heaven next to Jupiter's throne and that he received a kick from the god's right toe and was thrown down to earth.[25] Also seen as portents were some things that had happened just by chance slightly earlier that very day. 4 While sacrificing he was splashed with a flamingo's blood;[26] and the pantomime Mnester danced a tragedy that the tragic actor Neoptolemus had once performed during the games at which the Macedonian king Philip was assassinated; then there was the farce *Laureolus*, in which the main actor vomits blood when he falls running away, and several of the supporting cast competed to provide proof of their artistry and drenched the stage with blood.[27] Preparations were also under way for a night-time show in which underworld tales were to be presented by Egyptians and Ethiopians.[28]

The Final Conspiracy

Prodigies offer a wonderful insight into the way that ancients saw the world. They cannot of course be used as serious evidence for actual events, but in truth the earthly historical accounts seem at times scarcely more reliable than the heavenly portents. Conspiracies are by their nature secret, and all that we can say with confidence is that at the end of January, AD 41, Caligula was murdered by officers

Nero 37.1 [this last suggests that he was executed]). The sentence of death presumably became null and void after Caligula's assassination, another example of the last-minute rescue (see comments on Memmius: 6.27, and Petronius: 4.55), which makes the whole tale rather suspect.

[25] There is surely a humorous element to this story, especially the detail of being ejected by Jupiter's big toe. It is reminiscent of Dio's comment that on the day of his assassination Caligula learned that he was not in fact a god (8.13).

[26] The blood on his garment suggests that Caligula was also destined to become a sacrificial victim. This seems to be a garbled account of the incident. Josephus (Jos. *Ant.* 19.87) reports that it was in fact the garment of Publius Nonius Asprenas that was bespattered during the sacrifice. Subsequently Asprenas was the first to be killed in the moments after Caligula's assassination, and the same story seems to have been told about both individuals. Just before a battle Caligula's father Germanicus dreamt that he was bespattered by a victim's blood, and that Livia then provided him with a clean toga (Tac. *Ann.* 2.14.1).

[27] We can piece these events together by adding information from Josephus. He informs us that on Caligula's last day there was a performance of a mime involving a band of robbers, who were crucified. There was also a pantomime called the *Cinyras* (Jos. *Ant.* 19.94). This told the tragedy of the king of Cyprus, Cinyras, whose daughter developed an incestuous passion for him. Cinyras was killed (Myrrha turned into a myrrh tree) and there was much fake blood sloshing about (some of which may have splashed Caligula, although this is not mentioned). Josephus adds that the performance fell on the anniversary of the day when Philip II, father of Alexander the Great, was murdered. Suetonius' source has made a connection with Neoptolemus, a tragic actor, who performed for Philip at a state banquet and sang a piece that supposedly foretold the king's death (Diod. 16.92.3; Dem. *Peace* 5.5–7). Philip was assassinated as he entered the theatre at the wedding of his daughter in 336 BC. This in fact happened in the summer or autumn, not at the end of January. The *Laureolus* seems to have involved the story of a runaway slave who in the end was crucified. It was clearly a bloody affair. It may be that the writer Catullus is the celebrated love poet of the late republic, but this is far from certain.

[28] Presumably the oracle here consisted in the notion that Caligula would not need the performance, since he would be able to testify for himself what happened in the underworld.

of the Praetorian guard. The involvement of the Praetorians seems certain. Lurking behind them, however, there are other shadowy figures who may or may not be involved but whose names came to be attached to the assassination by later historical accounts. The overall picture seems to suggest an organized conspiracy involving a number of people in high places. But the evidence is opaque, and any conclusions are bound to be tentative in the extreme.

The leading role in the final act of Caligula's life was assumed by the Praetorian tribune, Cassius Chaerea. We first learn of Chaerea in AD 14 when unrest spread through the legions in Lower Germany after the death of Augustus. He appears in Tacitus as a hot-headed *adulescens* ("young adult" rather than our "adolescent"), cutting his way fearlessly through a wall of armed soldiers, seemingly in an attempt to restore order. By early AD 41 and the time of the assassination he is a tribune in the Praetorian guard, and he is now described as *senior* (Tac. *Ann.* 1.32.5). The sources claim that Chaerea had a partner, another tribune, Cornelius Sabinus (8.8, 12, 13) Additionally, Suetonius claims that Chaerea also enjoyed the support of the prefects of the guard (8.7). We know the name of only one of those prefects (if, indeed, there were two at this time), Marcus Arrecinus Clemens, who went on afterwards to enjoy considerable imperial favour (his daughter married the future emperor Titus). In perhaps the most extraordinary detail reported about the whole affair, Josephus claims that when approached by Chaerea to join the conspiracy, Clemens endorsed the plan in the warmest terms but asked to be excused on the grounds of age (Jos. *Ant.* 19.45)! The involvement of the Praetorians is remarkable, and it is hard to imagine that they would not have had a careful plan for what would come next. Given that they enjoyed considerable privileges by virtue of their membership of the emperor's guard, they would certainly have had no interest in the restoration of the republic.

Suetonius also mentions that Chaerea had the support of Caligula's most powerful freedmen (8.7). He offers no specific names, but there are suggestions in other sources of the possible identity of one of them, no less than one of the most notorious of the freedmen in imperial service, Callistus. As recorded earlier, the suspected conspirator Capito had, according to Dio, claimed that Callistus was plotting against Caligula, a charge seen at the time as absurd (8.3). But Dio explicitly states that Callistus was complicit (8.8). Also, Josephus expressly asserts that Callistus switched his allegiance to Claudius, and even later insisted that he had been ordered to poison Claudius but had made up excuses for delaying the act. Tacitus, in a later context, tantalizingly suggests that the historian had discussed Callistus' role in Caligula's death—unfortunately he would have done so in the part of the *Annals* that is now missing (8.10, 11) It is certainly the case that after Caligula's assassination Callistus became prodigiously wealthy and occupied a prominent place in Claudius' inner circle (Plin. *NH* 36.60). He clearly did very well out of the change of regime, and he would certainly have had no more interest than would the Praetorians in the restoration of the republic. If

Claudius' role in the events leading to his succession was less innocent than we are told, he might have found a very useful ally in Callistus.

8.7 Suet. *Cal.* 56.1 While he was in this perturbed and violent state, there was no lack of people considering an attack on him. But it was after one or two conspiracies had been uncovered and others were hesitating through lack of opportunity that two men came together and brought one off, not without involvement of his most powerful freedmen and prefects of the imperial guard, and although a charge made against these groups of participating in some conspiracy was groundless they nevertheless felt themselves suspected and hated by him. Indeed, he aroused much animosity by taking them aside, drawing his sword, and declaring that he would perish by his own hand if they thought he deserved to die; and from then on he never stopped denouncing one man to the other and setting them all against each other.

2 After they decided on mounting the coup at the Palatine games when he went out at midday,[29] Cassius Chaerea, a tribune of a Praetorian cohort, demanded the leading role for himself.

8.8 Dio 59.29.1 (*in epitome*) Now when he continued with all manner of madness, a plot was hatched against him by Cassius Chaerea and Cornelius Sabinus, although they were tribunes in the Praetorian guard. For there were many others who were involved in the conspiracy and plotting against him, including Callistus and the prefect.

1a Nearly all his retainers were roused to the call, both for themselves and for the common good. And those not part of the conspiracy did not disclose it when they learned of it and were also pleased to hear of a plot against him.

8.9 Jos. *Ant.* 19.17 Three paths to death were being prepared for Gaius, and a good man was to be in charge of each of them. Aemilius Regulus, who came from Cordoba in Spain, brought a number together, being anxious to see Gaius brought down either by their hands or by his own.[30] 18 There was also a second path being prepared, its leader the tribune Cassius Chaerea. And Annius Vinicianus was not the least significant of those preparing to fight the tyranny.[31] 19 Their motives for hating Gaius merged together: for Regulus it was anger over the general situation and hatred for his unjust actions;

---

[29] The Palatine games had first been instituted in AD 15 by Livia, as a memorial to Augustus, lasting then for three days (Dio 56.46.5). Late calendars provide the date of January 17 for the first day (*Inscr. Ital.* 13.2.239, 264), the anniversary of their marriage. At some point the festival was extended to five days.

[30] Aemilius Regulus of Cordoba is not attested elsewhere, and disappears from history at this point. It should be noted that his name, as often in Josephus' manuscripts, is hopelessly corrupted.

[31] The form of the name that appears in Josephus' text is Minucianus. The emendation to Vinicianus is generally accepted.

temperamentally he had a certain passion and love of liberty to the point of not even keeping his adherence to the plots secret (at least he shared the secret with a large number of people, both friends and others he thought men of action). **20** For Vinicianus it was revenge for Lepidus; he had been Vinicianus' best friend, whom Gaius had destroyed along with some of the citizens; partly also since he feared for his own situation because, when Gaius gave vent indiscriminately to any anger that was aiming at death he brought it to fulfilment.[32] **21** Chaerea felt dishonoured by Gaius' slurs on his unmanliness; and as he was every day at risk because of his close contact and service with him he assumed that bringing off Gaius' death would be an act worthy of a free man...[33]

8.10 Jos. *Ant.* 19.64 Then there was Callistus, a freedman of Gaius; he was a man who by the fear he inspired in everyone, and the enormous wealth he had acquired, had achieved the heights of power and actually exercised what amounted to despotic power. **65** For he was a bribe-taker and a man of unrivalled arrogance, whose manipulation of his authority was outrageous; and in particular he knew full well the intractability of Gaius' temperament and how he could never be diverted from any decision he had made, and that there were many reasons for him to be at risk, not the least of them being the extent of his finances. **66** He therefore even started fawning on Claudius, surreptitiously switching allegiance to him in the expectation that the empire would fall to him if Gaius were removed, and thus by an early demonstration of favour and kindliness he would be establishing for himself a foundation for high status and power. **67** At any rate, although ordered to see Claudius off with poison he made countless excuses for putting off the deed.

8.11 Tac. *Ann.* 11.29.1 Initially, Callistus, whom I have already discussed in connection with the assassination of Gaius Caesar, came together with Narcissus...[34]

---

[32] Annius Vinicianus belonged to a family that was solidly establishment but constantly at loggerheads with the current ruler. He and his father were charged with treason in AD 32 (Tac. *Ann.* 6.9.3) and he later became a friend of Lepidus, the brother-in-law, and ultimately victim, of Caligula. Some see Vinicianus as a key agent in the plot, with ambitious hopes of replacing Caligula. But in fact he showed little inclination to seize power after the assassination. He eventually became involved in the later revolt of Camillus, legate of Dalmatia, and committed suicide on its failure in AD 42. His son, also Annius Vinicianus, headed a plot against Nero, exposed in Beneventum in AD 66.

[33] The sources claim widely that Caligula teased Chaerea for his effeminate mannerisms (Suet. *Cal.* 56.2; Dio 59.29.2; Pausanias 9.27.4; Auson. *De Caes.* 1.4). Chaerea had reached a tribunate in the Praetorians, which would have been preceded by the legionary rank of centurion. Such progress through the ranks is difficult to reconcile with this image, especially given that Tacitus describes him as "ferocious of spirit" (Tac. *Ann.* 1.32.2: *ferox animi*).

[34] Tacitus here discusses the involvement of Callistus (along with the freedman Narcissus) in the downfall of Messalina, the disgraced wife of Claudius.

The Assassination

The assassination was carried out on the Palatine hill, where a temporary stage was set up each year for the celebration of the Palatine games, which began on January 17, AD 41,[35] attracting crowds of spectators jammed into the confined space. The festival had probably been running for a week (8.12) when Caligula started his last day in the temporary theatre erected for the event, where he conducted sacrifices in honour of Augustus, during which blood, ominously, spattered his garments. The sacrifices over, he joined his friends, eating and drinking and apparently in good spirits. Fruit was scattered to the crowds, and exotic birds collected for the celebrations swooped on it, leading to much boisterous fun as the spectators competed to capture them. Eventually Caligula left the scene and made his way through an underground passage to have lunch in one of the imperial residences on the Palatine. He was supposedly murdered at this point by the two tribunes. Since in one version of the murder he was asked by Sabinus for the new watchword, it seems most likely that Sabinus' cohort was in the process of taking over from that of Chaerea. The time that Suetonius provides, the seventh hour, about 1.00 p.m. (8.12), seems therefore generally reasonable.[36]

8.12 Suet. *Cal.* 58.1 At about the seventh hour on the ninth day before the Kalends of February (January 24),[37] Gaius was hesitant about getting up for lunch since his stomach was still playing up from overeating the previous day, but at his friends' urging he did finally appear. In a covered passageway through which he had to pass some boys of noble parentage who were brought from Asia to give stage performances were rehearsing their parts; and had their leader not said that he had a cold Caligula would have wanted to go back and have the show put on immediately. **2** After that there are two versions. Some report that as he talked to the boys Chaerea delivered a critical sword blow to his neck from behind, first crying out "Take that!"[38] after which one of his co-conspirators, Cornelius Sabinus, ran him through the chest from the other side. Others record that after having the crowd pushed back by some centurions party to the plot, Sabinus, following military protocol, asked for the watchword, and when Gaius said "Jupiter" he cried out "Take that!" and split his jaw with his sword when he looked back.

---

[35] See note 29.

[36] Mart. *Ep.* 10.48.1 gives the eighth hour for the change of guard in his time, but no doubt the procedure allowed for some flexibility; Jos. *Ant.* 19.99 places the assassination in the ninth hour.

[37] The date provided by Suetonius here for the deed, January 24, is generally accepted by scholars as very plausible.

[38] *Hoc age* (literally "do this thing!") is a common expression, found in a number of contexts, including the ritual language of sacrifice, spoken in response to the executioner asking if he should proceed.

3 As he lay prostrate with his limbs contorted and crying out that he was still alive, the others dispatched him with thirty strokes; for the sign given to everyone was "Get him again!" Some even drove their swords through his genitals. At the start of the melee his chair bearers came running with poles to help him, and soon his German bodyguards did the same, and these killed some of the assassins but also a number of innocent senators.

59.1 He lived for twenty-nine years and was emperor for three years, ten months, and eight days.[39] His corpse was secretly carried off to the Lamian gardens,[40] and after being half-burned on a makeshift pyre it was buried in shallow ground; and later it was dug up by his sisters on their return from exile, cremated, and interred. It is well known that before that was done his garden keepers were tormented by ghosts, and that in that house in which he met his end no night passed without some frightful occurrence, until the house itself was consumed by a fire.[41] Along with him died his wife Caesonia, run through with a sword by a centurion, and his daughter, who was smashed against a wall.[42]

8.13 Dio 59.29.4 (*in epitome*) This was how it was done. He was holding some party on the Palatine and staging a show, **5** and during it he was himself eating and drinking and hosting the others, while Pomponius Secundus, then a consul, was gorging himself while sitting at the man's feet and constantly bending over and kissing them.[43] Now Chaerea and Sabinus, though disgusted by such disgraceful bevaviour, held back for five days. **6** But when Gaius wanted to perform in a dance and a tragedy himself and for this proclaimed a three-day extension to the festival, Chaerea's associates could tolerate it no longer. They

[39] In fact Caligula would have been twenty-nine years old in the August of his final year.
[40] The Lamian gardens were close to the gardens of Maecenas, on the Esquiline hill, which stood opposite the Palatine, on the other side of the valley that ran from the forum to the site of the later Colosseum, and were outside the technical city limits. They have been tentatively identified and excavated: https://www.nytimes.com/2021/01/12/science/caligula-archaeology-rome-horti-lamiani.html, accessed December 30, 2022. We know that Caligula had a residence there, for it was where Philo's delegation met him (5.48: Philo *Leg.* 351). We are not told anything of the logistics of moving the body to that location, and it probably occurred some time later, when the furore had died down.
[41] This entertaining anecdote is baffling. The Palatine was severely ravaged during the Great Fire of AD 64, and the imperial residences destroyed or seriously damaged. Caligula was supposedly killed in an underground passage (Suet. *Cal.* 58.1). The story told by Suetonius may in fact refer to the section of the palace (unidentified) where Caligula's corpse was supposedly taken immediately after the assassination and tended by Herod Agrippa (Jos. *Ant.* 19.237).
[42] Jos. *Ant.* 19.190–200 identifies the agent as Lupus, a tribune rather than a centurion, who found Caesonia draped over her husband's corpse at the end of the day of the assassination. The murder of the mother and child would have been seen as one of political necessity, undertaken to avoid the danger of their becoming the rallying point for later resentment, and was presumably planned from the outset. Josephus' story of Caesonia draped over the body of Caligula is no doubt a poetic exaggeration.
[43] Quintus Pomponius Secundus made a show after the assassination of seeking to restore the republic, but eventually went over to Claudius' side, and, according to Jos. *Ant.* 19.263–4, received the new emperor's personal protection. He eventually joined the rebellion of Camillus, legate of Dalmatia, in AD 42, and may have died as a consequence.

kept an eye on him when he left the theatre to see highborn boys that he had sent for from Greece and Ionia to sing the hymn specially composed for him and then waylaying him in a narrow passageway they killed him. 7 When he fell nobody there held back, but even when he was dead they kept viciously stabbing him, and some even tasted his flesh. As for his wife and daughter, they also immediately killed them.

30.1 So after behaving like that over three years, nine months, and twenty days, Gaius learned from hard experience that he was no god.

1.a By people from whom he would receive obeisance even in his absence he was now spat upon; for those by whom he used to be called "Jupiter" and "god" he was now a sacrificial victim; and his statues and portraits were pulled down, the people well remembering their frightful suffering.

1.b All the soldiers of the German corps were in uproar and squabbling with each other, even to the point of bloodshed.[44]

1.c Those present remembered what he once said in addressing the people, "I wish you had just one neck," and now they were showing him that it was he who had only one neck, while they had many hands. 2 When the Praetorian guard then frantically ran around asking who had killed Gaius, the ex-consul Valerius Asiaticus calmed them in a remarkable way, climbing to a spot visible from all around and crying out: "I wish I'd killed him myself."[45] In amazement, they stopped their clamouring. 3 All those feeling any allegiance to the senate kept to their oaths and settled down. And while this was going on around Gaius, the consuls Sentius and Secundus promptly removed the money from the treasuries to the Capitol. They stationed most of the senate as custodians and a large enough group of soldiers for there to be no looting by the common people. Together with the prefects and Sabinus and Chaerea's adherents, they then began to consider what needed to be done.

---

[44] Augustus had initially recruited German bodyguards as his own private corps from among the Batavians, in the area at the mouth of the Rhine. They were distinct from the Praetorians, who were not a private unit but officially part of the Roman army. The German guard was noted for being particularly loyal, and particularly brutal. Suetonius claimed that Caligula launched his expedition in 39 in order to recruit Batavian bodyguards (7.18), which, while implausible, does suggest that he acquired some of them during this campaign. The Germans ruthlessly pursued any they suspected of being involved in the murder. Suetonius here seems to suggest that there was some internal friction about how to proceed.

[45] In claiming in public after the murder that he wished he could take credit for it Valerius Asiaticus was playing a familiar double game of parading his republican virtues while evading direct responsibility for the assassination. This pronouncement may have been the basis for the claim made some six years later, in AD 47, when he was brought down by Claudius' wife, the notorious Messalina. Tacitus reports that on that later occasion it was asserted that Valerius had masterminded an earlier conspiracy. Seneca claims that he held a personal grudge against Caligula for aspersions that the emperor cast on the sexual skills of Valerius' wife. Unfortunately beyond these indirect links we have no concrete evidence of what his actual involvement, if any, might have been (Sen. *Cons.* 18.2; Jos. *Ant.* 19.159; Tac. *Ann.* 11.1–3).

8.14 Suet. *Cal.* 60 The situation at that time one might also judge from this. Not even after word of the assassination spread was it immediately believed, and there was some suspicion that the report of the killing had been fabricated and circulated by Gaius himself so he could in this way discover what people thought of him; nor had the conspirators earmarked anyone for the imperial power; and the senate was so uniformly agreed on asserting freedom that the consuls called their first meeting not in the curia, since it was named "Julian,"[46] but in the Capitoline temple, and when their turn came for expressing an opinion a number of people recommended that all memory of the Caesars should be wiped out and their temples destroyed. It was also observed, and a note of it made, that all Caesars whose praenomen was Gaius had died by the sword, beginning with the one killed in Cinna's time.[47]

Aftermath

One of the most celebrated events associated with the name of Caligula occurred in fact after his death, in the immediate aftermath of the assassination—the succession of his uncle Claudius. The popular story is that while the soldiers were rampaging through the palace they found Claudius hiding there, and had the spontaneous brainwave that they should make him emperor, carrying him off to their camp where he reluctantly acquiesced in their demands. This account of the events, as related by Suetonius and Dio, and in one of the versions preserved in Josephus, is inherently implausible. As stressed earlier, the Praetorians clearly would have seen no advantage in bringing an end to the principate and restoring the republic. And it is inconceivable that they would have assassinated an emperor without some plan in place for what was to replace him.

It is, of course, a version of events that suited the interests of Claudius. He would not have wanted the reputation of a regicide, which might have suggested an uncomfortable precedent. It would be more in his interest to promote the notion that he had, as Suetonius words it, become emperor *mirabili casu* (8.17 "through an amazing stroke of fortune") and had reluctantly stepped forward in Rome's hour of need. But his behaviour immediately after he was supposedly coerced into becoming emperor suggests a man in firm control. He rewarded the Praetorians with a

---

[46] The task of building the Curia Julia was assigned to Julius Caesar in 44 BC but actually undertaken, or at least completed, by Augustus.

[47] Gaius Julius Strabo, the great-uncle of the famous Julius Caesar, was killed in 87 BC when Rome was under the control of Lucius Cornelius Cinna. People would also have had in mind Gaius Caesar, the grandson of Augustus, who died of wounds received in Asia in AD 4. But by contrast Gaius, the father of Julius Caesar, died suddenly, of no apparent cause, while putting on his shoes (Plin. *NH* 7.181). Moreover, Caligula's oldest brother, who died in boyhood, was called Gaius (Suet. *Cal.* 7, 8.2).

generous donative, then presented the senators with a *fait accompli*, making quite clear to them that they could forget any dream of restoring the republic.

8.15 Jos. *Ant.* 19.162 While this was happening Claudius was suddenly abducted from the house; for, holding a meeting, the soldiers had been discussing among themselves what needed to be done since they saw that democracy was incapable of managing very much to their advantage, **163** whereas with some new person coming to supreme power it could be a sorry situation for them not to have been supporting his assumption of power. **164** So while confusion reigned it was a good idea to choose Claudius as emperor: he was a kinsman of the dead man's father, and of those gathered in the senate none was more deserving of consideration because of his distinguished ancestry and academic prowess, **165** and if made emperor he would in all likelihood respect them and repay them with bounty. Such was their thinking and they put it into effect immediately.

8.16 Jos. *Ant.* 19.216 Claudius was standing in a spot that could be reached by a few steps, and he was shrinking back into the darkness. **217** And when Gratus, one of the soldiers guarding the palace, saw him there, he did not recognize his face in the darkness and did not pull back, since he judged it was some man lurking there, but instead he moved closer to him... "It's Claudius Germanicus," he said to the men behind him; "let's take him away and make him emperor." **218** Seeing them ready to carry him off and fearing that he would die for causing Gaius' death, he begged them to spare him as he was harmless and unaware of what had been happening.

219 Smiling, Gratus took his right hand and said, "Enough trivial talk about your life being spared; you have to think big about supreme rule, which for the benefit of the world the gods have wrested from Gaius and agreed to bestow on you in recognition of your virtue. **220** Go, then, occupy your ancestors' throne!" They then lifted him up, a man not wholly able to walk on his own two legs from fear and joy over what he had been told.

8.17 Suet. *Claud.* 10.1 Most of his life having been spent in these and similar conditions, Claudius came to power in his fiftieth year by an amazing stroke of luck. After he and the others were barred entry by Gaius' assassins as they pushed back the crowd, claiming he wanted seclusion, he had retreated into an annex called the Hermaeum; and not much later, terrified by reports of the assassination, he crept off to a solarium close by and hid among some drapes hanging before its door. **2** As he hid there, a regular soldier who happened to be rushing around noticed his feet, and wanting to find out who he was he then recognized him and pulled him out; and when Claudius fell in terror before his knees he saluted him as emperor. From there he led him off to his comrades who were drifting about and still in a state of frustrated rage. He was put in a litter by them, and because his own bearers had run off he was, dejected and fearful, taken to the camp on the shoulders of men who took turns, the crowd that met him pitying him as though an innocent man being rushed off for execution.

8.18 Dio 60.1.1 This was how Claudius became emperor. After Gaius' murder the consuls sent guards throughout the city, convened the senate on the Capitol, and many different views were put forward there; to some democracy seemed good, to others monarchy, and some were for one man, and some for another. **2** And because of that they frittered away the rest of the day and all night coming to no decision. Meanwhile some soldiers who had gone into the palace in search of plunder came upon Claudius hidden away in some dark corner **3** (for he was with Gaius when he left the theatre and then, fearing the uproar, had been crouching down), and at first thinking that it was someone else or that he had something valuable, they dragged him out. Then when they recognized him they declared him emperor and took him off to their camp; and after that, since he was from the imperial family and looked suitable, they and all the others conferred on him the supreme power.

Further Reading

Ash, R. 2016. "Never Say Die! Assassinating Emperors in Suetonius' Lives of the Caesars." In Writing Biography in Greece and Rome. Narrative Technique and Fictionalization, edited by K. De Temmerman and K. Demoen, 200–216. Cambridge: Cambridge University Press.

Hurley, D.W. 2014. "Rhetorics of Assassination: Ironic Reversal and the Emperor Gaius." In Suetonius the Biographer. Studies in Roman Lives, edited by T. Power and R.K. Gibson, 146–58. Oxford: Oxford University Press.

Power, T. 2015. "Caligula and the Bludgeoned Priest." *Mnemosyne* 68: 131–35.

Wardle, D. 1991. "When did Caligula die?." *Acta Classica* 34: 158–65.

Wiseman, T.P. 1988. "Killing Caligula." *Pegasus* 16: 1–9.

Further Reading

The emphasis in this bibliography is on works in English. Only a small number of key publications in languages other than English are included. Many of the items in this list have useful information on the topics dealt with throughout the book. In addition, there is appended to each individual chapter a small list of works that are relevant primarily to that specific chapter.

General Studies

Adams, G. W. 2007. *The Roman Emperor Gaius 'Caligula' and His Hellenistic Aspirations.* Florida: Brown Walker.

Balsdon, J. P. V. D. 1934. *The Emperor Gaius.* Oxford: Oxford University Press, repr. Westport, CN, 1977).

Barrett, A. A. 1990. *Caligula: The Corruption of Power.* New Haven: Yale University Press.

Barrett, A. A. 2015. *Caligula: The Abuse of Power.* 2nd revised edition. London: Routledge.

Barrett, A. A. 2008. "Caligula." In *Lives of the Caesars*, edited by A. A. Barrett, 61–83. Oxford: Blackwell.

Dabrowski, A. M. 1972. *Problems in the Tradition about the Principate of Gaius.* Dissertation: Toronto.

Ferrill, A. 1991. *Caligula: Emperor of Rome.* London: Thames & Hudson.

Fratantuono, L. 2018. *Caligula: An Unexpected General.* Barnsley: Pen & Sword Military.

Gelzer, M. 1918. "Iulius Caligula (133)." *RE* 10: 381–423.

Madssen, J. 2020. *Cassius Dio.* London: Bloomsbury.

Momigliano, A. 1932. "Osservazioni sulle fonte di Caligola, Claudio, Nerone." *RAL* 8: 293–336.

Pelling, C. 1997. "Biographical History? Cassius Dio on the Early Principate." In *Portraits: Biographical Representation in the Greek and Latin Literature of the Roman Empire*, edited by M. J. Edwards and S. Swain, 117–44. Oxford: Clarendon Press.

Power, T., and R. Gibson. 2014. *Suetonius the Biographer.* Oxford: Oxford University Press.

Wilkinson, S. 2005. *Caligula.* London: Routledge.

Willrich, H. 1903. "Caligula." *Klio* 3: 85–118, 288–317, 397–470.

Winterling, A. 2011. *Caligula: A Biography.* Berkeley: University of California Press; translation of *Caligula: Eine Biographie.* Munich: Beck, 2003.

Woodman, A. J. 2009. *The Cambridge Companion to Tacitus.* Cambridge: Cambridge University Press.

Yavetz, Z. 1996. "Caligula, Imperial Madness and Modern Historiography." *Klio* 78: 105–29.

Collections

Ehrenberg, V., and A. H. M. Jones. 1955. *Documents Illustrating the Reigns of Augustus and Tiberius.* 2nd edition. Oxford: Clarendon Press.

Smallwood, E. M. 1967, repr. 2011. *Documents Illustrating the Principates of Gaius Claudius and Nero.* Cambridge: Cambridge University Press.

Commentaries

Edmondson, J. 1992. *Dio, the Julio-Claudians: Selections from Books 58–63 of the Roman History of Cassius Dio*. London: London Association of Classical Teachers.

Humphrey, J. W. 1976. *An Historical Commentary on Cassius Dio's Roman History, Book 59 (Gaius Caligula)*. Dissertation: Vancouver.

Hurley, D. W. 1993. *An Historical and Historiographical Commentary on Suetonius' Life of Caligula*. Atlanta: Scholars Press.

Lindsay, H. 1993. *Suetonius, Caligula*. London: Bristol Classical Press.

Lindsay, H. 1995. *Suetonius, Tiberius*. London: Bristol Classical Press.

Maurer, J. A. 1949. *A Commentary on C. Suetoni Tranquilli, Vita C. Caligulae Caesaris Chapters I–XXI*. Dissertation: Philadelphia.

Smallwood, E. M. 1970. 2nd edition. *Philonis Alexandrini, Legatio ad Gaium*. Leiden: Brill.

Van der Horst, P. W. 2003. *Philo's Flaccus: The First Pogrom*. Leiden: Brill.

Wardle, D. 1994. *Suetonius' Life of Caligula: A Commentary*. Brussels: Collections Latomus.

Wiseman, T. P. 2013. *The Death of Caligula*. 2nd edition. Liverpool: Liverpool University Press.

Translations

Cary, E. 1924. *Dio's Roman History*, Volume 7. Loeb Classical Library. Cambridge, MA: Harvard University Press. Repr. Heinemann, London, 1968.

Edwards, C. 2008. *Suetonius, Lives of the Caesars*. Oxford: Oxford University Press.

Hurley, D. W. 2011. *Suetonius, The Caesars*. Indianapolis: Hackett.

Rolfe, J. C. 1964. *Suetonius, Lives of the Caesars*, Volume 1. Loeb Classical Library. Cambridge, MA: Harvard University Press. Revised, with new introduction by K. R. Bradley, 2014.

Yardley, J. C., and A. A. Barrett. 2008. *Tacitus, Annals*. Oxford: Oxford University Press.

See also Van der Horst, Smallwood (section "Commentaries" above).

Index

For the benefit of digital users, indexed terms that span two pages (e.g., 52–53) may, on occasion, appear on only one of those pages.